T0297901

# The OpenXP Solution

## For the **Strategic Consolidation** of **Multiple Diverse Perspectives** on **Agile Software Projects**

## Dr. Sandra Walsh

To order additional copies of this book, contact:
Xlibris
0800-056-3182
www.xlibrispublishing.co.uk
Orders@ Xlibrispublishing.co.uk

# The OpenXP Solution

for the **Strategic Consolidation**
of **Multiple Diverse Perspectives**
on **Agile Software Projects**

Dr. Sandra Walsh

# Contents

# Chapter 1 Introduction

## 1.1 Overview

This chapter begins by introducing the research problem under investigation. Section 1.2 briefly discusses the challenges reported in Requirements Engineering (RE). Agile Methods are also described and the key challenges for the customer role during requirements activities in Agile Methods (AMs), particularly XP are discussed in-depth. Section 1.4 presents an overview of the OpenXP solution, this is then followed by a brief description on how the remaining chapters in this book are organised.

## 1.2 Requirements Engineering

Software Engineering (SE) is a discipline that addresses all activities involved in the creation of software from project inception through to maintenance of the completed system (Sommerville 2001). Requirements Engineering (RE) is an important part of this. RE can be defined as *"a coordinated set of activities for exploring, evaluating, documenting, consolidating, revising and adapting"* the perceived needs of a target software system (Van Lamsweerde 2009).

It is widely acknowledged that requirements elicitation and management is crucial for successful software development. This is often attributed to project failure or systems not meeting user needs (Sutcliffe *et al.* 1999), (Coulin *et al.* 2005a), (Bell 2006), (Zhang 2007), (Berry *et al.* 2010), (Vijayan and Raju 2011). Developers have also described the *"requirements effort"* within their own organizations' as *"insufficient"*, a statement supported by a substantial majority of 71% (Neill and Laplante 2003). However, RE is not straightforward with numerous problems reported (Cheng and Atlee 2007), (Pandey and Mustafa 2010). While reporting that only 37% of software development projects are successful, the Standish Group (2010) highlights *lack of user involvement* as the key reason for project failure. Obtaining *"good requirements"* has also been closely correlated with high levels of user involvement (Verner *et al.* 2005a). Miller (2008) also identifies *lack of user involvement* and *changing user needs* as the *"top causes"* of software project failure. Significantly, and with some overlap, the root cause of failure attributed to the requirements stages include *incorrect assumptions, communication failure, inadequate conflict management* and *lack of provision of contextual detail* (Johnson and Holloway 2006). Clear requirements, objectives and goals and a realistic schedule have also been identified as critical success factors in software projects (Nasir and Sahibuddin 2011).

### 1.2.1 Requirements Challenges

Pressman (2000) identifies general problems that relate to stakeholders understanding of requirements, these include: customers have *conflicting priorities*, are *unsure* of what is needed; do not understand the *capabilities and limitations* of their computing environment; don't fully understand the *problem domain*; and have trouble *communicating needs* to the software engineer. Sommerville (2007) highlights that often *developers don't have implicit knowledge* of the problem domain, and also, that *political factors influence requirements*.

In addition to and with some overlap of these challenges, Nuseibeh and Easterbrook (2000), add that *stakeholders have difficulty articulating requirements*. Also, Grünbacher (2006) asserts difficulty in *accommodating multiple diverse stakeholders* coming from different backgrounds, culture and experience, which presents a challenge in finding a common language for communicating requirements during projects.

Requirements elicitation *"is widely regarded as one of the more challenging"* of all the RE activities (Coulin *et al.* 2005b). Elicitation occurs shortly after project inception but typically before preliminary planning and can involve establishing objectives from broad high level goals to specific system constraints. It is claimed that inaccurate elicitation of requirements is *"a major factor in the failure of 90% of large software projects"* (Davis C.J *et al.* 2006). Others recognise elicitation as the *"hardest and most critical"* aspect of the SE process (Rajagopal *et al.* 2005), (Pacheco and Garcia 2012). It has also been suggested that elicitation is not performed effectively due to a lack of customer commitment and participation (Taylor 2000). Significantly, *"a stronger focus on the customer at the problem definition stage"* during RE is clearly in demand (Mahaux and Mavin 2013a).

### 1.2.2 Requirements Techniques

Davis A. *et al.* (2006) report a shortage of empirical studies assessing the performance of requirements elicitation techniques in more than one setting. The authors found *"absolutely no agreement among experts"* about how elicitation should be conducted in practice (Davis A. *et al.* 2006). Advice still remains limited for the selection of appropriate elicitation techniques in specific situations (Dieste *et al.* 2008). Despite an abundance of techniques that exist for requirements development (Davis A. *et al.* 2006) and indeed, efforts made to classify them (Van Vleit 2000), (Easterbrook 2004), (Van Lamsweerde 2009), it is claimed that current techniques are inadequate (Zhang 2007), (Cheng and Atlee 2007), (McBryan *et al.* 2008). Indeed, McGee-Lennon (2008) suggests that a novel approach may be required, however, it is acknowledged that potential does exist if existing techniques could be modified to deal with a *"combination of multiple distributed and possibly conflicting stakeholder needs"* along with *"long term configuration and evolution of these needs"*, a balanced approach is needed that, for certain domains, should be *"lightweight enough to be useable yet rigorous so as to be justifiable"* (McGee-Lennon 2008).

Some suggestions for adapting current RE methods have been made. These include: gaining a greater understanding of the system context, involving relevant stakeholders, iteratively defining requirements, and the need for stakeholders to repeatedly negotiate requirements overtime (Grünbacher 2006). In addition to resolving potential conflict, requirements elicitation must endeavour to facilitate effective communication and negotiation amongst multiple diverse stakeholder groups (Nuseibeh and Easterbrook 2000), (Cheng and Atlee 2007). It has also been advised that challenges facing RE cannot be resolved by developing a new tool or selecting the appropriate process model, instead research needs to focus on *"the complex interplay between a number of organisational, cultural, technological and economical factors impacting the RE process"* (Zowghi *et al.* 2005d).

## 1.3 Software Development Models

In general, software development can be described as the *identification, analysis, design, coding, testing* and *maintenance* of requirements for a software system (Sharp *et al.* 2007). A software process model is defined as a *"simplified description of a software process presented from a particular perspective"* (Sommerville 2001). There is a wide range of software processes but they are generally categorised as either *plan-driven* or *agile* development.

Traditionally, formal plan-driven approaches promote extensive planning, documented processes and are reuse-driven (Boehm 2002). In contrast, Agile Methods (AMs) promote frequent delivery of fully developed software rather than conformance to a specific process, they also attempt to deliver business value quickly and accommodate changing user requirements (Abrahamsson *et al.* 2003). Generally, AMs promote stakeholder communication and collaboration and response to change, encouraging a greater emphasis on the working software product.

### 1.3.1 Plan-Driven Software Development

The traditional *waterfall* model, a typical example of plan-driven development, was derived from a hardware engineering model and adapted for software development in the late 1960s (Royce 1987). With this approach software is developed in consecutive phases, with each producing a clearly defined deliverable that must be validated before moving on to the subsequent phase (Van Vleit 2000). For example, the output of the requirements phase is usually a formal requirements specification, which is used as the input for the design phase. This method is most suited to situations where the problem domain is well defined, with requirements well understood and not expected to change (Highsmith 2002).

Another characteristic of this approach is that software development team roles are clearly defined for each distinct phase. For instance, the role of a *systems analyst* is to solely complete *requirements* activities, with no further involvement in any of the subsequent development phases. It is assumed that because the problem is well understood that there will be little need for feedback between the phases, which results in efficiency. However, one drawback in separating roles is that members of the team are only proficient in one aspect of the process and somewhat detached from activities involved in other phases. Another distinctive feature of plan-driven development is the role of the customer representative. Customer involvement is restricted and long periods of time can elapse between their initial involvement at inception and the eventual deployment of projects.

In many cases this led to efficiency and project success (Nerur *et al.* 2005). However, for less stable situations, requirements are difficult to understand, define and regularly change (Cheng and Atlee 2007) (Berry *et al.* 2010). Indeed, if problems with requirements are identified later in the project it is difficult and considerably more costly to return to earlier stages to rectify this (Boehm 1981), (Boehm and Papaccio 1988), (Urquhart 1999), (Berry *et al.* 2010). Another problem reported is that the approach lacks flexibility, when a requirement change occurs, it cannot be easily accommodated (Nerur *et al.* 2005). In such cases inappropriate application of plan-driven development has led to many reports of project failure (Cutter Consortium 2000), (Bell 2006), (Sutherland 2007a). This has led to the emergence of AMs in the late 1990s.

### 1.3.2 Alternative Development Approaches

A growing body of knowledge has now begun to recognise that highly innovative dynamically changing domains must regularly adapt to effectively respond to the needs of both *highly competitive* and *evolving business conditions* (Bello *et al.* 2002), (Finken 2005), (Cottmeyer and Lee Henson 2010), (Moniruzzaman and Hossain 2013). In Growing Systems for Emergent Organisations, Truex *et al.* (1999) differentiate between stable and emergent software systems describing stable systems as more closely aligned with traditional plan-driven software development approaches where requirements complete and clear delineation can be seen to exist between the beginning and the end of projects. The alternative emergent systems viewpoint claims that the presence of continuous change within business organisations calls for software systems within such organisations to adapt to what is termed *"organisational emergence"*, this concept refers to *"a theory of social organization that does not assume that stable structures underpin organizations"* (Truex *et al.* 1999, 2000), (Baskerville and Pries-Heje 2002).

Here, traditional plan driven approaches when applied in dynamic domains can impede rather than facilitate the natural way in which organisations evolve. For dynamic and innovative domains software development procedures need to more closely align with the characteristics of emergent systems development (Truex *et al.* 1999), (Zheng *et al.* 2011). Here emergent organisational needs are directly related to the requirements for software systems that reside within such dynamic domains (Alatalo *et al.* 2002).

This strongly suggests that dynamic organisations must place greater value in churning rather than controlling change for emergent software systems development. In other words, change is effectively controlled by facilitating continuous requirements churn. This idea of viewing business organisations as emergent aligns more closely with agile rather than plan-driven approaches to software development indicating that agile approaches may be better suited for fully exploiting the emergence of goal sets to be achieved within dynamic innovative business domains.

### 1.3.3 Agile Software Development

A number of AMs exist, these include eXtreme Programming (XP) (Beck 1999), Scrum (Beedle and Schwaber 2001), Lean Software Development (LSD) (Poppendieck and Poppendieck 2003a), Dynamic System Development Method (DSDM) (Stapleton 1997) and Feature Driven Development (FDD) (Palmer and Felsing 2002). Although each employ different practices, all adhere to the Agile Manifesto (Beck *et al.* 2001), which recommends:

*Individuals and interactions* over processes and tools;
*Working software* over comprehensive documentation;
*Customer collaboration* over contract negotiation;
*Responding to change* over following a plan.

While AMs value the items to the right of each statement above, they place greater emphasis on those items to the left, highlighted in italics. AMs value the skills and experience of individual team members rather than emphasising conformance to rigid processes and tools. This is achieved by building on trust and communication through regular face-to-face interaction between relevant stakeholders. Instead of relying on extensive documentation, the manifesto recommends short iterations of working software as the key indication of progress. This provides feedback to the development team and the customer representative. Having continuous customer collaboration throughout the project removes the need for extensive contract negotiation before the project commences. In turn, when change does occur it is embraced. These principles help to fulfil the ability to remain flexible and respond to change rather than the rigidity of adherence to a predefined plan. Regular customer feedback contributes toward high levels of adaptability where requirements can be regularly clarified and prioritized, according to *current business value* during development.

### *1.3.3.1 Agile requirements development*

To help overcome the problems associated with plan-driven development, AMs recommend Active Stakeholder Participation (ASP), a highly participative and iterative approach to requirements development (Ambler 2002). Initially, requirements are briefly documented through *user stories*. User stories represent a high level user request written by the customer on an index card or post-it note. Other relevant information such as story title, release date, order of priority, developers initials and time estimates are also included. Developers estimate how long the stories will take to complete and select the appropriate release dates. The customer then prioritizes each story according to business value. During iteration planning the stories depending on the order of priority are divided into iterations. During development, each story is then used to provoke an in-depth discussion between developers and the customer representative to examine each requirement in further detail (Astels *et al.* 2002).

### *1.3.3.2 Challenges for the customer role*

One oversight with early AMs included that customer involvement was often reduced to a single on-site customer with little guidance provided on how to implement this role. Many authors have expressed the importance of having the appropriate and relevant stakeholders on board, and strong customer involvement is needed for AMs to succeed (Chow and Cao D.B. 2008). For instance, in distinguishing between traditional and agile RE practice, Cao L. and Ramesh (2008) found that the "inability to gain access to the customer and obtaining consensus among stakeholder groups" were the most common challenges experienced in industry. New techniques have also been called for to support developers in understanding user needs (Kujala 2003).

Martin *et al.* (2009a) report a set of additional roles employed in successful projects to help facilitate *real customer involvement*. The authors illustrate the complexity of customer representation, identifying ten roles on a customer team, which had been informally created after little prior guidance existed to support the customer role. Each person on the customer team negotiates with and represents a widely diverse group of stakeholders.

In examining critical success factors in software development, Boehm and Turner (2003) found that customer representatives should be Collaborative, Representative, Authorised, Committed and Knowledgeable (CRACK), deeming these crucial attributes that customer representatives should possess in successfully implementing the role. This strongly suggests that performing the customer role in agile software development presents a challenging task. Also, it is considerably less than straightforward to determine which qualities stakeholder representatives possess during early encounters with the software development team.

## 1.4 Toward an evolutionary approach

With reference to existing approaches to the problem, the issues that must be addressed are as follows. For real customer involvement, practical support is needed for the emergence of relevant stakeholder representatives from the business domain, ideally those possessing CRACK skills and abilities. A suitable user involvement strategy must be developed to support ongoing ASP and self-organisation during team-customer interactions. This should consider support required to identify, negotiate and resolve conflict in order to assist stakeholders in developing consensus as early as possible in the development process.

It is also necessary to amalgamate multiple diverse stakeholder viewpoints into a collective and representative perspective of the problem to be addressed. This is important for the provision of accurate contextual detail needed during implementation. The development of a common language must also be addressed in order to promote mutual understanding between business and technology domains. This in turn will strengthen support needed for efficient and effective team-customer communication throughout development. This work examines the process of requirements elicitation and how this activity is generally conducted. The main objective is to create a novel evolutionary framework to facilitate requirements elicitation and link this to ongoing development in order to support the customer role, thereby enhancing AMs.

A framework can be defined as *"the identification and categorisation of processes or steps that constitute a complex task"* (Carnes 2011). An evolutionary framework can be described as a structure that is flexible enabling the steps to evolve according to the needs of the project. For example, the steps or indeed the sequence in which they commence can *change* when applied to *specific* development contexts. A framework may evolve in practice if in the first instance this supports a mutually beneficial outcome for the project. Essentially, this depends on the specific needs of the stakeholder group involved, the project context and the type of problem to be addressed.

To illustrate the proposed solution and to clarify some of the efficiency issues that may be involved, a specific evolutionary group interaction technique, Open Space Technology (OST) (Owen 1995), is offered together with a specific agile approach, eXtreme Programming (XP). As such, this work proposes a 3-phase framework, called OpenXP, which is developed to facilitate the link between the customer role and the development team in XP.

OpenXP is an evolutionary framework specifically designed to support the role of the customer during requirements elicitation in XP-based agile software development. The goal of OpenXP is to successfully combine *collaborative interaction* with *effective communication* between *relevant business stakeholders* on agile software projects. Originally, OpenXP was developed as part of a Ph.D. dissertation to address the numerous reports which highlight the significant difficulties experienced with the development of requirements in software projects. This solution is a 3-phased approach that consists of four broader facets presenting a unique combination of existing techniques and methodologies, which have been integrated into a unified framework in order to better facilitate the link between the customer role and the software development team in agile projects.

The first phase supports an initial OST investigation defining a collective and agreed upon understanding for the problem to be addressed. The third phase initiates XP activities associated with the creation of a Release Plan and User Stories, followed by the detailed definition of iterations and their implementation. Integrating OST and XP is a bridging phase, in which specific business improvement scenarios are identified as outputs generated from the OST investigation. The scenarios then serve as inputs for the creation of User Stories as part of the XP development method during phase three. This approach essentially combines the collection of values, principles and practices that link OST with XP through the use of scenarios. The novelty here is in the unique combination of OST, scenarios and XP in developing a framework that evolves during enactment according to the circumstances and constraints of specific development contexts.

## 1.5 Document Outline

The remaining sections of this book are organised as follows. Chapter two presents the research design adopted throughout this work with the justification for the specific strategy selected. Chapter three focuses on the current literature in RE. This presents an in-depth synthesis of existing RE approaches, techniques and methodologies with a particular focus on the key challenges reported for each. Three case studies have also been conducted for the purposes of this research, first an exploratory case study was conducted and this is presented in detail in chapter four.

Chapter five concentrates on explaining the OST interaction technique, while Chapter six focuses on drawing both the philosophical and practical links that can be made between OST and XP. This is followed by a short introduction to the two confirmatory case studies which were subsequently conducted to test the OpenXP framework. The confirmatory case studies are then presented in chapters seven and eight respectively.

An expert evaluation of the OpenXP framework is detailed in chapter nine where two relevant industry practitioners provide valuable feedback on the potential for the framework to be applied in practice. Chapter ten then concentrates on putting all the elements of the framework together, this includes focusing on the four broader OpenXP facets that underpin the framework as a whole. Finally Chapter eleven concludes with the key findings that have emerged throughout this work. This also discusses the research limitations and validity and provides specific recommendations for when OpenXP can be applied in practice.

## 1.6 Summary

Chapter one identifies an important research problem surrounding the issues of concern in requirements development. Plan-driven development is ideal when project requirements are well understood but lacks flexibility in situations where requirements change. AMs work iteratively overcoming this problem but challenges pointing toward people issues such as conflicting priorities, understanding the wider context of requirements and communication problems are still widely reported. AMs have the potential to improve on some of the shortcomings, however, support for the role of the customer is needed especially where this role involves multiple diverse representatives. A solution with the potential to address this problem is introduced and this suggests a collaborative group interaction technique OST, combined with a flexible software development method XP to support the link between suitable business representatives and the development team during elicitation. OST has been recommended for stakeholder collaboration, requirements elicitation and improved domain understanding during software development projects.

# Chapter 2 Research Design

## 2.1 Overview

This chapter presents the research methods section detailing commonly used approaches to research design and highlighting the differences and similarities between each. Potential research strategies for the purposes of this work are investigated and the following points then present the justification for the specific methodology selected.

## 2.2 Research Setting

This research has focused on the elicitation of requirements for the development of bespoke software solutions involving small development teams.

### 2.2.1 Research Question

The research question to be investigated here is:

*How can an evolutionary framework be developed to improve the facilitation of agile requirements elicitation?*

The research investigations which contributed towards the formulation of this question are detailed in the literature review in chapter three, the exploratory case study detailed in chapter four and the OST section presented in chapter five.

This research question has been examined by fulfilling the following set of aims and objectives.

### 2.2.2 Aims

- Develop an acute awareness of the issues to be addressed in requirements elicitation;

- Develop an increased understanding of the customer role in agile software development methods;

- Provide agile practitioners with a novel approach to obtain a contextual account of problem space needs to support the role of the customer in collaborative decision making.

### 2.2.3 Objectives

1. Investigate and classify the factors that affect the communication of requirements between developers and other stakeholders;

This first objective aims to gain a greater appreciation for the process of requirements elicitation in research and in practice.

2.  Investigate and classify agile software development approaches with particular relevance to the customer role;

    The second objective aims to develop a deeper understanding of agile software development methods focusing on the link with the customer role in communicating requirements between business and technology domains.

3.  Develop a suitable solution;

    Based upon the results of objectives one and two, an evolutionary framework is developed to support requirements elicitation in agile software projects.

4.  Evaluate the solution in an appropriate environment;

    The proposed solution is evaluated through two case studies with feedback obtained through observations, questionnaires and interviews. Two independent industry-based reviews are conducted in order to validate the framework.

## 2.3 Philosophical Perspectives

It is necessary prior to embarking on research to acknowledge the philosophical perspective that has influenced the research undertaken. Philosophical stances in research can vary depending on the perspective of the researcher, the nature of phenomena and the subject(s) under study. This is important to recognise since the type of knowledge that will be contributed can be clearly identified from the outset (Saunders *et al.* 2009).

### 2.3.1 Positivism

The *positivist* perspective focuses on the systematic verification of existing hypotheses based upon a set of directly observable facts (Guba and Lincoln 1994). The approach can be adopted when formal propositions have been identified, specific variables can be quantified, with results then logically derived from testing the predefined hypothesis or theory (Runeson and Host 2008). The positivist stance is therefore not adopted where hypothesis have not yet been developed and where the research problem includes a set of potentially unknown factors that are not directly observable for quantification. As such, this stance does not represent the research carried out here.

### 2.3.2 Realism

The *realist* perspective is closely aligned with the positivist view since it adopts a similar perspective of controlled deduction of measurable variables via predefined hypotheses (Saunders *et al.* 2009). The realist perspective holds that an objective and collective view of reality is wholly representative of truth. This philosophical viewpoint has been divided into two categories. Direct realism claims that the world is accurately portrayed by what is experienced by the senses (Saunders *et al.* 2009). Critical realism claims that what is perceived through the senses can be distorted causing a less than accurate picture of reality to prevail (Saunders *et al.* 2009). Due to the fact that realism also takes a hypothesis driven deductive approach, similarly to positivism, the stance is not considered representative of the research conducted here.

### 2.3.3 Pragmatism

The *pragmatist* perspective asserts that the practical application of research is driven primarily by the research question and that the choices made in a research design reflect primarily on the research problem being examined (Saunders *et al.* 2009). This supports the adoption of mixed methods which can be used to complement each other in designing a research strategy to befit a specific problem. A clear advantage for the pragmatic approach is that triangulation can be achieved by using mixed methods with the benefits of strengthening support for the results. The research problem described in this work was the primary catalyst for determining how the research would later be conducted. With consideration for the mixed methods also employed (described later), the research stance adopted for this work could be described as pragmatic.

### 2.3.4 Interpretivism

The *interpretivist* perspective aligns closely with *constructivism* since each focus on the process by which meaning is created, negotiated, sustained and modified (Andrews 2012). As such the interpretive perspective values how humans perceive, understand and interpret their world seeking to acquire meaning based upon this (Klein and Myers 1999). The research stance adopted for this work can be described as interpretive since data collected include synthesis of participants' understanding of how requirements elicitation is conducted in practice. Later, participant experiences in using the proposed solution also contribute. This stance is an appropriate approximation given that the factors contributing to this research problem are not fully understood and participant experiences that provide further insights are considerably valued.

## 2.4 Research Approaches

### 2.4.1 Deductive Research

Quantitative research takes a deductive approach where first hypotheses are drawn from a set of quantifiable dependent and independent variables identified in the research site. This approach gradually produces results using statistical analysis to measure the relationships between variables including how each reacts given a certain set of measurable circumstances (Trochim 2002). Fundamentally, quantitative research is concerned with data that can be quantified numerically, whereas qualitative research adds a contextual dimension providing rich descriptions that are not easily measured using quantitative methods alone (Trochim 2002).

### 2.4.2 Inductive Research

While quantitative research primarily focuses specifically on *what* can be measured, qualitative research, on the other hand, concentrates on *why* or *how* phenomena occur. The two methods differ in that while quantitative methods take a hypothesis driven deductive approach to research, qualitative methods take an inductive approach, where hypotheses can be drawn more toward the end of, or pending the outcome of the research conducted (Creswell 2009). Qualitative research investigates phenomena not directly measurable using quantitative methods alone. This research is inductive with results emerging over time hence a predominantly qualitative approach is taken.

### 2.4.3 Research Choices

Research choices fall into three categories, mono-method, multi-method and mixed method research (Saunders *et al.* 2009). For mono-methods, the data collection and analysis procedures conducted are either quantitative or qualitative. Multi-methods are employed if a study utilizes both quantitative and qualitative approaches. However, qualitative data collected can only be analysed using qualitative analysis and likewise, quantitative data collected can only be analysed using quantitative forms of analysis (Saunders *et al.* 2009). Mixed methods use both quantitative and qualitative approaches. However, this choice permits qualitative data collected to be analysed numerically (or quantitatively) and quantitative data collected may be analysed thematically (or qualitatively). Mixed methods also include a mixed model approach in which a research instrument, for instance, a questionnaire can include both quantitatively measured (multiple choice) and qualitatively measured (open-ended) question sets (Burke Johnson and Onwuegbuzie 2004).

For the purposes of this research, a mixed methods approach employing a mixed model research instrument uses both quantitative and qualitative strategies in addressing the research question. However, it should be noted that the methodology leans more towards the qualitative approach. The mixed model instrument (detailed later) is applied in a confirmatory capacity toward the latter part of the research conducted here.

## 2.5 Time Horizons

Time horizons classify whether research has been conducted over short or longer periods. As such, this falls into two categories, cross-sectional or longitudinal studies (Saunders *et al.* 2009). Cross-sectional studies are categorised as short term where research is conducted over a fixed or limited period of time. Longitudinal studies on the other hand conduct research over prolonged periods of time. This is suitable when it is possible and beneficial to monitor the subject(s) where long term gradual changes or the impact of a treatment can be measured overtime (Saunders *et al.* 2009). This research can be classified as cross-sectional since time constraints had influence over this considering that academic settings were used and the time available for practitioner participants involved, was also limited.

## 2.6 Research Strategies

Under qualitative research, seven main research strategies are commonly employed (Saunders *et al.* 2009). The suitability of each, for the purposes of this work is examined in the following section.

### 2.6.1 Experiment

Experimental research is a hypothesis driven deductive approach, appropriate when a set of dependent and independent variables can be detected, channelled and measured in a controlled environment (Creswell 2009). Generally an experiment group and a control group are defined, both follow an identical procedure however, during the procedure, the experiment group is deliberately exposed to a different treatment, the effect of which is then carefully measured (Saunders *et al.* 2009). Experimental design seeks to isolate the direct impact one variable may have on another, having being exposed to the specific treatment. Here, *cause* and *effect* relationships can be determined using quantitative research methods. A disadvantage is that the conditions must exist where all variables can be fully controlled in order to prove that the treatment given to the experiment group was actually responsible for the experimental result (Saunders *et al.* 2009). In cases where not all variables are known as is the case with this research, experimental research is considered not suitable.

### 2.6.2 Survey

Surveys are often used as quantitative strategy where a standard or uniform set of questions are designed, this can generate a set of responses that are relatively straight forward to categorise later during the analysis stage (Saunders *et al.* 2009). The survey strategy can also include instrumentation such as structured interviews (Saunders *et al.* 2009). Survey research can be an effective strategy for acquiring data from large numbers of respondents in a cost effective and timely manner. Surveying respondents entails collecting and statistically measuring data, and with a focused sample, results that emerge can later be generalised into a broader population (Creswell 2009). Survey research is considered a useful means to triangulate other sources of data (Saunders *et al.* 2009). This can help to determine relationships between concepts and ideas when a number of other sources of information are used. Under this strategy questionnaires have been selected as an appropriate method used during this research.

### 2.6.3 Ethnography

Ethnography is a form of qualitative research which originally stemmed from anthropological studies with the aim of more fully understanding the socio-cultural properties pertaining to a research setting (Atkinson and Hammersley 2007). Generally, ethnographers can spend a prolonged period of time becoming involved with the issues being experienced in their natural setting. Rich descriptions of participant experiences can be sought using strategies such as participant-observation, interviews and artefact collection in order to develop a holistic viewpoint of the issue being investigated (Atkinson and Hammersley 2007).

In particular, ethnography is used as a means to provide empirical context for the purposes of examining less well understood phenomena. However, the approach is typically longitudinal which can be time consuming and participants must be comfortable with the researcher immersing themselves for prolonged periods of time in their natural setting, also, it must be clear in advance that in using the strategy the research question and objectives can be fulfilled (Saunders *et al.* 2009). In the context of this research, the ethnographic strategy may restrict what can be observed to within a single organisation or setting, ethnography is thus considered unsuitable for this work. Although, it should be noted that techniques under the ethnographic strategy are employed, however, this is not considered ethnographic research due to the fact that this is conducted over shorter more limited periods of time in a cross-sectional context.

## 2.6.4 Action Research

Action research involves the researcher taking an active participatory role in the research setting. This includes carefully monitoring, documenting and analysing events that occur surrounding an issue to be investigated often in a real life working environment. The aim of the strategy is to positively influence the issue being examined where outcome of the research expects to change the existing situation through improvements recommended by the research carried out (Saunders *et al.* 2009). Conducting action research requires that researchers are actively involved in the everyday tasks being carried out where planning, observation and reflection continuously occur throughout the period of the study (Kemmis and McTaggart 2005). The strategy is considered a somewhat practical application of research which involves *"action, evaluation, critical reflection and based on the evidence gathered changes in practice are then implemented"* (Koshy *et al.* 2010). Here, outcomes including the improvements to be made from the results of an action research study are applied to the specific situational context rather than generalised across broader contexts.

For the purposes of this work, action research is not considered suitable since this strategy would limit the authors understanding of how requirements are elicited to within a single organisation or setting. For instance, this particular strategy may not provide a representative understanding of how requirements are elicited outside of the context of a specific location or setting, the approach is therefore considered unsuitable for the purposes of this research.

## 2.6.5 Grounded Theory

Grounded theory emerged as a research method through the work of Strauss and Glaser (1967) where it was first implemented in the social sciences. The strategy has since evolved through a number of versions that differ from the original implementation, typically known as the *Classic grounded theory* approach (Strauss & Corbin 1998), (Charmaz 2006), (Clarke 2005). Regardless of which variation of the approach is employed, a common set of practices characterise grounded theory research. These are: coding procedures (open, theoretical, axial, selective) used to disseminate, analyse and re-assemble data into a coherent understanding of the phenomena under investigation. Constant comparison is used to continuously compare and contrast emerging themes and categories grounded as data are collected. Memoing encourages the researcher to continuously examine emerging ideas by recording potential insights into the research question which are gradually developed and refined over time as the study proceeds toward completion. Theoretical sampling aims to target a specific sample considered adequately representative of the topic under investigation. Theoretical saturation has been reached when no new information emerges about the research question being investigated.

However, effectively achieving theoretical saturation is described a difficult task *"even for experienced researchers"* (Suddaby 2006). It has also been acknowledged that the positioning of the literature review in a grounded theory study has posed a number of practical problems in Ph.D. research (Glaser 1998), (Nathaniel 2006), (McGhee et al. 2007), (Dunne 2011). For example, grounded theory is difficult to implement:

> *"for Ph.D. students whose research funding, ethical approval and progression through the doctoral process is heavily dependent upon producing a detailed literature review prior to commencing primary data collection and analysis"* (Dunne 2011).

For this reason, grounded theory was not considered a suitable choice, particularly due to the fact that the research conducted in this work was originally developed as part of a doctoral research project.

## 2.6.6 Archival Research

Archival research is a strategy that utilizes existing documented records and artefacts as a primary source of data collected from the research setting. Saunders *et al.* (2009) argue that as a secondary source of data, archival records have originally been collected for a separate purpose, and although this can provide factual evidence, existing artefacts may be incomplete. This is important since it is necessary to determine from the outset if data relating to the research question can be obtained. In relation to third party usage of such data, issues of privacy and confidentiality may need to be established and addressed upfront (Saunders *et al.* 2009). Archival research can be a useful strategy where access to existing records is possible and the approach can benefit triangulation of results when used in conjunction with multiple sources of information (Easterbrook and Aranda 2006).

Archival research is however, not considered a suitable strategy for this research due to the fact that it may only reveal information that has been documented on the research problem. For instance, this research is focused on studying the process of elicitation and considering that many aspects of this problem may not be documented as yet, using archival research alone, in this context, could risk overlooking important aspects surrounding the problem under investigation.

## 2.6.7 Case Study

Case study research is defined as a strategy used to *"explore in-depth a program, event, activity, process, or one or more individuals"* (Creswell 2009). This strategy is used in situations where questions such as *how* and *why* need to be addressed. In particular, the case study approach has been recommended where the issue to be investigated does not exist in isolation from its context. In this sense the approach is best used when the topic is said to be bound by the context in which it occurs (Yin 1994, 2003), (Stake 1995), (Robson 2002). A strong advantage of case study research is that the collection of multiple sources of data are encouraged to support the triangulation of results. Easterbrook *et al.* (2008) distinguish between *exploratory* and *confirmatory* case studies. The former can be conducted during early investigations into phenomena, where hypotheses are not immediately clear and often drawn later to build theories. The latter expects fixed propositions to begin with where existing theories can then be confirmed. Single cases can investigate phenomena in-depth often bound to the specific context, while multiple cases show consistencies across more than one case with potential to increase validity. Considering the nature of the research problem being investigated here, the case study approach was considered the most suitable strategy. The following section presents the justification for this.

## 2.6.8 Justification for the use of Case Study research

Case studies are considered an appropriate strategy for the purposes of evaluating a software process (Kitchenham *et al.* 1997). This is considered suitable for this work since a focus on *process,* namely how requirements are elicited, could be maintained by studying the context in which this occurs across a variety of real world settings. A clear advantage is that different types of case studies can be applied depending on the nature of the investigation and this research required an initial exploratory phase to develop a more comprehensive understanding of requirements elicitation. To advance further in the field other types of case study including multiple cases could equally be employed. This suggests case study research as a suitable strategy for this research.

Three case studies were conducted during the course of this research. First an exploratory case study took place, and two confirmatory case studies were subsequently conducted. This consisted of collecting both primary and secondary sources of data. Secondary sources involved a review of the literature (Chapter 3) which helped to formulate the research question, aims and objectives. Primary data were then collected using participant-observation, interviews, direct observations, questionnaires and physical artefacts; this is explained in detail in section 2.8.

## 2.7 Case study sources of data

Case studies require multiple sources of data which are used to support the triangulation of results. These include documentation, archival records, interviews, direct observations, participant-observation and physical artefacts (Easterbrook *et al.* 2008). The specific sources used for data collection in this research are illustrated in Figure 1 and presented in greater detail in the following sections.

Figure 1 represents the research map where multiple sources of data were used during the three case studies conducted throughout the course of this work.

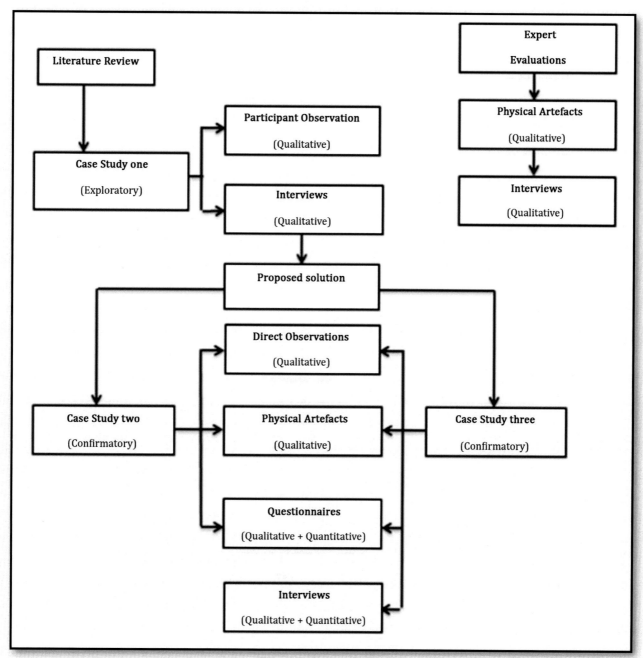

*Figure 1 Research Map*

## 2.7.1 Participant Observation

Two types of observation are discussed by Saunders *et al.* (2009). These are participant observation and direct observation. Participant observation is a technique that enables the researcher to directly observe events taking part in the activities being studied in the research setting. The technique originally stemmed from ethnographic research where the role has typically been used by researchers to act as independent observers in order to better understand the context surrounding the activities being studied in the research setting (Atkinson and Hammersley 2007).

In the context of an ethnographic study, participant observation is typically longitudinal taking place over long periods of time. However, the approach can also be conducted over shorter periods of time. Considering that this research is classified as cross-sectional, participant-observation was considered appropriate during the first exploratory case study (detailed in Chapter 4). This provided an opportunity to develop additional context about the role of the customer and the challenges experienced for an agile team.

## 2.7.2 Direct Observations

Unlike participant observation, direct observations do not involve the researcher partaking in the research setting. Rather, direct observations are passively recorded by documenting the activities that take place during the study. As noted by Saunders *et al.* (2009) it is important to maintain minimal interaction with participants throughout. Direct observations were used as a method to record the activities and interactions between participants that took place during each working session throughout both confirmatory case studies conducted.

## 2.7.3 Interviews

Interviews are a commonly used technique in case study research as a means to obtain rich descriptions of participant experiences. Generally, interviews can be unstructured, structured or semi-structured. For structured interviews a fixed question set is adhered to throughout with the same set of questions asked during each interview. Semi-structured interviews are used where some structure is needed to direct a general line of inquiry but this implementation enables researchers to also deviate if, for instance, the interviewee should mention something of potential interest to the research objectives that was not originally anticipated (Turner 2010). Semi-structured interviews can also inform a more structured approach that could be used as a follow up to responses. Interview questions can be *closed* requiring a response within a specific range, or *open ended* encouraging a more elaborate response from participants to emerge.

For the purposes of this work, semi-structured open ended interviews were used during the exploratory case study (Chapter 4), the second confirmatory study (Chapter 8) and the expert evaluations (Chapter 9). In the second confirmatory study, interview design included a single question which used the likert scale (Denscombe 2003) to weight responses. The likert scale was selected since this approach enables a weighted response to be determined. This is also beneficial for clearly determining extent to which participants agree or disagree with a given statement. The semi-structured interviewing technique provided a means for participants to elaborate on experiences in using the proposed solution, OpenXP. The structure of the interviews conducted is further detailed in section 2.8.2.

## 2.7.4 Questionnaires

Questionnaires are a research instrument in which a fixed set of questions are answered by a wide range of participants. The level of rigor in the design of questions asked is determined by the researcher and this generally depends on the matter to be investigated. For instance, a *closed* or *fixed* set of questions might take the form of multiple choice responses, one of which can be chosen by participants. This can be particularly useful for the purposes of analysis, however, on the other hand designing responses in this manner can also be a disadvantage as participant responses are constrained within a fixed and predefined set.

In the context of this research questionnaires were employed for the confirmatory case studies (Chapters 7 and 8) to obtain feedback from participants. A mixed-model approach was considered appropriate here since the nature of the instrument was to confirm the set of propositions that emerged from the literature review and the exploratory case study. The Likert scale was used to weight participant responses and after each question additional space was also provided for participants to further elaborate on their responses where necessary. The instrument also included a number of open-ended questions. This was helpful for encouraging participants to provide further contextual information surrounding their choice of response. This is explained in further detail in section 2.8.3.

### 2.7.5 Physical Artefacts

Physical artefacts commonly form part of, and contribute to, the analysis process during case study research (Easterbrook and Aranda 2006). Studying artefacts produced by participants contributes to the researchers understanding and subsequent analysis of the subject of research.

For the two confirmatory case studies physical artefacts were generated by participants as part of the process of implementing XP. Here, user stories written on index cards were organised by participants and placed on flipchart sheets of paper. Subsequently the artefacts produced were photographed. Also the order in which stories were implemented was depicted using flipcharts, which showed iteration plans indicating progression during the two projects along a timeline.

Physical artefacts were also photographed where the OpenXP framework was implemented. Here, in addition to the XP artefacts, A4 sheets of paper and flipcharts containing contextual information which captured the output produced from phases one and two were also photographed. These artefacts provided additional context which helped to visualise progression made by participants. The structure of the physical artefacts produced is detailed later in section 2.8.4.

## 2.8 Defining the research instrument

An initial exploratory study was suitable since it was necessary to develop a deeper understanding of the problem context surrounding the challenges reported in the literature and to determine how the process of requirements elicitation is conducted in practice. Also, a greater appreciation was needed for developing an increased understanding for how the customer role is performed. This entailed collecting data surrounding the interactions between developers and other stakeholders including the customer representative during elicitation. From an empirical perspective, first-hand practitioner experience presented an invaluable opportunity to collect information with the potential to describe the embedded context in which these interactions occur.

## 2.8.1 The Components of Case Study Research

Yin (1994) divides case study research into five components, these are explained in the following points:

1. The research questions;

2. Propositions;

3. Units of analysis;

4. Logic linking data to propositions;

5. Criteria for interpreting the findings.

First, the *research question* is generally known in advance and used to derive a set of *propositions* that guide and direct the research. However, an exploratory case study can often proceed without an initial set of propositions due to the fact that propositions are more likely to emerge as an outcome (Easterbrook and Aranda 2006). Propositions consist of a set of statements that a case study aims to examine. The *unit of analysis* provides the centre focus, which drives the study. The *logic* then links the data to the set of propositions and the *criteria for interpreting the results* are defined in advance.

In this research, secondary data collected from an initial review of the literature, contributed toward the formulation of the research question set out in section 2.2.1. In accordance with the first two aims listed in section 2.2.2 the literature indicated that the issues to be addressed in requirements represented a set of overlapping problems that predominantly surrounded people related issues in requirements elicitation. This appeared mainly to relate to the communication and understanding of requirements. Significantly, challenges for the role of the customer in AMs set out in section 1.3.3 required a more comprehensive understanding be developed.

To achieve this, the author played the role of participant-observer on an agile project, an opportunity that assisted in developing an in-depth appreciation for the roles and challenges for an agile team. In order to develop a deeper understanding of these problems, in their context, an industry-based study was also conducted. These steps collected primary data which provided additional information that contributed toward addressing the first two objectives set out in section 2.2.3. In accordance with the case study approach to research, a set of propositions emerged as a result of the literature review and the initial exploratory case study. This formed the basis for two confirmatory case studies which were later conducted. The confirmatory case studies addressed the third aim set out in section 2.2.2 and the third and fourth objectives listed in section 2.2.3.

In this research the unit of analysis focused on *the process of how requirements are elicited* which helped to focus the research question on determining how an evolutionary framework could be developed to improve the facilitation of agile requirements elicitation. With consideration for the proposed solution, propositions that subsequently emerged from the completion of the literature review and the first exploratory case study are as follows:

1.  Activities conducted prior to phase three would not be difficult for developers to understand and would not introduce a steep learning curve;

2.  Developers would use the framework steps as described;

3.  Activities conducted prior to phase three would assist the team in understanding the problem background;

4.  Artefacts generated prior to phase three can produce agile models;

5.  Artefacts generated prior to phase three would provide additional context for communicating the project status to an outside stakeholder.

For both confirmatory studies, the unit of analysis remained focused on how requirements are elicited and the aim of the first confirmatory study was to examine if the first three propositions were true. The second confirmatory study tested the fourth and fifth propositions and retested the second proposition. The criteria for interpreting the findings involved comparing the multiple sources of data collected, developing the logic behind this and determining whether the propositions set out at the start were proved or not. The exploratory case study is presented in chapter 4 and the confirmatory case studies are then detailed in chapter 7 and 8 respectively.

## 2.8.2 Structure of Interviews

An interview protocol was initially established for the interviews conducted in industry. This consisted of participant information which included the purpose of the study, the expected duration for each interview, a statement ensuring confidentiality, the declaration of informed consent and background information collected from participants in advance of each interview. Data were recorded during each interview and later transcribed.

Due to the flexible nature of semi-structured interviewing, this was considered an appropriate technique for the first exploratory case study during the industry-based interviews. The interview guide consisted of semi-structured open ended questions focusing on the process of eliciting requirements in practice. This was divided into two subsections. The first set of questions specifically focused on objective one shown in Figure 2:

> **Objective 1:** *Investigate and classify the factors that affect the communication of requirements between developers and other stakeholders*

*Figure 2 Objective one*

The second section of the interview guide focused on probing the role of the customer as part of objective two as shown in Figure 3:

**Objective 2:** *Investigate and classify agile software development approaches with particular relevance to the customer role*

*Figure 3 Objective two*

Prior to the development of specific open ended questions, a general question focus was first established which helped to guide the direction of inquiry and to maintain focus on the process of how requirements are elicited in practice. The design of questions thus involved developing the following different types of questions as recommended by Kvale (1996) (Examples of actual questions asked are illustrated for demonstration here in quotes and italics).

- Introducing questions – *"Could you explain to me about how requirements are elicited?"*

- Follow up questions – "nodding, mm, repeating significant words"

- Specifying questions – *"What did you do when you realised that the requirements were not what the stakeholders wanted?"*

- Direct questions – *"Have you ever experienced a situation where stakeholders were not the most appropriate people to involve on a project?"*

- Indirect questions *"In your opinion, what impact did this have on the project?"*

- Structuring questions *"I would now like to focus on customer involvement on projects"*

- Silence – carefully pause to give interviewees enough time to answer by breaking silence themselves;

- Interpreting questions – *"Would it be accurate to say that meetings are used?"*

Lutters and Seaman (2007) argue for a storytelling approach known as a *"war stories"* interviewing technique to be incorporated in qualitative software engineering research. Probed in the context of eliciting requirements, this was adopted in the design of a number of questions in the interview guide, two examples are shown as follows:

- *"Could you tell me about a time when communication was successfully channelled?"*

- *"Could you tell me about a time when communication broke down or was constrained?"*

The duration for each interview was approximately one hour in length. Interviews were recorded and transcribed and the summary of responses for each interview was later verified by participants.

### 2.8.2.1 Industry interviews setting

The research setting involved nine participants all of whom specialised in a combination of engineering, developing and testing requirements for bespoke software solutions. Table 1 shows each participant, the number of years of experience alongside where their primary experience lay. Also included in Table 1 are the specific markets for each participant. This spanned across the Telecommunications, Health Care and Pharmaceuticals, Transportation, Industrial Goods and Services and Consumer Services segments.

*Table 1 Industry study participants*

| Company Pseudonyms | Participant Pseudonyms | Experience in Years | Primary Experience | Market Sector |
|---|---|---|---|---|
| SoftCo | Andrew | Eleven | RE | Telecommunications, Transportation, Financial |
| Flyberg Technologies | Marcus | Twenty-one | RE | Industrial goods and services |
| Optimal Development | Elaine | Four | RE | Financial, Telecommunications, Consumer services |
| VeriTech | Rachel | Five | RE | Financial |
| Smart Solutions | Greg | Eighteen | Test Management | Industrial goods and services |
| NA | Karl | Eleven | RE | Financial |
| | David | Sixteen | RE | Healthcare & pharmaceuticals |
| TrentCo | Oran | Fifteen | Development, Testing | Financial |
| | Alex | Twenty-four | Test Management | Financial |

### 2.8.2.2 Confirmatory case study three interviews

In addition to the feedback from observations and questionnaires, interviews were also conducted with participants in the third confirmatory case study. The open-ended semi-structured interview format was also used. The XP-only team were asked four open ended questions. The OpenXP team were asked five open ended questions and for one question participants were asked to rate responses according to the likert scale (Denscombe 2003).

### 2.8.2.3 Expert interviews

Two expert interviews were conducted in order to validate the OpenXP framework. The interview guide consisted of twenty two questions. The expert participants provided feedback on each step in the OpenXP framework for both confirmatory case studies conducted. This exercise also provided a synthesis of expert opinion on how the framework might perform if it were to be applied in industrial practice.

## 2.8.3 Structure of the questionnaires

Questionnaires were considered the most appropriate technique for collecting feedback from participants in both confirmatory case studies. For these studies, the XP-only team were required to answer eleven questions while the OpenXP team answered seventeen. Extra questions included for OpenXP focused on collecting data specifically in relation to using OpenXP. The Likert scale was used to determine a weighted response which indicates the average opinion from participants. The order in which responses were organised is as follows: 1 [Strongly Disagree], 2 [Disagree], 3 [neutral], 4 [agree], 5 [Strongly Agree]. The questionnaires also included extra space for the participants to elaborate on each response where necessary. A number of open-ended questions were also included. One question for the OpenXP team required a binary response.

## 2.8.4 Structure of the physical artefacts

During both confirmatory case studies the physical artefacts generated were also collected. For the OpenXP team, phase one artefacts consisted of the themes, the four principles, the law of mobility and the concerns raised by the participants. During phase two flipchart and A4 sheets consisting of the improvements generated from phase one and scenarios were also collected. Phase three artefacts consisted of the user stories created, design artefacts and the iteration plan for each project. Photographs were also taken of each artefact generated throughout the course of both confirmatory studies. The structure of the artefacts produced from each phase are shown in Table 2.

*Table 2 Artefacts produced during each phase*

| Phase One | | Phase Two | | Phase Three | |
|---|---|---|---|---|---|
| Theme | Principles | | | User Stories | Design Models |
| | | Improvements | Scenarios | | |
| Law | Concerns | | | Iteration Plan | |

## 2.8.5 Relationship between the Case Studies

For the remainder of this book, chapters 4, 7 and 8 present the three case studies conducted. For each case study, the single unit of analysis remained focused *the process of how requirements are elicited* as this is a central aspect of the research question.

Chapter 4 presents the exploratory case study which addresses the process of how requirements are elicited in practice. This is achieved by assessing requirements elicitation, first from the perspectives of a small agile team in a student setting, and second, from the perspectives of nine practitioners operating in bespoke software engineering in industry. The findings from both the literature review and the exploratory case study inform the design of five propositions which are then later tested using the two confirmatory case studies as detailed in chapters 7 and 8 respectively.

In relation to how the studies link with the propositions, chapter 7 presents the first confirmatory case study. This tests the first three propositions which focus on (i) assessing the learning curve for developers in understanding and using OST, (ii) the extent to which developers adhere to the nine framework steps as described, and (iii) assessing whether activities conducted in OST, prior to phase three, would assist the team in understanding the problem background.

Chapter 8 then presents the second confirmatory study, this re-tests the second proposition, namely whether developers adhere to the nine framework steps as described. Proposition four is assessed and this is focused on determining the extent to which the artefacts produced by participants could be described as agile models. Finally, proposition five tests whether the OST artefacts generated prior to phase three, can provide additional context for communicating the project status to an unexpected outside stakeholder joining the project late.

Overall, the propositions are linked to the process of elicitation as the main unit of analysis in the case studies since they focus primarily on communication and understanding as an important part of elicitation, and the extent to which tangible artefacts produced can seamlessly integrate as agile models for creating user stories as part of the XP development process.

## 2.8.6 Summary

In summary, as shown in Table 3, this research began with a pragmatic interpretivist perspective. An inductive approach was used which enabled results to gradually emerge over time. The specific strategy consisted of cross-sectional case study research. Among multiple sources of data collected, this also included survey instrumentation. The specific sources of data for objectives one and two were fulfilled in part by conducting a review of the literature. This was followed by an exploratory case study which also contributed to fulfilling the first two objectives. The specific sources of data for the exploratory study consisted of open-ended semi-structured interviews conducted with practitioners in industry. The second objective was also fulfilled in part via participant observation conducted separately with an agile team in a student setting. The third objective was fulfilled solely based upon the findings from the literature review and the exploratory case study. Finally, the fourth objective was addressed by conducting two confirmatory case studies.

The sources of data for these studies consisted of mixed model questionnaires, direct observations, physical artefacts and mixed model interviews. Separately, interviews were also conducted for the expert evaluation as part of the fourth objective; however, an open-ended semi-structured mono-method was employed here. The physical artefacts produced by the participants from both confirmatory studies were also used as part of the demonstration during the expert validation.

*Table 3 Research design*

| Perspective and Approach | Strategy | Type | Sources of data | Objective 1 | Objective 2 | Objective 4 |
|---|---|---|---|---|---|---|
| Interpretivism Pragmatism Inductive | | | Literature Review | X | X | |
| | | Exploratory case study | Participant observation | | X | |
| | | | Interviews | X | X | |
| | Cross-sectional Case study Research -Including Survey Instrumentation | Confirmatory case studies | Questionnaire – *mixed model* | | | X |
| | | | Direct observation | | | X |
| | | | Physical Artefacts | | | X |
| | | | Interviews – *mixed model* | | | X |

## 2.9 Validity

Four main criteria for validity are relevant to evaluating case study research. These are: construct validity, internal validity, external validity and empirical reliability (Easterbrook and Aranda 2006). The following sections explicate in detail how each type of validity was addressed throughout the course of this research.

### 2.9.1 Construct validity

For case study research *"the construct validity of a procedure refers to the extent to which a study investigates what it claims to investigate"* (Gibbert and Ruigrok 2010). Wright *et al.* (2010) state that for empirical research the studied parameters must be relevant to the research questions in order to ensure a high level of construct validity. As part of the research question, the unit of analysis focused carefully on developing a deeper understanding of how requirements are elicited drawing inferences from multiple sources of data throughout the study. Relying on multiple sources of data is a method for increasing construct validity. The authors' interpretation of participant responses from the industry interviews were also later verified by participants.

The interview protocol also consisted of two particular questions designed to ascertain whether participants felt that the appropriate questions had been asked with regard to the reality of requirements elicitation in practice. For instance, at the end of each interview the following questions were asked: *"Is there anything else you would like to add? Is there anything you feel I should have asked?"* Responses to these questions reiterated context surrounding the replies to questions that had already been obtained earlier during the interview and one participant replied that that questions asked were *"very relevant"* to elicitation as conducted in practice. No new information emerged from the responses to these last two questions. This confirmed that the questions were representative of the reality of the process of requirements elicitation in practice, reflecting a valid construct for examining the unit of analysis.

### 2.9.2 Internal validity

Internal validity ascertains whether the treatment applied actually caused the outcome rather than the outcome having been influenced by other potentially unknown confounding factors (Feldt and Magazinius 2010). Primarily, an internally valid study seeks to isolate variables measured in order to disprove this threat. As pointed out by Easterbrook and Aranda (2006), internal validity is not relevant to exploratory case studies, however, confirmatory case studies must to the best of the researcher's knowledge be internally valid. Every effort was made to manage the potential threats to internal validity during the course of the two confirmatory case studies. In each case two teams address the same problem, in the same research setting using two different development methods. This aimed to contribute toward isolating any potential difference between the performance of one method over another. Also, the participants involved in both groups reflected equally diverse cultural backgrounds and equally consisted of mixed age and gender. Simultaneously measuring the performance of two teams given an identical problem, in an identical setting but using two different methods served as a precaution in this research to enable a clear and balanced comparison. This also aimed to reduce the potential for unknown confounding factors to pay influence.

A potential threat to the internal validity of the confirmatory studies conducted which should be addressed is that student subjects may be additionally pressurised due to a busy academic year. To address this threat every effort was made to minimize this risk and it was also planned that both confirmatory case studies would be conducted in the penultimate semester to minimize the potential for additional pressure to have an impact on the research conducted. This measure has been recommended by Trochim (2006) as a means with which to strengthen the validity of research conducted specifically with student subjects.

### 2.9.3 External validity

External validity addresses the extent to which the results of a study can be generalised in other settings outside the context in which it was originally conducted (Feldt and Magazinius 2010). A study is said to be externally valid if *"the conclusions hold throughout the study domain"* (Wright *et al.* 2010). For case study research external validity is strengthened by the use of multiple cases in which the results replicate overtime (Easterbrook and Aranda 2006). A limited number of case studies were conducted in this research, it would therefore be considerably beneficial in strengthening the external validity of this research if additional case studies focusing on the process of requirements elicitation could be conducted in practice.

Also, the confirmatory studies conducted here took place in a student setting and it would be considerably beneficial to repeat these studies in a real development setting to compare the potential difference in implementing OpenXP within a live development environment. External validity could then be strengthened based upon the outcome of further research. Although, it is acknowledged that conducting the confirmatory studies in a student setting may differ considerably to doing so in an industrial real world setting, it should be noted that particularly for research conducted in AMs the participation of undergraduate students is a widely accepted approach (Müller and Tichy 2001), (Syed-Abdullah *et al.* 2003), (Abrahamsson 2003), (Erdogmus *et al.* 2005), (Cau 2005), (Rundle and Dewar 2006).

### 2.9.4 Empirical Reliability

A study is said to be empirically reliable if *"the operation of the study can be repeated with the same results"* (Easterbrook and Aranda 2006). This can be strengthened by careful documentation of protocols used throughout the research such that this can be reapplied with reliable results. Every effort has been made to include the instrumentation and protocols used in this study and to present a clear chain of evidence explaining as clearly as possible how this research has been conducted (further details of the specific protocols used can also be found in Walsh 2014). To the best of the author's knowledge, no evidence exists to suggest that this work could not be considered empirically reliable.

## 2.10 Summary

This chapter presented the research methodology, the research stance and the justification for the strategy adopted for this work. This research is inductive, predominantly taking a qualitative approach. The research stance stems from both pragmatism and interpretivism. First a pragmatic perspective is taken considering that this research was driven by the specific research problem. An interpretivist stance then draws inferences from participant experiences on how requirements are elicited and subsequently participant experiences in using the proposed solution. As such the research strategy considered most suitable is case study research. First a review of the literature and an exploratory case study is conducted followed by two confirmatory case studies used to evaluate the proposed solution.

# Chapter 3 Requirements... Grasping the Problem?

## 3.1 Overview

This chapter presents a review of the current RE literature, this begins by defining RE and the stakeholder roles that can be involved during software projects. Particular attention is paid to the importance of RE in Dynamically Adaptive Systems (DAS) using HCS characteristics as an exemplar to examine the specific RE needs for this domain. Commonly reported challenges are discussed identifying the factors that affect the communication of requirements on projects. Existing RE approaches are also presented outlining the benefits and challenges reported for each, techniques used to elicit requirements are then described and categorised. AMs are then discussed focusing on the challenges reported in the literature including the role of the customer in XP.

## 3.2 Requirements Engineering

A requirement is defined as *"a condition or capability needed by a stakeholder to solve a problem or achieve an objective"* (IEEE 1990). Requirements are divided into two categories: *functional* and *non-functional requirements*, functional requirements are defined as *"the functional effects that the software-to-be is required to have on its environment"* (Van Lamsweerde 2009). An example of a functional requirement might be to *search for a list of modules on a selected course*. Non-functional requirements are defined as *"the constraints on the way that the software-to-be should satisfy its functional requirements"* (Van Lamsweerde 2009). For example, *a response to a query will take less than three seconds*. Non-functional requirements can be identified as the attributes of functional requirements such as qualities and constraints (Alexander and Beus-Dukic 2009).

RE involves the development and subsequent management of requirements as shown in Figure 4 (Wiegers and Beatty 2013).

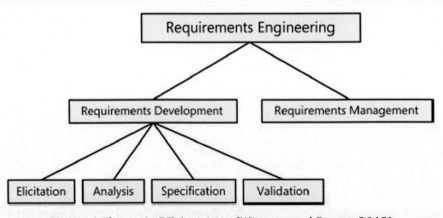

*Figure 4 The main RE Activities (Wiegers and Beatty 2013)*

Requirements development completes four main activities; the first of these is *elicitation,* which is defined as *"the process of seeking, uncovering, acquiring, and elaborating requirements"* for software systems (Zowghi and Coulin 2005c). During elicitation, a wide range of techniques are available to investigate and clarify requirements (Davis A. *et al.* 2006). Zowghi and Coulin (2005c) identified five steps involved during elicitation:

1. Understanding the application domain which consists of developing a clear comprehension of the problem space to be addressed;

2. Identifying sources of requirements involves identifying stakeholders and other sources such as existing artefacts in the domain, competitive requirements through marketing studies, or existing systems the solution may be required to integrate with;

3. Analysing the stakeholders involves developing a clear understanding of stakeholder needs and perspectives;

4. Selecting an appropriate set of techniques, approaches and tools to use;

5. Eliciting the requirements from stakeholders and other resources.

Requirements elicitation is intricately linked to *"the specific characteristics of the project, the organisation and the environment"* to be addressed (Zowghi and Coulin 2005c). Once requirements have been identified, *analysis* is performed where it is necessary to reduce or eliminate potential conflict and ambiguities from requirements. Requirements must also be appropriately documented. The format that documentation takes usually depends on many factors including the nature of the project and the level of formality required by stakeholders. This can range from very formal documents to informal verbal agreements. *Specification* produces the formal requirements document. Here, each requirement is described in detail, typically including diagrams, which illustrate precisely the behaviour for each feature requested for the improved system. The detailed specification must then be *verified* by customers to ensure that requirements are accurate before design can commence. Once verified, the specification is used to inform the design phase.

A critical component in RE is the *management* of requirements throughout subsequent phases. Requirements management concerns how a requirement is identified, developed, modified and traced through the project lifecycle (Sommerville 2007). Traditionally, following the waterfall approach each activity is performed sequentially. However, a previously verified requirement may still need to change later in the development process and this needs to be carefully managed.

### 3.2.1 RE for Dynamically Adaptive Systems (DAS)

A DAS can be defined as a system that *"alters its behaviour or composition in response to changes in its environment"* (Welsh and Sawyer 2008). Particular systems that require DAS solutions include automotive systems, web services, new network topologies, smart homes, video surveillance, ecosystem monitoring, disaster management and Search Based Software Engineering (SBSE)

(Welsh and Sawyer 2008), (Archer *et al.* 2009), (Fox and Clarke 2009), (Fredericks *et al.* 2013), (Harman *et al.* 2012).

In this emerging field of ubiquitous computing, *"the interaction space is ill-defined, unpredictable and emerges opportunistically"* (Coutaz *et al.* 2005). Requirements that depict the particular context of use rely upon *"the emergence of information and cooperation rather than the sophistication of individual components"* (Coutaz *et al.* 2005). Given the volatile characteristics expected of large scale ubiquitous computing environments, context is considered *"too complex to be programmed as a fixed set of variables"*, and the particular behaviours of adaptive systems are *"not always precisely specifiable in advance"* (Coutaz *et al.* 2005).

The challenges unique to this emergent domain further include: *new interaction techniques* which have been called for to reduce the potential for *"mismatches in the mental models between users and systems"* (Coutaz *et al.* 2005). Goal oriented approaches are considered inadequate, since they are limited to modeling steady-state systems (Goldsby *et al.* 2008), and eliciting the specific context with regard to *"user groups, their tasks, goals and the operational environment"* requires significant attention from researchers (Sitou and Spanfelner 2007).

In the four levels of RE for DAS as defined by Berry *et al.* (2005), human activity is prominent since this relates to requirements elicitation and analysis for the DAS on level 1. Level 2 refers to RE conducted by the system itself at runtime to detect and select which configuration to apply for a given adaptation (Goldsby *et al.* 2008). Levels 3 and 4 again require human decisions regarding potential target programs including which features the system should adopt, and the specific functionality required for each (Berry *et al.* 2005). Alongside early prototyping, scenario-based approaches have been explicitly recommended for the development of systems expected to dynamically adapt in specific situational contexts (Sitou and Spanfelner 2007). In particular the development of adaptation scenarios is a main contributor to the four levels of RE (for DAS) as defined by Berry *et al.* (2005). However, additional support is called for *to model RE concerns* for this domain (Goldsby *et al.* 2008).

In this work, HCS is used as an exemplar for a DAS, since the particular features required for this domain indicate that a DAS is needed to provide an appropriate solution. The following points briefly outline the motivation behind research in HCS and the specific characteristics defined for a desirable approach to RE in this domain are then discussed.

### 3.2.1.1 HCS as an exemplar for DAS

According to the World Health Organisation (WHO), the population of over 60s in developing countries is expected to triple from *"400 million to 1.7 billion"* over the next forty years (WHO 2010). Rising healthcare costs and lack of resources in terms of hospitals and the availability of skilled doctors and nurses mean that by 2050, this situation will become unsustainable. In Ireland 11% of the population is currently over 65 and this is expected to double over the next 25 years, in particular a threefold increase in those aged 80 and above is expected (Roberts *et al.* 2007).

Accommodating the ageing population is and will continue to be an increasing challenge. For example, Technology Research for Independent Living (TRIL) report that 40% of older people are prematurely institutionalised due to injuries sustained from falls in the home (TRIL 2010). In general it is beneficial to develop alternative approaches to prevent or delay the institutionalisation of older people, enabling the elderly to remain at home. This has subsequently required an increase in the need to develop HCS.

A HCS can be defined as the *"potentially linked set of services of either social care, health care, or both that provide or support the provision of care in the home"* (Mc Gee-Lennon 2008). Software developed for HCS (also known as Ambient Assisted Living, Aged Care and Ageing in Place) can be described as emergent since these interactive systems are expected to continuously evolve throughout development, and must regularly adapt to consistent change long after deployment in a given target domain. These systems also refer to the technologies required *"to support and realise activities of a network of care, providing the means to collect, distribute, analyse and manage care related information"* (Gururajan *et al.* 2005).

### 3.2.1.2 Interaction Evolution (IE)

The IE model developed by McBryan *et al.* (2008) is a fruitful approach designed primarily to manage multiple sources of change in the HCS domain. This is an iterative model consisting of four main steps described as follows:

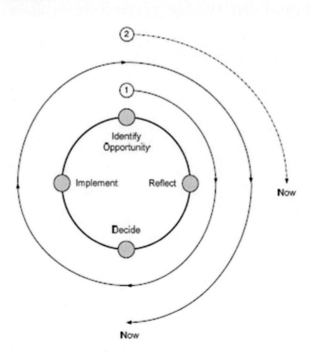

*Figure 5 The IE process (McBryan et al. 2008)*

As shown in Figure 5, the first step in IE is to identify an opportunity for change. It is anticipated that the need for change will consistently emerge from a variety of *"rapidly changing circumstances"* causing the system to gradually evolve over time (McBryan *et al.* 2008). The second step focuses on reflecting on all potential alternative options that could be taken to develop an appropriate resolution to the situation. The third step involves making a decision with regard to what action will be taken in addressing the problem. The fourth step then concentrates on implementing the change to be made (McBryan *et al.* 2008). However, due to the fact that a HCS is an *"inherently multi-user"* system, significantly, additional support is called for to effectively facilitate collaboration between the multiple diverse stakeholder groups involved in the decision-making process for this domain (McBryan *et al.* 2008).

### 3.2.1.3 Compliancy Mapping for a Desirable RE Method with AMs

Considering that a potential solution may be found with the principles and practices suggested by agile development, it also appears that the characteristics of agile development closely match the desirable qualities of a requirements development approach for interactive systems such as HCS. The following section elaborates on this.

In developing the IE model for the HCS domain, McBryan *et al.* (2008) also identified ten desirable characteristics RE methods should possess in order to meet the criteria needed for developing requirements in HCS. Table 4 investigates the suitability of AMs for the development of a new or adapted requirements approach in HCS. Column 1 presents a summary of the desirable HCS characteristics as defined by McBryan *et al.* (2008), column 2 demonstrates the extent to which AMs comply with these. Two ticks indicate that AMs comply fully with the characteristic, one tick indicates partial compliance and an 'x' indicates that no compliance exists for the characteristic. The following points then describe the capacity for AMs to address each of the desired characteristics.

*Table 4 Compliancy mapping of RE characteristics vs. AMs*

| HCS Characteristics | AMs |
|---|---|
| Iterative development | ✓✓ |
| Prioritization | ✓✓ |
| Correlation with other processes | ✓✓ |
| Appropriate stakeholders | ✓ |
| Participatory elicitation | ✓ |
| Identification of conflict | ✓ |
| Resolution of conflict | ✓ |
| Retention and traceability | ✓ |
| Annotation (negotiation and trace-ability) | ✓ |
| Distributed elicitation | ✓ |

*Iterative development:* As circumstances change in HCS, requirements are expected to evolve based on stakeholder input. Due to the short development cycles, perhaps even as short as two weeks, this is a characteristic that AMs can be considered fully compliant with.

*Prioritization of requirements:* The requirements elicited from multiple diverse stakeholders may need to be given different priorities depending on a variety of circumstances that may not be known in advance. AMs are fully compliant with the prioritization of requirements as user stories are prioritized by the customer at the beginning of each development cycle.

*Correlation with other processes and work practices* is a characteristic that calls for immediate benefit from solutions required. This is entirely consistent with the agile approach which promotes the early delivery of high quality working software to satisfy the customer's business objective, this characteristic is therefore fully compliant with AMs.

*Identification and engagement of appropriate stakeholders* is partially compliant as AMs recognise the need for this, however, no generalised procedure as such can be applied here since realizing this depends on constraints and circumstances often unique to each situation. Identification and engagement of stakeholders can also depend on accessibility to relevant stakeholders in a given domain which is difficult to determine in advance of projects.

*Participatory elicitation* is partially compliant as ASP is encouraged in AMs but achieving this remains problematic. Regular communication is needed for HCS to ensure that requirements remain closely aligned with changing stakeholder needs. However, problems exist where timely feedback is not always received and this can bring projects to a standstill. This characteristic is therefore given partial compliance in Table 4.

*Identification of conflict* partially complies since AMs encourage conflict to be aired as soon as possible but this is often challenging if relevant stakeholders are not actively involved or only identified during the latter stages of development. Hence, AMs only partially comply with this characteristic.

For *resolution of conflict,* AMs again partially comply because although the need to air and resolve conflict early is well recognised, successfully achieving this depends on heavy interaction between relevant stakeholders and developers throughout the project. Although AMs promote ASP only one customer represents all *non-developer* stakeholders and achieving consensus in the short development cycle is challenging where more than one stakeholder group is concerned. Hence, Table 4 indicates partial compliance on this characteristic.

*Retention and traceability of requirements overtime* is partially compliant because throughout the project the user stories are retained and can be traced through their acceptance tests, however, over long periods this information is not generally permanently retained. Also temporary models such as use case diagrams can be drawn to help investigate a feature but these are rarely retained. The artefacts are usually held for the duration of the project, recorded on wall charts or as automated tests. Traceability incurs cost and overhead so AMs only recommend it if stakeholders specifically request a need for it.

*Annotation* of requirements to enable negotiation and traceability is also partially compliant because physical story cards can be annotated, or the annotation could be incorporated as an important part of the user story. If the user story becomes difficult to understand due to extra information like annotations being added, agile practitioners would simplify this by breaking the story down into a series of further stories or tasks so as to understand it more clearly.

*Distributed elicitation* and negotiation is also necessary. Originally AMs were recommended for use with small (up to 10 people) co-located teams. Recently, various tools have helped to support distributed input from stakeholders. Although face-to-face communication is predominantly advised, agile teams can and do improvise where distributed stakeholders are concerned.  For instance, other means such as web conferencing and shared online spaces such as wikis improve collaboration efforts in cases where stakeholders are geographically dispersed.  This characteristic hence partially complies.

The above points illustrate that three characteristics of a desirable approach to requirements for the HCS domain are fully compliant with AMs. The remaining seven characteristics show partial compliance with AMs indicating that further support is required to assist AMs in improving on these particular aspects.

### 3.2.2 Classification of Stakeholders in RE

A stakeholder in a software system is defined as *"anyone who could be materially affected by the implementation of a new system or application"* (Leffingwell and Widrig 2003). Stakeholder identification  is defined as *"a process that  contributes to the identification of relevant stakeholders in RE"* (Conger 1994), (Macaulay 1996), (Finkelstein 2000), (Zowghi and Paryani 2003), (Pacheco and Garcia 2012).  A number of stakeholders can be involved in a software development project. As shown in Figure 6 (Alexander and Beus-Dukic 2009), different types of stakeholders involved can be structured using the *stakeholder onion*.

The *product or service* to be developed alongside the developer role is situated in the centre circle of the onion. Stakeholders relevant at the *business system* level are represented on the next layer, alongside the operational and maintenance roles depicted in the model in Figure 6, these might include business analysts or other domain specialists. The *wider business layer* then represents other typical roles such as distributors or systems integrators who will purchase the system. The outer layer depicts roles relevant to the *broader environment,* this typically includes end users in the domain and regulatory bodies to which requirements standards might need to comply.

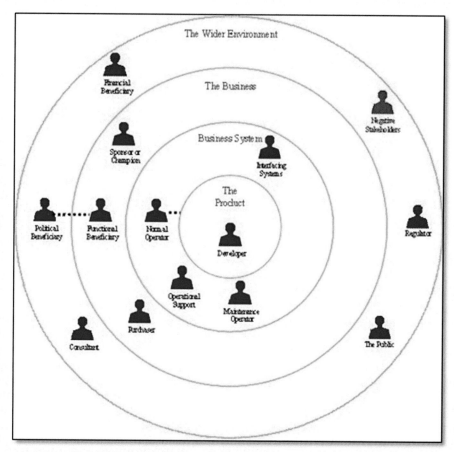

*Figure 6 The stakeholder onion model (Alexander and Beus-Dukic 2009)*

Stakeholder identification is recognised as one of the earliest activities conducted in RE (Glinz and Wieringa 2007). Once identified, an appropriate balance between business needs must then be achieved, where the most critical requirements always receive the highest priority in order to remain closely aligned with the most important business objectives throughout development.

Power (2010) provides an example where primary stakeholders are identified at the centre of the onion as those who accept software after small releases and secondary stakeholders from a wider perspective as those who accept software after quarterly releases. Therefore, in practice, the stakeholder onion model should be adapted accordingly to the stakeholder roles relevant to specific development contexts. However, Blomkvist (2006) describes a common stumbling block as the lack of clear distinction between customers, users and other stakeholders, *"all too often they are regarded as one and the same"* (Blomkvist 2006). Also, understanding stakeholder roles and relationships is considered a complex task (Sharp *et al.* 1999), (Phalp *et al.* 2007), (Fricker 2010a). In addition to this *"no guidelines or proper standards"* currently exist *"to help and guide software engineers in stakeholder identification"* (Pacheco and Garcia 2012). For example, a systematic literature review conducted on stakeholder identification methods in requirements elicitation has reported that:

> *"Effective practices, or standards such as CMMI, SWEBOK, BABOK, AND ISO/IEC 12207*
> *(SEI 2006, IEEE 2004, IIBA 2009, ISO/IEC 12207 2004) have the following limitation: they*

*do not explain how to define the entire set of stakeholders. Furthermore, this process is not always self-evident, and so an organisation must be analyzed in order to identify all possible stakeholders. Hence, the application of a stakeholder identification method becomes indispensable"* (Pacheco and Garcia 2012).

While Pacheco and Garcia (2012) point out that further research is still needed to develop a method or model to conduct stakeholder identification in RE, the authors have nevertheless established that any given stakeholder identification method must be capable of:

i)   Allocating appropriate stakeholder roles,  using *"group dynamics and personality tests"* (Pacheco and Garcia 2012);

ii)  Establishing constructive interaction between all stakeholders to manage conflict arising from communication between different viewpoints;

iii) The classification of requirements according to an evaluation of  stakeholder priorities relating to the overall project goal.

In this research, the stakeholder term is intended to mean the business stakeholder roles who contribute toward problem space understanding, for the purposes of communicating implicit domain context, of the requirements to a software development team. And the term customer representative is intended to mean those who directly interact with a software development team, communicating requirements on the behalf of stakeholders who cannot be present. Both stakeholders and customer representative perspectives are equally important here, since either one may directly or indirectly convey requirements detail to a development team.

### 3.2.3 Communication Structure in Business Organisation

The existing communication structure for a given business domain is typically established by studying the organisation chart during elicitation. This resource helps to understand different stakeholder roles, relationships between these and the path of communication throughout hierarchical business domains. In general, *"the formal organizational chart defines the relationships that should exist in the core of the organization"* for instance this formally indicates *"who should speak to or communicate with whom."* (Molina 2001).

An informal organizational network (ISN) on the other hand, is defined as *"a network of relationships that employees form across functions or divisions to accomplish tasks quickly"* (Krackhardt and Hanson, 1993), (DeToni and Nonino 2010). While it is widely acknowledged that rather than arguing the difference between formal vs informal organisation and so forth, it is much more important to understand and establish a symbiotic co-existence between these seemingly separate yet intricately intertwined approaches to human organisation (Ali 2011).

For example, one disadvantage in *solely* focusing on roles and relationships as depicted on the formal organisation chart is that considerable opportunities are missed by not picking up on the potential for ISNs as an additional valued source of information. However, a key challenge in tapping into this resource is that due to the informal nature of ISNs, they are difficult to detect, model and visualize (without introducing more complex approaches such as Social Network Analysis (SNA)). As a result, the presence of ISNs for emergent business domains may go unnoticed. This is a particularly problematic challenge since it is now widely recognised that ISNs play a crucial role in *"gaining the competitive advantage"* for knowledge-based industries (Kurland and Pelled 2000), (Cross *et al.* 2001), (Awazu 2004), (Hoffman *et al.* 2005), (Plickert *et al.* 2007), (DeToni and Nonino 2010), (Ali 2011).

## 3.3 Requirements Engineering Challenges

Echoing the work of Boehm (1981), Berry *et al.* (2010) point out the practical implications that up to *"85% of defects found in running software"* continue to trace back to RE, and up to the same percentage of project cost is attributed to rework or new requirements. A persistent problem in RE is *"the gap between what the customer wants and what the analyst thinks the customer wants"* (Niknafs and Berry 2012). Many challenges thus relate to bridging this gap and recommendations tend to move toward, supporting the development of a joint understanding between domains in relation to the requirements that must be addressed by a software system to be delivered.

### 3.3.1 Challenges Reported in the Literature

In generic requirements engineering, Pressman (2000) points out that business stakeholders have *difficulty articulating requirements* and are *unsure of what is needed*. The author also asserts difficulty with *conflict identification and resolution* and *continuously changing requirements*. Nuseibeh and Easterbrook (2000) published a roadmap for requirements engineering research identifying a number of challenges to be addressed. The issues raised here are *identifying and engaging multiple diverse stakeholder groups* alongside *conflict identification and resolution,* they also found that business stakeholders have *difficulty expressing requirements*.

Sommerville (2007) highlights a number of challenges including the need to address *changing requirements* and *conflict identification and resolution.* Also, he asserts that often *stakeholders are not sure of what is needed*, have *difficulty articulating requirements* and *developers lack implicit domain knowledge.* Decker *et al.* (2007) highlight the need to effectively manage challenges involving *differing stakeholder backgrounds*, perspectives and objectives on projects. The authors adapted wiki-based support with the aim of improving collaboration and the coordination between multiple documents that can be produced during elicitation. Although their approach assists in the process of detecting inconsistencies it does not provide a means to directly manage conflict (Decker *et al.* 2007).

Zhang (2007) asserts that *multiple diverse stakeholder backgrounds* present challenges in finding a common language to communicate requirements. The author points out that understanding the nature of a technique is important in appropriately determining how best to apply the technique in practice. Relevant to this is the nature of the problem domain, the organisational context and the sources of requirements within each organisation.

Vijayan and Raju (2011) also highlight problems such as *conflict identification and resolution*, *lack of implicit domain knowledge, difficulty for users in expressing requirements, stakeholders not understanding what is needed* and *difficulty managing continuous change* in requirements scope.

Specifically in AMs, Ambler (2009a) asserts that challenges exist for *managing conflicting stakeholder requirements, identifying the appropriate stakeholders* for projects pointing out that *stakeholders are not sure of what is needed* and *developers lack implicit knowledge* in the business domain, *limited access* to stakeholders is also problematic.

Grünbacher (2006) focuses on highlighting requirements challenges specifically experienced in the development of internet/web-based applications. These include *identifying, accessing and engaging multiple diverse stakeholders*. The application of traditional approaches to elicitation is considered inadequate and requirements are expected to *continuously change*.

McBryan *et al.* (2008) concentrate on challenges specific to the emerging Home Care Systems (HCS) domain. Challenges here include *identifying, accessing and engaging multiple diverse stakeholder groups, changing requirements* and *managing multiple conflicting stakeholder priorities* which are expected to continuously evolve over time. They also assert that *stakeholders are not sure of what is needed* in addressing requirements for this domain. The authors developed the *interaction evolution* model to manage sources of change, however, they do not elaborate on how this could be integrated with a software development process.

Raatikainen *et al.* (2011) identify challenges for requirements engineering specific to the nuclear energy domain: *managing conflicting requirements, requirements change, prioritization*, transferring *implicit knowledge, communicating efficiently* with stakeholders with different backgrounds crossing organisational borders and ensuring knowledge integrity requires a new method to *understand relationships between requirements* across organisational boundaries, hence, the authors assert that it is necessary to determine how to represent several *cross cutting concerns* in requirements.

Cheng and Atlee (2007) assert that further advancements are needed in RE to support the development of a *shared mental model* of the problem space between *multiple diverse stakeholder roles. Conflict identification and resolution* is described as a grand challenge since requirements must be understood and represented from differing levels of abstraction. Another point made here is that entirely new approaches are called for to *manage consistent levels of uncertainty and incomplete requirements* which are expected to *continuously evolve over time*.

Jørgensen *et al.* (2011) report challenges in managing *conflicting perspectives* of *multiple diverse groups* consisting of up to twenty stakeholders in practice. The stakeholder group changed and also expanded throughout the duration of the project. Balancing *changing perspectives* of multiple stakeholder representatives proved problematic. Also, effective communication, getting the right requirements and knowing which stakeholder is the most important are described as significant challenges.

Bjarnasan *et al.* (2011) investigate the causes and consequences of RE challenges predominantly identifying communication gaps that currently exist. These include complex product development in large organisations which causes difficulty in *reaching agreement* on requirements presenting *a lack of a complete requirements overview*. There is little understanding between different roles and a *common language* is needed to effectively communicate. *Limited access* to certain roles is problematic and a distinct *lack of clear business priorities* resulted in difficulty establishing a collective vision of the overall project goal.

Qadir *et al.* (2009) identified challenges which include *managing multiple diverse roles* and responsibilities, *managing change*, *lack of implicit knowledge* presents difficulties for long term tacit knowledge transfer, *lack of informal communication* has an impact on customer expectations considered to be better managed in informal settings, and *trust management* is considered a challenge. Success factors include establishing a clearer understanding of requirements and balancing business priorities in a cooperative manner with customers involved, detecting problems earlier, visualisation of project status and constant communication. Significantly, an evolutionary RE process is called for (Qadir *et al.* 2009).

In addressing communication problems in RE, Marczak and Damian (2011) identified that requirements *clarification* and *communication of changes* are the most predominant reasons for regular communication and one challenge for collaboration driven by interdependent requirements involves significant cross-functional interactions between *multiple diverse roles*. In their study, the actual communication structure showed significant informal backchannel communications and the *absence* of some stakeholders input had disrupted collaborative efforts during requirements activities.

In Market-Driven RE (MDRE), Lehtola *et al.* (2007) highlight a need to develop a holistic long term view of *multiple diverse stakeholders needs* to create a shared overall business goal. MDRE faces a difficult challenge and requires new approaches to support the *prioritization* of requirements in line with business goals. The authors report that developing explicit links between business decisions and requirements engineering decisions presents a significant challenge and have suggested that it is necessary to broaden narrow technical viewpoints into wider business oriented perspectives to strengthen this link. Also in MDRE, Kabbedijk *et al.* (2009) call for more adequate methods to *involve customers* in the requirements activities on software projects and advocate the use of *customer participation sessions* to accommodate inclusion of the customer perspective.

Toçi (2012) also discusses challenges specifically for MDRE. These include problems emerging when market research does not adequately reveal customer preferences. In the absence of direct interaction with a wide and diverse end customer base, problems have emerged for identifying the right requirements. New methods are called for to support the *prioritization* of requirements for a largely unknown or inaccessible customer base. In MDRE the diverse range of technical stakeholder backgrounds particularly for games development, presents challenges in *communicating between different disciplines*. This has resulted in *difficulty managing conflict*.

Figure 7, summarises the common challenges for requirements development as reported in the literature. Each row indicates the challenges reported by specific authors, these are organised beginning with the most common. The column on the left indicates the reporting authors while the presence of a '✓' indicates that the referenced author has identified the specific challenge indicated. A blank cell shows that the author has not expressed the particular challenge.

Pressman (2000), Nuseibeh and Easterbrook (2000), Sommerville (2007), Decker *et al.* (2007), Zhang (2007) and Vijayan and Raju (2011) report challenges for generic requirements engineering, while Ambler (2009a) states more specifically challenges experienced for agile requirements engineering. The focus of Grünbacher (2006) is on Web Engineering (WE). Raatikainen *et al.* (2011) report challenges found specifically in the nuclear energy domain. McBryan *et al.* (2008) concentrate on challenges in requirements engineering for HCS. The remaining authors in Figure 7, Cheng and Atlee (2007), Jørgenson *et al.* (2011), Bjarnasan *et al.* (2011), Qadir *et al.* (2009), Marczak and Damian (2011), Lehtola *et al.* (2007), Kabbedijk *et al.* (2009) and Toçi (2012) all focus on challenges for scaling requirements for large or globally distributed software systems.

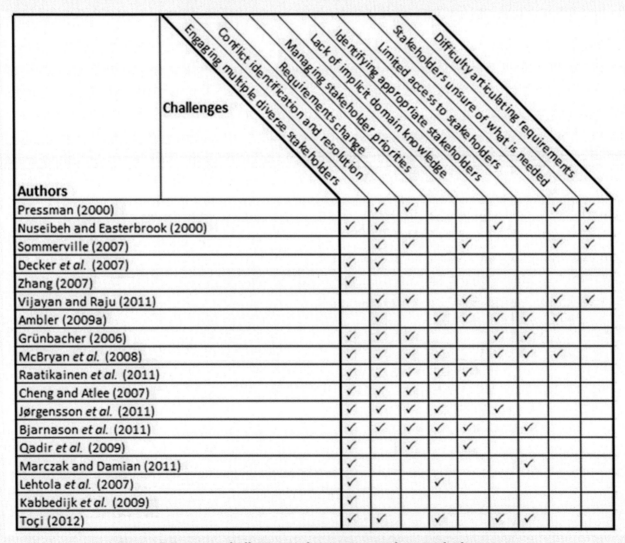

| Authors | Engaging multiple diverse stakeholders | Conflict identification and resolution | Requirements change | Managing stakeholder change | Lack of implicit domain knowledge | Identifying appropriate stakeholders | Limited access to stakeholders | Stakeholders unsure of what is needed | Difficulty articulating requirements |
|---|---|---|---|---|---|---|---|---|---|
| Pressman (2000) | | | ✓ | ✓ | | | | ✓ | ✓ |
| Nuseibeh and Easterbrook (2000) | ✓ | | ✓ | | | | ✓ | | ✓ |
| Sommerville (2007) | | | ✓ | ✓ | | ✓ | | ✓ | ✓ |
| Decker *et al.* (2007) | ✓ | | ✓ | | | | | | |
| Zhang (2007) | | | ✓ | | | | | | |
| Vijayan and Raju (2011) | | | ✓ | ✓ | | ✓ | | ✓ | ✓ |
| Ambler (2009a) | | | ✓ | | ✓ | ✓ | ✓ | ✓ | ✓ |
| Grünbacher (2006) | ✓ | ✓ | ✓ | | | | ✓ | ✓ | |
| McBryan *et al.* (2008) | ✓ | ✓ | ✓ | ✓ | | ✓ | ✓ | ✓ | |
| Raatikainen *et al.* (2011) | ✓ | ✓ | ✓ | ✓ | ✓ | | | | |
| Cheng and Atlee (2007) | ✓ | ✓ | ✓ | | | | | | |
| Jørgensson *et al.* (2011) | ✓ | ✓ | ✓ | ✓ | | ✓ | | | |
| Bjarnason *et al.* (2011) | ✓ | ✓ | ✓ | ✓ | ✓ | | ✓ | | |
| Qadir *et al.* (2009) | ✓ | | ✓ | | ✓ | | | | |
| Marczak and Damian (2011) | ✓ | | | | | | ✓ | | |
| Lehtola *et al.* (2007) | ✓ | | | ✓ | | | | | |
| Kabbedijk *et al.* (2009) | ✓ | | | | | | | | |
| Toçi (2012) | ✓ | ✓ | | ✓ | | ✓ | ✓ | | |

*Figure 7 Common challenges and respective authors in the literature*

Figure 7, illustrates that the most commonly reported challenge is *engaging multiple diverse stakeholders* discussed across fourteen contributions. This is closely followed by *conflict identification and resolution* reported by thirteen. Ten have raised *requirements change* as challenging while seven report difficulty with *managing stakeholder priorities*. This is closely followed by *lack of implicit domain knowledge, identifying appropriate stakeholders* and *limited access* to stakeholders reported by six. Then five discuss *stakeholders being unsure of what is needed* and finally, four contributions have reported that *stakeholders have difficulty articulating requirements*.

The set of challenges that have been consistently reported across many authors in the literature are thus considered representative of the set of factors that affect the communication of requirements between developers and other stakeholders. What can also be discerned is that these factors predominantly surround people issues on software projects. In this research they are classified as a set of *human related problems* that must be better managed in order to improve the communication of requirements during elicitation.

Many authors have conducted research on the development of viewpoints, an approach with the potential to manage multiple stakeholder perspectives on projects (Finklestein *et al.* 1992), (Kotonya and Sommerville 1992), (Kotonya 1997), (Goedicke *et al.* 2000), (Arao *et al.* 2005), (Salem 2010). A strong advantage of the viewpoint oriented approach is that inconsistencies between stakeholder viewpoints can be tolerated, however, a challenge still remains in managing this as systems scale (Easterbrook *et al.* 2005). Also, although Easterbrook *et al.* (2005) found that viewpoints provide further insights, the analysis was extremely time consuming. More fundamentally, viewpoints have tended to focus on the analysis of existing information rather than the *elicitation* of this information from various stakeholder perspectives in a given problem space. An important point here is that it is first necessary to establish a collective understanding of multiple stakeholder perspectives upfront.  Darke and Shanks (1996) point out that no single viewpoint can capture a holistic perspective of the requirement, therefore multiple interrelated perspectives simultaneously exist, change over time and must be managed.

Numerous valuable contributions have focused on detecting and resolving conflict (Moreira *et al.* 2005), (Giorgini *et al.* 2006), (Niu and Easterbrook 2007), (Fricker and Glinz 2010b), (Salay *et al.* 2012). However, a key problem is that little attention has been paid to how consensus can be reached (Niu and Easterbrook 2007); very few systems development methods directly support collaborative face-to-face interaction (Reinikainen 2001), and even less attention is focused on directly engaging stakeholders to facilitate the necessary negotiations to achieve mutual agreement. This is not just relevant to the start of projects, it also appears relevant when inconsistencies have been detected in existing documentation for example, since this still requires negotiation on the part of the relevant stakeholders to reach an amicable agreement with regard to how such inconsistencies could be resolved.

## 3.3.2 Systematic Bias in Software Development

Significantly, attention has also been drawn to a set of systematic biases found to be responsible for a series of high profile software development failure in practice (Shore 2008). This illuminates a set of serious pitfalls occurring outside of the engineering process and more so in the managerial aspect of software development. Regardless of this, the problems are nevertheless directly related to the outcome of projects in terms of success or failure. For all intents and purposes, it has become crucial to address how cultures can be changed to discourage systematic biases from influencing software development as a whole (Shore 2008). The following points elaborate on this:

*Available Data* is a systematic bias that occurs when decisions are made based only on readily or conveniently available data, this prevents a wider variety of sources from contributing to the decision making process (Shore 2008). When this bias occurs it results in situations where the scope of the project is defined by decision makers who *"limit their knowledge to internal data in contrast to widening the data collection process to include customers, suppliers and competitors"* (Shore 2008).  For development in competitively changing domains, this bias immediately introduces risk to a project since it prevents the inclusion of broader interdisciplinary stakeholder groups from the outset. As a result, the requirements specific to each of these broader groups may not be met.

*Conservatism* is defined as *"the failure to consider new information or negative feedback as a project unfolds"* (Shore 2008). Echoing the work of Bazerman (1994), Shore (2008) points out that this bias occurs when *"managers close down paths of communication, especially when those paths are likely to produce data or information that is inconsistent with their view of a situation".* This bias results in a situation where the manager does not proceed with an objective view of the project. As such, the Conservatism bias immediately puts the project at risk by disrupting communication with potential alternative sources, and the failure to effectively process negative feedback during development jeopardises the accuracy of the requirements delivered as a whole.

The *Group Think* bias refers to a situation where group members are *"put under pressure to think alike, to politicize their views in contrast to the views of others, and to resist evidence that may threaten their view"* (Shore 2008). This bias creates a type of destructive group dominance where *"less desirable contributions of powerful participants overwhelm useful ideas from others"* (Wood and Silver, 1995), (McGill 2005). This results in a situation where all stakeholders do not contribute an independent perspective to the problem. Resisting alternative sources of evidence also prevents decisions made from being fully informed. Additionally, if the information produced as the output of a group interaction (affected by groupthink), later serves as a source of information for development, then the requirements produced are compromised since they reflect only the perspectives of one or more dominant individuals. This presents a risk to the project since development proceeds without a balanced objective view of the business need.

The *illusion of Control* is defined as a bias that *"occurs when the projected likelihood of success is higher than an objective evaluation of the situation would warrant"* (Martz *et al.* 2003), (Shore

2008). Echoing the work of Langer (1975), Shore (2008) suggests that this bias occurs due to the fact that *"people are motivated to control their environments, because they may have a need to feel competent, or because it is appealing to believe that they can control chance events"*. As such, The Illusion of Control introduces risk by encouraging a potentially misinformed evaluation of the project to prevail throughout development.

*Overconfidence* occurs when the actual evidence of project success does not support the level of confidence expressed (by a manager) in the project (Shore 2008). This presents a further less than objective evaluation since the project becomes negatively affected by the narrow perspective of a manager. According to Bazerman (1994), this particular bias is attributable to the fact that *"we [as humans] are more inclined to be overconfident in areas outside our own expertise"* (Shore 2008). This suggests a need to address the inclusion of specific and relevant expertise to prevent the decision making process from being adversely influenced by the overconfidence bias of a single individual.

*Selective Perception*, also known as *Frame Blindness* (Russo and Shoemaker 1989), occurs when *"several people can perceive the same situation differently"* (Shore 2008). For example, this bias affects promoted managers who experience difficulty *"leaving behind the perspective of the previous position"*, as a result, decisions made are *"still influenced by their previous roles"* (Dearborn and Simon 1958), (Shore 2008). The problem with this bias on projects is that the decisions made on the broader business level, are disproportionally affected by the managers tendency *"to remain loyal to their former constituents"* (Gauthier-Villars and Michaels 2007), (Shore 2008). As a result, the managers' attention is not focused on delivering an overall balanced and objective evaluation.

In summary, this set of systematic biases repeatedly shows an underlying problem reflecting the negative impact that *narrow perspectives* can have on projects. These challenges were predominantly found among management positions; however, clearly due to the substantial level of risk they introduce, it is necessary to constructively work toward circumnavigating or ideally preventing the propagation of these systematic biases for projects to realistically succeed.

## 3.4 RE Approaches

A number of RE approaches have been developed which predominantly support the gradual development of a more formal transition between business stakeholder needs (in the problem domain) and the requirements for a software solution to be delivered. This is important considering that the existing approaches aim to increase stakeholder involvement during requirements activities on projects (Mathiassen and Nielsen 1989), (Maqsood *et al.* 2001), (Phalp *et al.* 2007), (Fu *et al.* 2008) (Grimm *et al.* 2008). The following section elaborates on the main RE approaches proposed in the literature focusing the benefits and limitations reported for each.

### 3.4.1 Business and Information Technology (IT) alignment

Business and IT alignment is primarily concerned with determining the *business impact* of integrating change, accurately projecting the expected cost and resources involved and ensuring that *business value* will be achieved by developing a new or adapted software system (Weiss and Anderson 2004) . Enterprise wide governance of business and IT alignment consists of the implementation of processes that enable business and IT practitioners to conduct their tasks in a manner that supports the creation of value from business investment (Van Grembergen and De Haes 2010).

However, business and IT alignment is widely regarded as a significant challenge to be resolved in software development (Sabherwal and Chan 2001), (Peak and Guynes 2003), (Cumps *et al.* 2006), (Luftman *et al.* 2006), (Babar *et al.* 2010).  A key point made by Hiekkanen *et al.* (2012) is that the perception of organisations and technology as *"static, mechanistic and segmented"* misleadingly presumes that a logical separation between business and IT functions can be obtained. This rather mechanistic perspective does not adequately represent the rich and dynamic or interdependent relationships within contemporary organisations as a whole (Hiekkanen *et al.* 2012).

Another significant challenge reported is in the assumption that, to some degree, business strategies already exist and as such, available models can be readily mapped to the processes within IT organisations (Chan and Reich 2007), (Fu *et al.* 2008). Also, linking immeasurable, unstated and conflicting goal sets between domains remains problematic (Santana Tapia *et al.* 2012). It has been established that under the broader category of communication, the key contributing factors to achieving business and IT alignment are *mutual understanding* alongside *mutual appreciation* of IT, (between business and IT people) as an innovator of business between the two domains (Silvius 2013).

In research however, a distinct shortage of focus on the role of people in business and IT alignment has been reported (Hiekkanen *et al.* 2012).  An important goal in Business Process (BP) modeling is improving comprehension of the models produced, while another challenge emphasises that *formal validation* is needed to determine the accuracy of the practitioner's interpretation of the reality of the domain to be modeled (Si-Said Cherfi *et al.* 2012). Primarily, for the purposes of developing reusable system components, BP models aim to develop *"a complete description of underlying business processes"*, however, BP modeling is a difficult task (Perjons 2011) involving complex notations and requires specialist expertise to conduct (Si-Said Cherfi *et al.* 2012).

### 3.4.2 Model driven approaches

Model driven approaches promote the use of formal models as the primary source for the analysis, documentation, design, implementation and maintenance of software systems (Truyen 2006). Originally developed as part of the Model Driven Architecture (MDA) (OMG 2014), model driven approaches also aim to increase the involvement of stakeholders in requirements activities (Phalp *et al.* 2007), (Grimm *et al.* 2008). In order to reduce development time and cost, this approach aims to match models of stakeholder needs with the set of currently available component models that can be extended or reused (Chung *et al.* 2006).

However, Lussenburg *et al.* (2010) assert that empirical evidence on the application of model driven approaches in practice is relatively scarce. In their work, the use of hand-written code as an extension to existing models was still found to be instrumental in refining the details of specific functional requirements. A number of significant challenges for model driven approaches include managing the number and diversity of the stakeholder groups involved, organising and integrating the artefacts produced (Grimm *et al.* 2008) and managing the diversity of stakeholder requirements (Demchak and Krueger 2012).

In addition to this, numerous examples have been published illustrating the transition between different model classifications using the MDA (Phalp *et al.* 2007), (Grimm *et al.* 2008), (Martin and Loos 2008), (Rech and Schmitt 2008), (Poernomo *et al.* 2008), Overall however, examples given do not make explicit reference as to *how* the contents of the models should be elicited from business stakeholders in a given domain (Kanyaru *et al.* 2008). Model driven approaches are focused on reuse driven development (Chung *et al.* 2006), relying heavily on the completeness of models produced, with a strong emphasis on formal languages such as the Unified Modeling Language (UML), this has also introduced a steep learning curve for those not familiar with adopting the approach (Den Hann 2008), (Fu *et al.* 2008).

### 3.4.3 Soft Systems Methodology (SSM)

SSM is another approach with the potential to support stakeholders in achieving a common understanding of the problem situation during early RE (Maqsood *et al.* 2001). Checkland and Scholes (1990) specifically distinguish between *hard* and *soft* systems approaches to development. A hard systems approach can be applied when *"well-structured technical problems can be precisely defined"* with clear statements derived for a proposed solution, on the other hand, a soft systems approach can be applied to *"ill-structured problems that cannot be precisely formulated in the first instance"* (Mathiassen and Nielsen 1989), (Patel 1995). SSM emerged from action research in practice and is generally recommended for addressing the *soft* problems which often surround the human aspect of existing systems within organisations (Mathiassen and Nielsen 1989), (Checkland and Scholes 1990), (Patel 1995), (Fennessy and Burstein 2000), (Sensuse and Ramadhan 2012).

SSM consists of a seven step process where an initially ill-defined problematic situation is first identified. The problem is then expressed using rich pictures, a free drawing graphical technique, which aims to capture a visual representation of the situation to be addressed (Biggam 2002). Once the problem has been expressed, a root definition of relevant systems is established. This consists of a concise statement describing the core activities of the system to be modeled (Bjerke 2008). A set of conceptual models are then produced to illustrate how the current system could be improved (Young 2009), this consists of a diagrammatic representation describing the main activities involved. The conceptual models are then compared with the expressed problem. Any necessary changes are then made over a series of iterations until the models align accordingly. Based upon this analysis, action is subsequently taken to improve the situation.

SSM can however, take time to conduct (Mathiassen and Nielsen 1989) and specialist skill is required to correctly implement the approach (Bustard and Greer 1997). While the literature on SSM provides an abundance of detail including valuable feedback from practice on how the methodology works, *"grasping the case with SSM"* is a complex task and little or no advice is given on *how* to elicit information such as the criteria needed to fulfil the models (Bjerke 2008). Another problem reported is that SSM practitioners lack implicit domain knowledge and key to the successful implementation of the approach is that practitioners establish a clear understanding of the problem situation during step one (Bjerke 2008). However, the proponents of SSM do not elaborate on *any* particular techniques used to support implicit knowledge transfer or *how* this can be initially achieved (Bjerke 2008).

### 3.4.4 Problem Frames

The problem frames approach explicitly distinguishes between the problem space where requirements are situated in their environmental context and the solution space yet to be designed and developed (Jackson 2001). As such, problem frames suggest the need to separate the problem to be addressed from the software solution. The approach can be used as *"the means to reason about requirements, specifications and their relationships"* (Li 2007).

Cox *et al.* (2005) published a roadmap identifying future research directions for the problem frames approach. The authors assert that in general, tacit knowledge is assumed to be available and specific skill is required particularly for problem decomposition. Also, the majority of problems are considered too complex to fit the basic problem frames originally defined (Cox *et al.* 2005). It has also been reported that the problem frames approach may not be scalable to industrial software problems (Phalp and Cox 2000).

Research on problem frames has progressed by developing increasingly more formal representations including complex mathematical notations to depict the transition between requirements and specifications (Gunter *et al.* 2000), (Lencastre *et al.* 2006), (Hall *et al.* 2010). However, Jackson (2001) acknowledges an important limitation describing formal models at best as *"a simplified approximation to the real world"*. This has suggested that misunderstandings can arise during the transition between informal to more formal representations, this in turn can present a mismatch between the perceived reality and the conceptual models produced, a challenge that should not be underestimated in RE (Li 2007).

### 3.4.5 Goal based approaches

Goal Modeling Languages (GML) relevant to the early stages of requirements have shown that inconsistencies between existing documentation can indeed be detected (Anton 1996), (Yu 1997), (Chung *et al.* 2000), (Letier 2001), (Van Lamsweerde 2003), (Bresciani *et al.* 2004), (Sabetzadeh and Easterbrook 2005), (Duboc *et al.* 2008). However, the identification of stakeholder goals is recognised as a complex task (Regev and Wegmann 2005) and difficulty remains in bridging the gap between the goal and business layers (Lemaire and Andersson 2010).

While goal based approaches do provide support for elicitation, a number of considerable drawbacks in their application have been acknowledged. For instance, these representations take time to implement, become difficult to manage as systems scale, are considered incomplete for describing problem context, and the relationships between goals and the problem context can be difficult to determine due to the assumption that goals should be structured in a hierarchical manner (Mohammadi *et al.* 2013).

### 3.4.6 Summary

In summary, clear challenges stand out with respect to the approaches discussed here. For instance the specific artefacts needed as inputs for business and IT alignment, model driven, SSM, problem frames and goal based approaches, take time to develop, requiring specialist skill and must be sufficiently complete in order to fully exploit the benefits of using any one of these approaches. Complex formal notations are also introduced which creates a steep learning curve for those considering adopting the approaches. Particularly for integration with AMs, this significantly reduces the ability to remain flexible during RE. A fundamental problem reported is that existing RE approaches have suffered from a lack of exploration (prior to their initial development) into the usability needs of RE practitioners, as a result, the extent to which current RE approaches are considered *practically usable* has been described as *"a major concern for practitioners"* (Winbladh *et al.* 2009).

As yet, there is very little discussion in the literature overall about *how* the contents of the artefacts needed as inputs for each of the approaches should be *elicited*. This suggests that regardless of the RE approach adopted, practitioners still need to separately select a set of suitable techniques to elicit the specific problem domain context for each situation. This further suggests that existing approaches to RE are largely independent of the techniques used during elicitation.

## 3.5 Categorisation of RE Techniques

In software projects an extensive range of techniques are used for eliciting requirements. An investigation was undertaken to help understand the range of elicitation techniques available and how best to select between them. Of particular interest, was in which circumstances would each be most useful. Van Vleit (2000) suggests thirteen techniques that are commonly used. Upon studying this classification, a number of techniques were found to encompass parts of other techniques for instance, Van Vleit (2000) describes, form analysis, natural language descriptions, the use of reference models, synthesis of requirements from existing systems and domain analysis as separate techniques. However, the description suggests that these particular techniques are all forms of domain analysis and for this reason they have been included singularly under domain analysis here. Also, Business Process Re-engineering (BPR) is now considered an overall strategy rather than a separate technique as described by Van Vleit (2000). As a result of this, eight rather than the original thirteen techniques from the Van Vleit (2000) classification have been focused on here. These are described in the following points.

### 3.5.1 Interviews

Interviews can be conducted in a structured, semi-structured or unstructured manner. Using the structured approach a predefined set of questions are designed which help to direct elicitation, this is most beneficial where *specific information* must be clarified (Preece *et al.* 2002). Alternatively interviews can be unstructured where no predefined agenda is followed, this is favourable if during the interview, an intriguing response needs to be further probed (Turner 2010). Semi-structured interviews utilize the advantages of both structured and unstructured approaches where some structure can be applied and any potentially interesting avenues of inquiry that may emerge during the interaction can also be pursued (Zowghi and Coulin 2005c). Interviews can be used to provide a rich collection of information, investigate responses in-depth and conduct follow-up inquiries. Limitations include that the technique is difficult to conduct requiring specialist skill and the interviewer must also select the most appropriate stakeholders (Escalona and Koch 2004). The technique is time consuming for establishing an overall perspective of the requirements and in discovering the most important issues that must be addressed (Alexander and Beus-Dukic 2009).

### 3.5.2 Delphi Technique

The Delphi technique is used to develop consensus between a group of purposefully sampled experts where the synthesis of specific expertise are required to inform development in a given domain. The Delphi technique is an iterative approach where a series of questionnaires are distributed, to a selected group of domain experts (Gordon 1994). Once the first questionnaire has been returned each subsequent questionnaire is developed based on the results and refined feedback from the previous questionnaire, gradually a consensus is reached when no new information surfaces indicating all participating experts are satisfied that the syntheses of information are accurate (Linstone and Turoff 2002). Also, participants can remain anonymous and are free from personality influence and individual dominance (Gordon 1994). However, care is needed as judgements are those of a selected group and must consist of a representative sample, as such, the appropriate experts must be identified in advance. Also the technique is time consuming and continuous participation is required for a complete consensus to be achieved (Gnatzy 2011).

### 3.5.3 Brainstorming session

Brainstorming is a creative problem solving technique that consists of problem understanding, idea generation and the development of plans for action (Maiden and Robertson 2005). The technique is used to *"generate, refine and develop ideas"* (Sharp *et al.* 2007), and is recommended for developing creative or innovative solutions to existing problems in a collaborative manner (Preece *et al.* 2002). Brainstorming works by focusing on a problem, and then purposely coming up with as many solutions as possible, expanding the ideas generated as far as possible. The approach encourages creativity and enables different perspectives of a common problem to be conveyed (Raghavan *et al.* 1994), (Gunda 2008). Brainstorming is best suited where ten or less stakeholders are involved and this includes the role of facilitator (Escalona and Koch 2004). Limitations include that outcomes can rely on the ability of the facilitator to maintain a dynamic atmosphere, and the approach is conducted informally, which depending on the domain, may not be suitable in the case where a more formal technique is required by stakeholders.

### 3.5.4 Task Analysis (TA)

TA is a systematic method used to develop a detailed understanding of each step involved in completing a task, where a user requires further support to improve how they currently achieve specific goals (Kieras 2004). TA is divided between *Action oriented techniques* which model directly observable behaviour, and *cognitive techniques* which focus on understanding the mental models of users, such as how they solve problems and make decisions as each step proceeds through to the completion of a task (Embrey 2000). The approach provides crucial input for Human Computer Interaction (HCI) components since TA is well suited to recognizing interaction issues that must be understood prior to making important decisions about the requirements for interface design (Crystal and Ellington 2004).

Clear benefits exist in having a detailed account of how users interact with the tasks they complete. However, some drawbacks in applying the approach are in the specialist skill required and the length of time to conduct TA, since users must be involved in developing an understanding and accurately identifying the specific steps (Embrey 2000). Considering that TA focuses solely on how users interact with a task, the technique is less well suited for situating tasks and overall goals in the wider organisational context (Hughes *et al.* 1994). TA is a retrospective technique since only interaction with tasks in an existing system as-is can be analysed in such meticulous detail, thus for developing entirely innovative approaches to conducting tasks, the technique may not be a suitable approach (Sharp *et al.* 2007).

### 3.5.5 Scenario-based analysis

A scenario can be described as an *instance* of a task (or a sequence of tasks) being executed, where a narrative is used to describe how tasks are carried out and goals achieved in their specific context (Escalona and Koch 2004). Scenarios can be used to capture both current and foreseeable needs and can represent *"the collective and agreed upon understanding and expertise of a wide variety of stakeholders"* (Waltzman *et al.* 2007). Scenario-based analysis is also consistent with *Use Case Analysis*.

The Cooperative Requirements Engineering With Scenarios (CREWS) model provides a scenario classification framework defining scenarios as multifaceted objects where properties and attributes relevant to the usage of a given scenario can be collected. For instance, the CREWS framework depicts a given scenario which has the properties: purpose, contents, form and lifecycle. By dividing scenarios into these four views, the contents are distinguished from the form, purpose and lifecycle enabling a useful meta-narrative about the scenario to be recorded (Rolland *et al.* 1998). Scenarios can therefore link important context to goals and tasks and serve as a useful tool in planning for future situations. Sharp *et al.* (2007) point out that when written by stakeholders, scenarios can help to establish a common language since the approach fosters a storytelling mode between stakeholders during communication. Limitations include there is no systematic approach to validate scenarios and no clear indication of when a sufficient number of scenarios have been elicited (Widya and Bults 2009).

### 3.5.6 Ethnography

Ethnography originally emerged from the social sciences and has increasingly been recommended as a requirements elicitation technique because it enables rich descriptions of human activity to be to be studied over a period of time in a natural setting (Hughes *et al.* 1994). This approach permits the ethnographer to participate in the customer domain, similarly to a trainee and experience first-hand the daily work activities of the group under study.

However, an important issue in conducting this technique is that participants whose activities are being studied must be comfortable enough to permit the presence of the ethnographer for potentially long periods of time and care should be taken that the ethnographers presence does not alter the normal flow of activities being studied (Atkinson and Hammersley 2007). Also, active participation on the part of the group being studied is considered low in ethnographic studies, and significant time and skill is also required (Preece *et al.* 2002). Ethnography is expensive to conduct and results in large amounts of qualitative data that can be difficult to analyse (Kujala 2003). Hughes *et al.* (1994) report problems where the technique attempts to scale from small to larger settings and Keller (2011) discusses problems in translating the resulting rich ethnographic analyses into concrete requirements which are needed for development.

### 3.5.7 Domain Analysis

Domain analysis is described as discovering, categorising and representing relevant information from existing systems, including knowledge elicited from domain experts, documented artefacts and emerging technologies in a specific domain (Jatain and Goel 2009). This technique builds a bank of requirements for the purpose of reuse in specific domains. This gradually evolves into a reference model that can behave as a skeleton to be adapted for other similar systems to be developed (Reinhartz-Berger and Sturm 2008). Domain Analysis is beneficial since components from related systems can be reused and domain specific knowledge including the terminology used by stakeholders can be ascertained, this is a particularly useful technique for improving or re-engineering existing legacy systems (Zowghi and Coulin 2005c).

However, a drawback is that since domain analysis is a retrospective approach, the technique is less well suited for emerging domains where no such previous reference model exists as yet. This can also inadvertently introduce design constraint, which overlooks the possibility that a unique or fresh approach might be needed. Another pitfall reported is, where the knowledge-base for an existing domain has not been sufficiently developed, the reference model may be either too broad or too restrictive in scope to be adapted for specific situational contexts (Khurum and Gorschek 2009).

### 3.5.8 Prototyping

Prototyping develops a limited set of early system requirements into a *prototype* which is used to demonstrate working software to stakeholders in an iterative manner (Mannio and Nikula 2001). Prototypes can provide early and quick feedback and are particularly suited to validating requirements for a new system with dynamically changing needs (Escalona and Koch 2004).

The technique is beneficial for exploring unclear requirements, for instance, paper prototypes can also be used to develop stakeholder ideas during elicitation (Vijayan and Raju 2011). Throwaway prototypes can be used to explore and validate requirements and evolutionary prototypes can develop further eventually forming a fully operational solution (Gunda 2008). Limitations include that prototypes can be difficult to scale if the initial intended purpose was to explore and clarify requirements, rather than to build a robust system, also, stakeholders can make the false assumption that the full quality system will be developed within the same short time frame (Fu *et al.* 2008).  Another pertinent drawback is that the technique is difficult to effectively apply if stakeholders do not provide regular and timely feedback.

### 3.5.9 Classification of techniques

Table 5, summarises a comparison of the techniques described in sections 3.4.1 to 3.4.8. Here criteria used to consider each are as follows. Under *'Main Source of Information'*, each technique is separated into two subcategories that indicate whether its main source of information comes from the *domain* itself or the *users* of the domain. The category *'Strong on',* is divided into two further subcategories that indicate whether each technique is most suitable for determining *current* or *future* business needs. These categories are taken directly from Van Vleit (2000). Further, two criteria *Iterative* and *Collaborative* are added, since these are key characteristics for elicitation in agile development.

Table 5, indicates that interviews are strong on eliciting information for current business needs. This is neither an iterative nor a collaborative approach and does not consider future business needs. The delphi technique is an iterative approach that elicits current business needs, however, since participants are physically isolated while taking part in the approach, this technique is weak on direct collaboration.

Brainstorming is an iterative and collaborative approach, involves users and is strong on eliciting both current and future business needs. Task Analysis, while user based and strong on current needs, does not iterate or focus beyond current needs and collaboration with stakeholders occurs only at the beginning of projects. Scenario-based analysis in an agile context is an iterative and collaborative approach, strong on eliciting both current and future needs.

Ethnography is a domain based approach that elicits current needs but is weak on iteration and collaboration and does not focus on future needs. Domain analysis is not iterative, collaborative and does not elicit future needs. Finally, prototyping is iterative, collaborative, user based and strong on eliciting both current and future business needs.

*Table 5 Categorisation of elicitation techniques (Adapted from Van Vleit 2000)*

| Technique | Iterative | Collaborative | Main Source of Information | | Strong on | |
|---|---|---|---|---|---|---|
| | | | Domain | User | Current Requirements | Future Requirements |
| Interview | | | | ✓ | ✓ | |
| Delphi Technique | ✓ | | | ✓ | ✓ | ✓ |
| Brainstorming Session | ✓ | ✓ | | ✓ | ✓ | |
| Task Analysis | | ✓ | | ✓ | ✓ | |
| Scenario (use case) Analysis | ✓ | ✓ | | ✓ | ✓ | ✓ |
| Ethnography | | | ✓ | | ✓ | |
| Domain Analysis | | | ✓ | | ✓ | |
| Prototyping | ✓ | ✓ | | ✓ | ✓ | ✓ |

Given that a new or adaptive approach needs to demonstrate agility, candidate techniques will support both iteration and collaboration. Since specific emphasis is placed on stakeholder involvement in the literature, greater importance is given here to techniques whose main source of information is the user. Support for the discovery of future business needs is imperative to an evolutionary approach. Thus, techniques exhibiting this quality are particularly favourable. Considering the above criteria, an inspection of Table 5, shows that three candidate techniques stand out. These are *brainstorming sessions*, *scenario analysis* and *prototyping* which are iterative, collaborative, user-based and capable of eliciting both current and future needs. These techniques demonstrate the potential necessary for a novel or adapted approach.

It should be noted that the above list is not exhaustive, but is intended to illustrate the diversity of elicitation techniques and where best they could be applied. Easterbrook (2004), for example, expands on these by including Joint Applications Development (JAD) (Wood and Silver 1995), Rapid Applications Development (RAD) and Focus Groups as additional *collaborative* techniques, along with Card Sorting, Laddering, Repertory Grids and Proximity Scaling as additional *Knowledge Acquisition* techniques. Easterbrook (2004) also includes socio-technical approaches such as SSM (Checkland and Scholes 1990) as candidate techniques in certain situations. The author then organises techniques under *traditional, cognitive, collaborative* and *contextual* approaches. This classification includes sixteen techniques, a number of which directly overlap with the Van Vleit (2000) categorisation. While traditional, cognitive and contextual approaches are clearly advantageous, considerable limitations for their application in AMs include that these techniques are time consuming and heavily reliant on practitioner skill.

Van Lamsweerde (2009) provides an additional classification organising techniques into *artefact driven, concept driven and stakeholder driven techniques*. Artefact driven techniques focus on existing system artefacts such as system prototypes, data samples and bodies of reusable knowledge. For instance, Van Lamsweerde (2009) recommends a background study to explore and learn more about the domain, marketing data and/or short experimental studies using questionnaires to acquire relevant facts and investigating existing domain models to encourage knowledge reuse. The author also recommends storyboards and scenarios to facilitate *exploration of the problem world* and prototyping and mock-ups to provide *quick feedback* from stakeholders. Also, conceptual laddering, card sorts and repertory grids are described as *concept driven techniques* in his classification. *Stakeholder driven techniques* then focus on the interaction between stakeholders and developers, here, interviews, observation, ethnographic studies and group sessions such as JAD are advised (Van Lamsweerde 2009).

Despite the fact that numerous techniques exist, experts do not agree on how best to elicit requirements or what techniques are best suited to any particular setting (Davis A. *et al.* 2006). Technique selection can be influenced by different criteria such as the learning curve involved in using the technique, its cost, the quality of information elicited and time required to apply the technique (Escalona and Koch 2004). Hence, the choice of technique also depends on each situation. An empirical study conducted by Davis A. *et al.* (2006), reports on the shortage of comparative studies that analyse the potential of one technique against the capabilities of others in same setting. The authors found that traditional interviews were one of the most effective elicitation techniques in a wide range of domains and situations, card sorting and thinking aloud were less effective than interviews.

Particular disciplines within software development suggest moving away from text based requirements elicitation to accommodate multiple diverse stakeholder needs, essentially, *"an explicit user-inclusion strategy is required"* (Verner *et al.* 2005b). In complex situations with numerous stakeholders, it is difficult to comprehend multiple documents and therefore necessary to move away from this heavily documented approach. For example, in multimedia development, Bruegge *et al.* (2008) proposed Video-Based Requirements Engineering (VBRE) which emphasised the inclusion of end user feedback. The authors express that the perception of how complex a scenario is will be determined by the *audience* and not the authors of that scenario. With this in mind they proposed the use of VBRE to foster creative thinking and to enrich communication possibilities with the intention of *eliminating potential misunderstandings* that can arise with written documentation.

Further, Williams and Alspaugh (2008) recommend performing elicitation through the development of comic-book style scripts to encourage stakeholders to articulate requirements sooner. This is a fruitful option since it maximises design capability by encouraging stakeholders to explore possible alternative paths to a solution early in the development process (Williams and Alspaugh 2008). Here, there is no learning curve as such for stakeholders involved as using comic styles takes advantage of human cognitive ability. Also comic style drawings can behave as throw away prototypes where ideas can be easily refined without stakeholders presuming that early designs must initially be fixed (Williams and Alspaugh 2008), this is particularly useful if stakeholders are not sure of how existing problems could be approached. In this sense the technique encourages many alternative paths to a potential solution to be fully explored before fixing important decisions about the requirements. Effectiveness of the comic styles approach does however present a disadvantage if a skilled artist is not involved.

In HCS Newell *et al.* (2006) used live forum theatre to stimulate discussion between users and designers, this is achieved through an experienced script writer and scenes enacted by professional actors to which much of the success of this novel and interesting idea is accredited. In contrast to an agile setting, a bottleneck here is in the specialised skill required, the cost and time consumption particularly in transcribing the sessions.

McBryan *et al.* (2008) developed Interaction Evolution, an iterative model (described earlier in section 3.2.1) to manage sources of change in HCS. This model is clearly ideal for requirements engineering in HCS and has the potential to be applied in RE across other dynamically adaptive domains. However, the authors' make no reference as to how the model could be actually integrated into a software development method.

Collaborative elicitation techniques such as focus groups and JAD are group intensive focusing on the engagement of stakeholders. However, as previously mentioned, a drawback for integration with AMs, is that these techniques require time to prepare and skill to conduct the sessions. Also, it may be incorrectly presumed that stakeholders relevant to the problem domain have been recruited (Coughlan and Macredie 2002). JAD in particular is more focused on design, highly structured and a skilled facilitator is required to direct participants toward a predefined goal (Duggan and Thachenkary 2004). A number of problems associated with power relations between participants have also emerged from JAD in practice (Reinikainen 2001). These include *the abilene paradox*, a situation where conflict is only superficially addressed after group decisions are made, which do not reflect the genuine opinions of all relevant stakeholders present (Kettelhut 1993). Another problem reported is the lack of proactive participation between stakeholders during the sessions (Carmel *et al.* 1995), (Reinikainen 2001).

In drawing inferences between methodology and practice, Coughlan and Macredie (2002) found that JAD does not necessarily improve communication. They assert that to achieve and share understanding, effective communication must first be in place considering this is a key prerequisite to the success of JAD. Scepticism in the use of the methodology in practice has been reported and participants have difficulty taking responsibility for communication and negotiation of requirements during JAD sessions (Coughlan and Macredie 2002).

In general, facilitated workshops have distinct drawbacks when dealing with more than a small number of stakeholders and particularly groups of a heterogeneous nature (Voigt 2004), (Hess 2007). For instance, challenges that typically emerge from diversity in groups include *"the intricacies of language issues, different cultures, communication styles and work patterns"* (Jain 2012). Therefore a problem is that group interaction techniques currently recommended, do not lend themselves well to effectively managing multiple diverse stakeholder perspectives on projects. Further, it should be noted that existing group interaction techniques have typically been used during the early stages of the development process where traditionally, requirements are expected to complete. This does not address support for continuous interaction between interdisciplinary stakeholders throughout the development cycle or the temporary nature of requirements which are expected to continuously evolve overtime. These rather fundamental limitations suggest a move away from the traditional plan-driven assumptions of development may be necessary. As such, the potential for alternative approaches to development should be considered.

## 3.6 Alternative Development Paradigm

### 3.6.1 Amethodical Systems development

In the alternative development paradigm, Truex *et al.* (1999) re-examine the meaning of method and illuminate what they term its privileged position in the development of information systems. The authors achieve this by investigating evidence suggesting an alternative *amethodical* way in which systems are also developed. They define the methodical view as *"the ordered, rational and universal way in which we interpret, represent and subsequently develop systems"*. Alternatively the amethodical view is defined as the development of systems *"without order, sequence rationality or claims to universality"*. The latter acknowledges unpredictability in systems development claiming that development efforts are *uniquely dependent on a variety of volatile factors* that cannot be predetermined prior to a system being developed.

Baskerville and Pries-Heje (2002) claim that software systems are not built within a single project that completes upon deployment, instead systems are being *"grown"* to adapt to the emergent organisations in which they reside. Here, the authors state that *"an amethodical development activity is unique and unpredictable for each systems requirement"*. The authors conducted an empirical investigation identifying five general differences between traditional and web development approaches to requirements engineering.

1.  Analysis should be different because requirements for web development are fluid and ambiguous.

2.  They assert that good architecture is required as *"an enabling basis for the survival of the software system"* (Baskerville and Pries-Heje 2002).

3.  Detailed design is different since it is based upon components and tool suites that are specific to each situation.

4.  A focus on coding and implementation behaves as a substitute for unambiguous requirements.

5.  The viewpoint on maintenance differs since it was found that maintenance in web development settings was generally ignored.

The above practices are described as an amethodical exemplar responding to emergent software system needs (Baskerville and Pries-Heje 2002). The authors conclude that this package of practices is a type of methodology but not in the traditional sense of process steps or stages, in this context it is considered a methodology for guiding developers in innovating *"unique techniques which primarily depend on a set of imperatives and constraints"* Baskerville & Pries-Heje (2002).

Gallardo-Valencia and Elliot Sim (2007) examined the extent to which software engineers follow a software process and subsequently the extent to which engineers improvise during the enactment of the process. The authors classified two different types of process, formal and informal and found that engineers improvised throughout both. Here formal processes were identified as methodical whereas informal processes were identified as amethodical. Because engineers improvised throughout the use of both types of process the authors concluded that amethodical processes were in fact processes too. The authors assert that informal processes used by participants should also be considered processes explaining that *"due to the marginalised position of amethodical processes, they have not received enough attention from researchers, thus, this fact could be considered a point of failure in process research"* (Gallardo-Valencia and Elliot Sim 2007). The authors suggest their work could be used by agile researchers or investigators of other amethodical processes to provide amethodical software practitioners with tools and process models that support improvisation providing the resources to innovate while still using a software process.

Elliot Sim et al. (2007) continue along this line of inquiry with a second empirical study focused more specifically on amethodical requirements engineering. This work identifies five amethodical RE practices listed below:

1. Requirements engineers act as bridges between different worlds;

2. Good communication is key;

3. Good process can help but being flexible in its application was found to be more important;

4. With the appropriate abstraction less is more;

5. Good requirements are driven by customer value not technical elegance.

In this work the authors utilize techniques borrowed from Gestalt psychology to present a figuration of requirements engineering claiming that requirements have both a methodical and an amethodical perspective however difficulty remains in gaining the holistic view whereby each perspective could be viewed simultaneously.

### 3.6.2 Emergent Systems Development

It has been recognised that for ill-structured problem domains practitioners typically engage with an *"unpredictable, opportunistic, improvised process"* (Nguyen and Swatman 2003), (Mahaux *et al.* 2013b). Requirements elicitation has also been specifically identified as a *"collaborative and emergent"* activity in software development (Coughlan and Macredie 2002), (Mahaux *et al.* 2013b). Indeed, emergent systems thinking has gradually overturned the original assumption set that historically underpinned plan-driven software development (Finken 2005), (Virili and Sorrentino 2008). This has resulted in the definition of a new goal set for dynamically adaptive software systems based on this emergent systems viewpoint (Truex *et al.* 1999), (Alatalo *et al.* 2002), (Bello *et al.* 2002). This new assumption set consists of five goals that organisations must strive to achieve in order to appropriately facilitate dynamically changing needs, these are defined as follows (Truex *et al.* 1999):

1. *Always analysis* suggests that analysis of requirements is a continuous maintenance activity which consistently occurs in parallel with other software development activities throughout the life span of a software system.

2. *Dynamic requirements negotiations* suggests that no particular set of complete and unambiguous requirements can be obtained since requirements are the result of an ever changing list of needs expected to continuously conflict between stakeholders within the

domain. Here a *"healthy degree of conflict"* between stakeholders is preferred (Truex *et al.* 1999).

3. *Incomplete but usefully ambiguous specifications* suggests that for the purposes of modification, the way in which requirements are documented must necessarily reflect the need for requirements to constantly adapt to such ever changing business needs. In this context it is considered futile to produce a fixed requirements specification. Instead, flexible requirements specifications are considered most favourable.

4. *Continuous redevelopment* suggests that software projects do not have a beginning or an end, instead systems continuously redevelop in order to appropriately respond to consistent organisational change. Here regular analysis activities occur throughout the systems life span where new requirements are constantly implemented, this in turn gradually prevents the need for stakeholders to ever arrive at the conclusion that a new or replacement system should be required.

5. The fifth and final assumption is *adaptability orientation* which asserts that in order to readily respond to emergent requirements, underlying system architectures must be designed such that components become easily modifiable since the ability to adapt a software system is key to addressing continuously changing, hence emergent organisational needs.

Alongside the above goals, Truex *et al.* (1999) also identify three specific levers that stimulate emergence in order to appropriately facilitate dynamically changing needs. These are summarised in the following points:

1. *Shared reality construction* claims that the reality of any organisation is defined by whatever stakeholders in that organisation currently believe to be real. Here organisational reality refers collectively to the existing belief systems of stakeholders in the domain. It is therefore necessary for stakeholders to develop a shared perception of reality which can be embraced through a process of continuous reconstruction of the organisations reality. Any process by which an organisations reality can be continuously reconstructed is particularly favourable here.

2. *Self-reference and organisational identity* involves continuous reference to historical or previous versions of the organisation. Organisations reconstruct with reference to previous versions of self from which the identity of the organisation develops – this also includes making reference to the shared perception of reality as defined by stakeholders in the domain. Here, the authors place particular importance on the need to facilitate a state of continuous adjustment in dynamic business environments.

3. *The dialectics of organisational autopoiesis* is defined as *"the process by which organisations emerge"* (Truex *et al.* 1999). Here organisational meaning is constantly renegotiated and specifically this lever claims that conflict is the result differing versions of reality that

exist between the belief systems of stakeholders in the domain. Embracing conflict over consensus is considered important in this regard since a shared view of the organisations reality *"becomes easier to reconstruct"*, this in turn creates the environment in which organisations can effectively emerge (Truex *et al.* 1999).

In summary, emphasis in the research is now moving in the direction of placing greater value on the benefits of collaborative group decision making over individual decision making during RE. This is evidenced by a growing trend in the research community on the need for both business and technical stakeholders to dynamically co-create requirements in a collaborative manner throughout projects (Fischer 2004), (Maiden and Robertson 2005),(Nguyen and Cybulski 2008),(Racheva *et al.* 2010), (Ralph 2010; 2013), (Mahaux *et al.* 2013b).

Business domains are typically identified as emergent if the particular company is *"in a state of constantly seeking stability, while never achieving it"* (Truex *et al.* 2001). As evidenced by the above points, emergence within business organisations includes *"every feature of the social organisations culture, relationships, decision making, and how meaning is socially negotiated and consensus reached"* (Truex *et al.* 2001). This suggests that it is necessary to further assess how communication can be structured in the context of emergent business domains.

### 3.6.3. Key Differences between Perspectives

An examination of the broader view shows that the set of original assumptions underlying both traditional plan-driven and alternative systems development are fundamentally rooted in the differences between the rationalist and empiricist worldviews (Ralph 2013). This is important to grasp, since depending on the perspective of individual practitioners, either approach may be adopted as the process by which software is developed. The following points made by Ralph (2013) present a summary of the key differences between the rationalist and empiricist perspectives of development:

Three formulations of the Rational Paradigm have been identified as follows (Brooks 2010):

1.  the mechanical-engineering view of design as a methodical, orderly process, as described by Pahl and Beitz (1996);

2.  the artificial-intelligence view of design as a search for satisfactory alternatives given goals and constraints, by a designer exhibiting *"procedural rationality"*, as formulated by Simon (1996);

3.  the managerial view of design as a sequence of weakly-coupled phases, i.e. the Waterfall Model (Royce 1970).

Further, in contrast to the rational perspective, three formulations of the Alternative Paradigm are also evident (Ralph 2013):

1.  Reflection-in-Action (RiA) – the view of designer as a *"reflective practitioner"* alternating between problem framing, adjusting a design concept and evaluating the adjustment's consequences (Schön 1983);

2.  the view of the designer as a creative agent whose attention oscillates between an ill-defined problem concept and a tentative solution concept (coevolution), gradually developing an understanding of both (Cross *et al.* 1992), (Dorst and Cross 2001);

3.  the view of design as a political process characterized by interpersonal conflicts,

4.  disagreement over goals, politicking and the supremacy of emotional considerations over efficiency (Kling 1980),  (Levina 2005).

As shown in Table 6, Ralph (2013) differentiates between the core components of the rational and alternative design paradigms. The author identifies the model of design as technical problem solving, with the planning model as the theory of action and the predominant development method as plan-driven for the rational paradigm. This is discussed in contrast to the alternative paradigm which employs Reflection-in-Action as the model of design, with the improvising model used as the theory of action and the development method identified as predominantly amethodical within the empiricist paradigm (Ralph 2013).

*Table 6 Core Components of the Rational and Alternative Paradigms (Adapted from Ralph 2013)*

| Dimension | Rational Paradigm | Alternative Paradigm |
|---|---|---|
| Epistemology | Rationalism | Empiricism |
| Model of design | Technical problem solving | Reflection-in-Action |
| Theory of action | Planning model | Improvising model |
| Development method | Plan-driven | Amethodical |

The alternative paradigm adopts Sense-making-Coevolution-Implementation Theory (SCI). Coevolution therefore in the context of the alternative paradigm, does not assume the rational perspective that a set of well-known software engineering activities can be directly mapped to the requirements specification,  instead it:

> *"refers to the mutual exploration of the [problem] context and design alternatives, where participants oscillate between conceptual models and design models, where changes in one, triggers changes in the other and vice versa"* (Ralph 2013).

Due to the fact that SCI includes *"interviewing stakeholders, writing and organising notes, reading about the domain, investigating potential technologies, sharing insights and acceptance testing"*, it can be stated that SCI is intricately linked with requirements elicitation for software projects that closely align with this alternative paradigm (Ralph 2013).

### 3.6.4 Summary

In summary, software projects that do not use a specifically defined software development method can be identified as those who use an amethodical development process. This does not imply *"anarchy nor chaos"*, instead, it *"implies management and orchestration of systems development without predefined sequence, control, rationality, or claims to universality"* (Truex *et al.* 1999, 2000), (Baskerville and Pries-Heje 2002), (Madsen and Kautz 2002), (Finken 2005), (Pries-Heje *et al.* 2008), (Ralph 2010, 2013). Elliot Sim *et al.* (2008) claim that Amethodical concepts *"are not rejections of method, but rather those concepts that are marginalized and left out of prescriptive methods for carrying out a procedure"*, furthermore, *"amethodical does not mean careless or without a procedure, but rather, beside or outside of method"* (Elliot Sim *et al.* 2008).

Amethodical systems development has been identified as more consistent with Reflection-in-Action which views software design as a *"reflective conversation between a designer and situation where problem understanding and solving are intermingled"* (Ralph 2010). In summary, an alternative amethodical development paradigm more closely aligns with the empiricist perspective as evidenced by the fact that this approach to development:

> *"rejects the proposition that project actors can anticipate future problems, phases and changes. As actors will not know what will happen until it does and is available to sensory perception, the logical approach would be to cultivate the capacity to adapt and respond quickly to unexpected changes, i.e., to maximize agility"* (Ralph 2013).

It has also been suggested that while plan-driven development predominantly invokes rationalist logic, amethodical development on the other hand, invokes empiricist logics, significantly, for the purposes of this research, Agile Methods have the potential capacity to combine both these approaches to software development (Ralph 2013).

## 3.7 Agile Methods (AMs)

AMs have been widely adopted in industry, the top reported benefits include an accelerated time to market, improved management of changing priorities and better alignment between IT and business domain goals (VersionOne 2013). More specific areas for improvement in AMs include further in-depth research on people management issues for handling cross cutting concerns to provide much needed *"relevant and valuable insights"* into future AM research and development (Wang *et al.* 2009). Also, some particular AMs including FDD, DSDM and Crystal methods are reported to be less widely adopted and discussed (Maurer and Hellmann 2013). Overall, a greater number of high quality studies have been called for to develop a more comprehensive empirical assessment on AMs in practice (Dybå and Dingsøyr 2008).

VersionOne (2013) reported on the factors contributing to failed attempts in the adoption of AMs in industry. 34% reported that this had been due to a failure to integrate the right people on projects, while 30% attributed this problem to communication issues between the development team and the business domain. In a survey conducted by Kurapati *et al.* (2012) a combination of agile practices across AMs were found to be more widely adopted than practitioners adhering to individual AMs. The application of agile practices such as iterative development and regular communication across both project and organisational levels has positively influenced customer satisfaction, particularly when regular timely feedback was received and the output from frequent delivery of software produced favourable results (Kurapati *et al.* 2012).

### 3.7.1 Lean Software Development

Lean concepts originated from the Japanese automotive industry where lean manufacturing was first introduced. Lean Software Development (LSD) is considered the only strategic AM that takes a *top down* approach to the purposeful elimination of waste across organisations as a whole (Highsmith 2002). Although LSD is often viewed as a type of AM and clear similarities exist between Agile and Lean concepts, some distinctions have been made suggesting that LSD actually underpins AMs by concentrating on the reduction of waste and the production of value stream organisational processes (Poppendieck 2002). When combined with AMs, implementing LSD provides support for the effective adoption of AMs required at upper organisational level (Wang *et al.* 2010).

Early adoption of Lean concepts in software development emerged from industry in response to a need to better manage risk in software projects (Anderson 2011). LSD is still considered an emerging concept and more empirical studies reporting on its implementation in practice are needed (Dybå and Dingsøyr 2008), Conboy and Duarte (2010) also point out that academic research in LSD has yet to begin. However, some include Staron *et al.* (2012) and Petersen (2012). Experience reports of LSD used in conjunction with AMs can be found in Wang *et al.* (2010), Rodriguez *et al.* (2012) and Lane *et al.* (2012). LSD recommends seven principles, in the context of requirements elicitation, four specific principles are relevant to this research:

1. *Eliminate Waste* requires that waste is recognised by developing a keen understanding of what *value* means to a customer. Any activity or artefact produced that does not directly relate to this value is considered waste and as such should be eliminated. By reducing waste, value is maximised. The end to end process from inception to delivery is perceived as a value stream which undergoes continuous optimization and once refined, the process is considered to be lean;

2. *Amplify Learning* recommends that tacit knowledge on software teams should be retained and effectively used as a means to inform a collective knowledge base, and improve both current and future development efforts (Tatum 2005);

3. *Empower the team* asserts that software development is a knowledge based activity and as such, self-organisation and respect for the competence and technical ability of developers is encouraged (Poppendieck, T. 2003b). This includes empowering developers to implement necessary changes where a process or part of a process could be improved;

4. *Build Integrity In* states that integrity is measured by value brought to the customer. This is divided into conceptual and perceived integrity. Perceived integrity focuses on the customer perception of value which is managed through regular communication and feedback, and conceptual integrity concentrates on how well the system integrates architecturally as a whole (Lunesu 2013).

## 3.7.2 eXtreme Programming (XP)

XP as originally defined by Beck (1999), had twelve practices, fifteen principles and four values. The approach was based upon Beck's experience with colleagues developing software in practice. In 2005 an updated version known as XP2 was published (Beck and Andres 2005). The second edition made some changes to the original XP development method that incorporated new insights which subsequently emerged based upon feedback from the application of the method in industry.

Evolution from XP to XP2 saw an additional value of respect added, two of the original practices were removed, a number of other practices renamed and a set of corollary practices were also introduced. The separation of practices aimed to help practitioners to focus on achieving the primary set first to provide guidance on adopting and developing the fundamentals of XP. These are considered the essential practices to establish first for companies new to XP. XP adoption has an impact on the culture of the organisation, therefore, the corollary set introduced secondary practices that could be progressively developed overtime. The XP process is considered to have matured for a given organisation after each of the practices are gradually implemented overtime.

XP2 now involves five values, fourteen principles, eleven primary practices and thirteen corollary practices which provide guidance on how the approach should be implemented.

### 3.7.2.1 XP values

*Communication* is the first value which recognises that problems can quickly manifest as a result of lack of communication between the team and the customer involved (Marchesi 2005). Regular communication is therefore valued to promote an effective and collaborative effort between business and technical stakeholders during development. This is achieved by introducing practices that support paired and collective team activities.

Second, *simplicity* revolves around the question *"what is the simplest thing that could possibly work?"* (Beck and Andres 2005). Applying simplicity involves judgement being made based upon information that is currently available. Future complexity can be prematurely assumed by developers leading to designs that unnecessarily consume the efforts of developers.

The third value is regular *feedback* which is important for effectively managing change (Beck and Andres 2005). Keeping feedback cycles as short as possible ensures that requirements can be reprioritized as business value changes. Another benefit is that with only a limited amount of time to manifest, any potential problems can be quickly resolved by maintaining a regular flow of information (Jeffries *et al.* 2001).

The fourth value is *courage* which was introduced to mitigate the problem of developers feeling fear in cases where it is necessary to resist the pressure to deliver low quality code in order to meet immovable deadlines (Melis 2006). This value also empowers developers to make necessary adjustments later than expected in a project, in situations where fundamental problems are discovered and resolving this, results in delivering higher quality code. This also requires courage needed to throw away existing code if it is not productive.

The fifth value is *respect* which was later introduced to complement the previous four values. This states that respect should be equally afforded to the effort and contribution being made by other developers on the team. By fostering a culture of equal worth, the methodology succeeds because the team care about each other, the needs of the customer and the project throughout development (Marchesi 2005).

### 3.7.2.2 XP principles

The first XP principle is *humanity* which primarily acknowledges that software is developed by people for the purposes of addressing human needs. As such, humanity is recognised as an important aspect to be embraced during software development.

The principle of *economics* emphasises that software is primarily developed for the purposes of producing business value. Requirements developed remain closely aligned with business goals and decisions.

*Mutual benefit* asserts that software developed should benefit all stakeholders who are affected or concerned by a solution to be deployed. Achieving the appropriate balance with this principle is considered valuable since this helps to build and maintain healthy relationships between software developers producing code. Also, mutually beneficial solutions strengthen external relationships with customers such as business stakeholders and the software team.

*Self-similarity* is a principle that asserts that *"nature continuously uses fractal structures which are similar to themselves but at various scales"* (Beck and Andres 2005). Beck and Andres (2005) claim that this concept should be applied to software development, for the purposes of reusing similar solutions in a variety of different contexts.

Continuous *improvement* is a principle considered key to successful XP projects. This states that during each iteration, software produced gradually improves in quality and functionality through certain mechanisms such as feedback obtained from the customer representative, automated tests and the XP team itself (Beck and Andres 2005).

The principle of *diversity* values diverse stakeholder backgrounds since solutions to problems are better informed when multiple perspectives of the problem are involved. A new or alternative viewpoint as to how a problem might be addressed is beneficial and as such, teams that consist of multiple diverse skill sets are particularly valued. Beck and Andres (2005) acknowledge that with diversity comes conflicting views. However, this is not problematic since conflict is treated as an opportunity for embracing potential alternatives. Here, a favourable outcome of assembling diverse teams is *"creating the most valuable software possible within the time frame available"* (Beck and Andres 2005).

The principle of regular *reflection* on progress made suggests that XP teams frequently reflect on questions such as how and why work is being done for the purposes of continuously improving the development effort and the performance of the team.

The *flow* principle recommends regular deployment of small software releases by maintaining a consistent flow between streams of development activities. Keeping iterations as short as possible with frequent integration limits the scope for potential problems and supports the flow for incremental improvement of solutions under development (Beck and Andres 2005).

The principle of *opportunity* recognises that from a positive perspective, all problems encountered during development can present new opportunities for growth. As such, problems that emerge should be treated as opportunities where a necessary change could positively impact an existing process.

*Redundancy* is a principle which suggests that where possible every effort should be made to minimize redundant activities during development. A number of XP practices aim to reduce waste particularly for handling defects.

*Failure* should be embraced in order to positively react to situations in which developers do not succeed. Communicating and examining this situation *"imparts valuable knowledge"* to the developer (Beck and Andres 2005). Understanding the factors involved and the context in which a failure has occurred promotes learning and has the potential to prevent future similar situations from recurring.

The principle of *quality* encourages XP teams to produce the highest quality software that can be delivered within the available means. Jeffries *et al.* (2001) strongly suggest that developers take responsibility for enforcing this principle which includes resisting pressure to deploy in situations where low quality code is at risk of being prematurely delivered.

*Baby steps* are encouraged for the successful deployment of short regular increments of working software. Taking many small steps can steadily improve solutions and this is preferred since integrating big changes increases the likelihood of problems emerging. This principle helps to contain and solve problems quickly in a short space of time, for instance regular short builds help to isolate and resolve defects quickly.

*Accepted responsibility* states that *"responsibility cannot be assigned, it can only be accepted"* (Beck and Andres 2005). This principle promotes a holistic perspective of requirements to be adopted since developers are expected to estimate, design, implement and test their own user stories. Developers commit to this by signing their initials on the user stories they intend to develop, this also communicates to the rest of the team, who is responsible for developing which user stories in the current iteration.

### 3.7.2.3 XP practices

To support the XP values and principles, twenty four practices provide more concrete advice for implementing the approach. As mentioned earlier, the XP practices are divided into two categories where each is considered either a primary or a corollary practice. The primary set should be achieved first while the corollary set is gradually accomplished after the primary practices have begun to mature within the software organisation.

Collectively, the set of practices provide further guidance on implementing XP. Marchesi (2005) provides a classification of each of the practices dividing these into four specific areas: *requirements analysis and planning*, *team and human factors*, *design* and *software coding and releasing*. This classification is reproduced in Tables 7 to 10 where the first column indicates the practice number, the second column shows the practice name, the third column briefly describes each practice and the fourth column indicates whether each practice belongs to the primary (P) or corollary (C) set. For the purposes of completeness, all practices are briefly described in the following tables, however, only those practices relevant to this research are explained in further detail.

*Table 7 Requirements analysis and planning (Adapted from Marchesi 2005)*

| No. | Practice | Description | Type |
|-----|----------|-------------|------|
| Requirements Analysis and Planning | | | |
| 1 | User stories | Requirements should be described using user stories to provoke a discussion between the customer and developers | P |
| 2 | Weekly cycles | Lengthy development cycles can increase the complexity of problems encountered during deployment so weekly cycles are encouraged to mitigate this | P |
| 3 | Slack | Minor tasks are introduced which can be dropped later if necessary, this discourages a culture of over commitment in favour of maintaining cycles of genuinely predictable throughput | P |
| 4 | Quarterly cycles | For larger projects where it is not suitable to deliver weekly, work should be divided into quarterly cycles | P |
| 5 | Real customer involvement | Those who are directly affected have the most representative perspective of the problem and should be involved with the team throughout development | C |
| 6 | Incremental deployment | Software should be incrementally deployed to avoid problems associated with large deployment efforts | C |
| 7 | Negotiated scope | While fixing time, costs and expected quality, project scope should be negotiable to facilitate adaptation of functionality according to changing business value | C |
| 8 | Pay-per-use | Charging customers each time the system is used has the advantage of providing solid reliable feedback | C |
| 9 | Team continuity | Effective teams remain intact however, a sensible amount of rotation is encouraged to support knowledge transfer between teams | C |
| 10 | Shrinking teams | As teams develop knowledge and skill over time, while keeping workload constant, the number of members are gradually reduced with extra members then integrated onto new teams | C |

### 3.7.2.4 Requirements analysis and planning

In requirements analysis and planning, the practices of user stories and real customer involvement are relevant to this research. Requirements should be written in the form of *user stories*. Stories are natural language representations of requirements that encourage communication between customers and developers, (Marchesi *et al.* 2002). The general format of a user story is as follows:

As a *<role>*, I can *<activity>*, so that *<business value>*

Where the role represents the person performing the action, the activity represents the task the system should perform and business value represents what value will be achieved (Leffingwell 2011). User stories are written by the customer and intended as a place holder for further discussions surrounding the context of the business need to be addressed by each user story created. Considering that this is the primary mechanism for eliciting requirements in XP, expressing requirements as user stories is relevant to this work.

The second practice relevant under requirements analysis and planning is *real customer involvement*. This practice makes a distinction between indirect customer proxies or representatives and a customer who will actually use the system claiming that real customer involvement ensures that requirements developed most closely represent the needs of users in a given domain.

Originally XP was designed to accommodate a single onsite customer (Beck 1999), and although this practice in the revised version emphasises having a directly experienced customer (Beck and Andres 2005), it was not envisaged that multiple stakeholder roles may need to be involved in clarifying the problem context surrounding the requirements. A number of challenges have emerged for XP as a result of this which suggests that room for improvement for team-customer interaction is needed (Sharp and Robinson 2006), (Wang *et al.* 2008), (Mohammadi *et al.* 2009), (Cao L. and Ramesh 2008), (Martin *et al.* 2009a), (Martin *et al.* 2009b), (Hoda *et al.* 2010a), (Hoda *et al.* 2010b), (Racheva *et al.* 2010), (Fraser *et al.* 2010). These challenges are further elaborated later in section 3.7.2.6.

Table 8 lists the practices categorised under team and human factors, the leftmost column shows the practice number, the second column indicates the name of the practice, the third column provides a brief description for each practice and the fourth indicates whether each practice belongs to the primary (P) or corollary (C) set.

*Table 8 Team and human factors (Adapted from Marchesi 2005)*

| Team and Human Factors | | | |
|---|---|---|---|
| **No.** | **Practice** | **Description** | **Type** |
| 11 | Sit Together | Teams should sit together and work in an open space to support open, collaborative and effective communication between members | P |
| 12 | Whole team | Teams should consist of the relevant expertise, a set of a diverse roles are necessary to effectively complete a given project | P |
| 13 | Informative workspace | This practice encourages the use of the wall to post informative artefacts such as user stories and wall charts depicting progress including potential problems that require attention keeping everyone informed | P |
| 14 | Energized work | Developers are encouraged to develop a sustained working pace to contribute effectively to the rest of the team and the project | P |
| 15 | Pair programming | Developers should sit together and code in pairs as this supports tacit knowledge transfer and proactive learning between team members | P |

Three XP practices categorised under team and human factors in Table 8 are also relevant to this research. These are *sit together, whole team* and *informative workspace.*

Teams should sit together and work in an open space. This practice fosters open communication between developers suggesting developers be physically located in an *"open workspace"* (Beck and Andres 2005). Considering that the customer role is part of the development team in XP, this practice is important to provide support for communicating requirements and problem space understanding between the members of the team.

Whole team implies that a sense of belonging encouraging shared responsibility is important on teams. Here teams should be made up of developers with diverse skill sets to bring a variety of perspectives to problem solving activities.

Informative workspace promotes a working environment where artefacts such as posters are used to inform the team about the project status, progression, tasks completed and those yet to be performed.

Table 9 lists the set of practices categorised under design. The practice number is indicated on the leftmost column, the second column indicates the name of each practice, the third column provides a brief description and the fourth indicates whether each practice is part of the primary (P) or corollary (C) set.

*Table 9 Design (Adapted from Marchesi 2005)*

| Design | | | |
|---|---|---|---|
| No. | Practice | Description | Type |
| 16 | Incremental design | Designs should be incrementally developed which supports change and the need to adapt designs in a cost effective manner | P |
| 17 | Test first development | This practice focuses developers on writing test criteria prior to coding to verify that the code will behave as expected and ensures that code written is directly testable with the benefit of acceptance criteria for each story established in advance | P |
| 18 | Root cause analysis | Rather than solving a problem that is likely to recur, the root cause of the problem should be determined to permanently resolve persistent issues | C |

One practice categorised under design and relevant to this work is *root cause analysis.* This is a practice that encourages developers to proactively seek out the root cause of defects as they emerge to prevent the same type of defect from recurring in future situations.

The remaining practices categorised under software coding and releasing are not directly relevant to the purposes of this research, hence, these are briefly summarised in Table 10, where the first column indicates the practice number, the second column shows the practice name, the third column provides a brief description and the fourth indicates whether each practice belongs to the primary (P) or corollary (C) set.

*Table 10 Software coding and releasing (Adapted from Marchesi 2005)*

| No. | Practice | Description | Type |
|---|---|---|---|
| **Software Coding and Releasing** | | | |
| 19 | Ten minute build | Integrate work with automated system builds of ten minutes as any longer is likely to discourage a culture of regular builds | P |
| 20 | Continuous integration | Integration problems can take longer to solve than actual development time so software should be integrated completely as often as every two hours | P |
| 21 | Code and tests | Code and tests are considered to be the only permanent artefacts since they closely correlate with customer-derived functionality. Here it is recommended that only these artefacts are to be consistently maintained and any other documentation required should be generated from these artefacts | C |
| 22 | Shared code | Developers are encouraged to take collective responsibility for code developed with each member able to modify any code regardless of the author | C |
| 23 | Single code base | Multiple code streams become increasingly problematic for scalability so a single code base is encouraged | C |
| 24 | Daily deployment | Software developed goes into production at the end of each working day gathering quick feedback on implemented requirements | C |

### 3.7.2.5 The process

Requirements are expressed as user stories, represented as short narrative descriptions of expected system behaviour from the perspective of the user (Jeffries et al. 2001). Initially, user stories identify a high level plan for each release of the project. The customer representative prioritizes each story according to business value. Attention is then focused on the first release with a number of prioritized stories used to identify the first short iteration. Developers further divide the stories into tasks and estimate a timeframe to complete each task. Writing requirements in this format ensures that the effort to complete the requirement is also estimated as soon as possible. Figure 8 below illustrates an example of a typical user story.

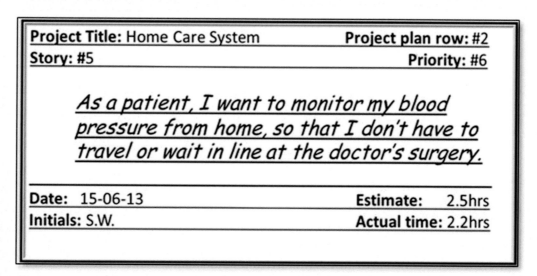

*Figure 8 Sample user story*

*Planning poker* is an agile practice often used to estimate the time to complete user stories (Sletholt 2011). In using this technique, each developer is presented with a deck of cards where the number on each card represents a time estimate. A user story is read aloud and each developer assigns a card to the story where the number on the card indicates the time each developer thinks it will take to implement the story. Cards are initially placed face down on a table and when all developers have made a choice the cards are turned over. If the estimates are relatively even, it suggests that the developers are in agreement and the given estimate is considered reasonably accurate. However, if the difference between estimates is significant then a discussion is held to negotiate the reasons for this and once differences are aired the process then repeats until consensus on estimates is reached (Grenning 2002).

User stories and their associated tasks are placed together on the story board. The board referred to as *"the wall"* by Sharp *et al.* (2006), is the main focal point of the room. Developers choose a story to complete from the board and commit to this by signing their initials on the card and taking it down from the story board for development. When the user story is complete, the developer ticks the card and returns it to a new position on the story board. Alternatively if the story is not fully complete, the card is considered to be still pending and is returned to the same position on the board. Complete stories become features of the system where they can be further developed in upcoming iterations.

The story board, populated with user stories and tasks, provides a clear indication of what work has been done and what work has yet to be completed. Stories placed with their tasks also allow developers to envisage dependencies, essentially providing a visual representation of the work plan to the team. The colour of a card also carries specific meaning and can be used to convey warning signs. Some examples from Sharp *et al.* (2006) showed:

- Green cards signified stories, white for tasks;

- Blue cards related to features for staff;

- Orange flags indicated incomplete acceptance tests;

- Pink cards described bugs.

The positioning of the cards on the story board can also communicate specific meaning. The top three rows for instance in Figure 9 taken from (Pietri 2004) contained recently completed stories. From the fourth row and to the left of the board were scheduled stories and to the right were unscheduled stories.

*Figure 9 Storyboard organised by Pietri (2004)*
*Photograph courtesy of James Home*

A more comprehensive set of examples which further illustrate the useful nature of the storyboard in practice can also be found here: http://williampietri.com/writing/2015/the-big-board/

### 3.7.2.6 Challenges for the customer role in XP

As mentioned previously a number of challenges have emerged for the role of the customer in XP. These are discussed in the following points:

Sharp and Robinson (2006) identified a clash between the culture of the customer and the development team during continual team-customer interaction. This had a negative impact on the project indicating room for improvement needed during these interactions.

Wang *et al.* (2008) discuss a number of pitfalls for the role of the customer, *none* of which are addressed by XP. These include the potential for problems that emerge due to inadequately low levels of customer participation, a heavy burden being placed on the customer, difficulty writing good quality user stories, inadequate customer preparation, the timeframe for feedback and overcoming communication problems.

Mohammadi *et al.* (2009) highlight challenges for the customer role which include partial access to an onsite customer, the gap in terminology presenting difficulties finding a common language to communicate, full time active participation may not be possible due to time constraints of the customer, also, customer engagement is likely to decrease when a direct interest in the tasks being conducted is not perceived.

Cao L. and Ramesh (2008) report considerable challenges obtaining access to the customer and in reaching consensus. The authors identified seven agile RE practices and described the benefits and challenges of each. One challenge relevant is that customer representation is difficult and face-to-face communication relies on *"intensive interaction"* between the customer and developers at the start. Where more than one customer group is involved, *reaching consensus* in the short development cycle is considerably difficult.

Martin *et al.* (2009a) identified ten customer specific roles that have been adopted in XP practice where the role of the customer has expanded into teams of multiple representatives. The authors classify these roles into three categories involving direction setting, skill specialists and collaboration guides. Here, each person on a customer team negotiates with and represents a widely diverse stakeholder group.

Additionally, Martin *et al.* (2009b) further highlight the complexity of the customer role by identifying eight customer focused practices in industry relating to three XP practices of *whole team*, *real customer involvement* and *energized work*. These include customer apprentice, onsite programmer, roadshow for demonstrations, customer pairing, customer boot camp and big picture up-front. These additional practices were informally created by practitioners and found to be successful in supporting the role of the customer in XP.

Hoda *et al.* (2010a) identified a distinct gap between business and technical terminology during team-customer collaboration on agile projects. This was improved through the use of a translator role which was informally created in practice to facilitate more effective communication. The role of the translator involved developing a dictionary of terms documenting business terminology, using user stories and iterative reasoning to clarify that implementation detail clearly aligned with business logic it intended to address. Also, promoting cross-functionality was another responsibility undertaken which fostered understanding between multiple viewpoints. Significantly, the authors conclude that regular interaction between diverse cross-functional roles has the capacity for all team members to learn from a given domain becoming proficient in translating business terminology used to communicate the requirements.

Hoda *et al.* (2010b) found that lack of customer involvement was a significant challenge experienced in industry. A set of practices which emerged from their work, known as *"agile undercover"*, are used to address this problem. These include *Changing Priority*, a practice used where developers demote stories that have not received the appropriate level of clarification from customers. *Risk Assessment Up Front* involves a questionnaire being filled prior to the commencement of a project to gauge the level of involvement customer representatives are likely to commit. *Story Owners*, a practice that involved multiple customer representatives being assigned to stories to mitigate the potential of lack of availability of a single representative. The *Customer Proxy* was beneficial for coordinating between customers and the team. *Just Demos* in some cases were the only means of obtaining regular collaborative stakeholder engagement. *E-Collaboration* included communicating via web conferencing, phone calls and email. *Extreme Undercover* is a practice where teams followed agile practices internally unbeknown to the customer. This was used to mitigate *"the extreme consequences"* of loss of business (Hoda *et al.* 2010b).

Hoda *et al.* (2011) identified that senior management support is critical for effective self-organisation within teams. Factors include creating and maintaining an open and informal organisational culture, negotiating agile friendly contracts, providing financial sponsorship and managing human resources in a manner that supports self-organisation. Indeed, where these factors were not present among the organisations studied, self-organisation was challenging and in some cases, had been disabled on teams.

Racheva *et al.* (2010) found that prioritization is conducted differently than expected in practice. This work identifies that *a joint effort* is needed between customers and developers in *creating business value* and the authors point out that support is needed to further extend this.

Fraser *et al.* (2010) claim that face-to-face communication requires *"catalysts such as facilitation to overcome challenges such as sustaining trust, avoiding false consensus and ensuring diversity of opinion is sustained"*. In this work facilitating improvisation and negotiation are described as key factors in developing high trust relationships for agile projects. They assert that creating an environment where *"collaboration can flourish"* involves supporting informative workspaces, visible artefacts depicting progression along a time continuum and staying in close contact with the customer claiming that self-organising teams cannot effectively operate in the absence of these conditions. The authors suggest that achieving effective and efficient interactions between stakeholders are highly sought after, considered *"the gold standard"* in agile software development. Significantly, they point out that very few contributions focus on the important aspect of fostering collaboration between stakeholders indicating that this merits significant attention from researchers.

In summary, a series of critical issues have remained unaddressed with regard to the role of the customer in XP. This strongly suggests that explicit support is required to facilitate team-customer interaction during requirements elicitation on XP projects.

The specific challenges to be addressed for RE in XP can therefore be described as follows:

- Additional support is required for self-organisation and ASP to succeed on teams;

- Limited access to relevant stakeholder representatives must be addressed;

- A common language must be created for effective communication between diverse domains;

- Multiple diverse viewpoints must be consolidated into a collective perspective of stakeholder requirements for development;

- An informative workspace is required for writing and prioritizing user stories in a collaborative manner.

This research will address these challenges by focusing primarily on the following key points:

1. A suitable *user inclusion* strategy must be developed to support ongoing *ASP* during team-customer interactions, this should consider further direction needed to proactively encourage *self-organisation* including the role of the customer on teams;

2. The limited amount of time representatives have to commit to projects suggests that the *time frame* available must be more *effectively and efficiently utilized;*

3. *Implicit knowledge transfer* between relevant representatives requires the development of a *common language* to promote *mutual understanding* of the issues to be addressed during face-to-face communication;

4. In developing *consensus* a practical solution is in demand for *collaborative negotiations* particularly in the case where multiple diverse stakeholders are involved. This is also relevant for consolidating the set of diverse viewpoints into a more *collective and representative perspective* of the problem to be addressed;

5. *Writing and prioritizing user stories* can be supported through the provision of *contextual detail* at the upper business level, it is therefore necessary to explicitly provide a means with which to develop a more *informative workspace* to support this need.

This research will therefore focus on developing a suitable solution to these issues for the purposes of strengthening support needed to achieve efficient and effective team-customer interaction during requirements elicitation on XP projects.

### 3.7.2.7 Justification for the choice of XP

The existing set of defined AMs show that some provide more extensive guidance than others. One such AM that stands out with regard to this is XP. Communication, simplicity, feedback, courage and respect are values that could support the needs of multiple diverse stakeholder groups and specific reference is made to the importance of nurturing mutually beneficial solutions in adequately addressing the needs of stakeholders concerned.

In contrast to the other AMs, the practices defined by XP under team and human factors specifically provide additional guidance for a collaborative development effort. Root cause analysis under design aims to surface key sources of problems as soon as possible. With reference to the factors that affect the communication of requirements between developers and other stakeholders, XP is the only AM that makes explicit reference to the importance of nurturing diverse backgrounds on teams. However, support is required to extend these benefits to include the customer domain.

Scrum, Crystal Methods, FDD, DSDM and AUP all advocate the definition of specific roles on agile projects. However, Cohn (2003) warns that the predefinition of specialised roles can cause members to *"shirk"* rather than accept responsibilities that are not explicitly stated under particular role definitions, this is counterintuitive to accepting responsibility for the system as a whole (Cohn 2003). While Scrum only lightly defines specific roles, it subsequently falls short on providing additional concrete guidance. In contrast, XP advocates a team of generalised specialists and only broadly defines the role of the customer. This suggests that an XP team would have the greatest potential to fully accept responsibility for a system to address the needs of stakeholders as a whole. However, a distinct challenge duly noted here is that XP does not address how the consolidation of interdisciplinary stakeholder perspectives could be managed for effective customer involvement on teams. While XP provides the most concrete guidance, the method proceeds with the least amount of rigor and the greatest level of flexibility applied during elicitation. As such, this particular AM appears to exhibit the most suitable characteristics for an evolutionary approach.

## 3.8 Requirements for an evolutionary framework

With reference to the characteristics of a desirable approach to RE in DAS as detailed in section 3.2, considering the frequently reported requirements challenges discussed in section 3.3, the shortcomings of existing RE approaches as detailed in section 3.4, the candidate techniques for a novel or adapted approach and suggested improvements investigated in section 3.5, the challenges raised for the role of the customer in section 3.7, the following set of criteria with the potential to support the development of an evolutionary approach to RE can be seen to emerge.

1. The candidate approach will exploit brainstorming, scenario analysis or prototyping. Indeed a combination of any or all of these techniques has potential;

2. Due to challenges relating to difficulties understanding and to improve and support face-to-face communication, the candidate approach should support stakeholder interaction and involvement through a visioning or exploration phase prior to writing requirements;

3. Due to inevitable changing conditions, iteration is a prerequisite;

4. The candidate approach should exploit the use of simple tools to support the development of a common language in communicating requirements. As such a steep learning curve should not be introduced;

5. Support is needed to identify appropriate stakeholders since clearly stakeholders relevant to the problem context must be present and involved;

6. The candidate approach should support stakeholder negotiation including the identification and resolution of requirements conflict;

7. Annotation of requirements where necessary should be possible. This includes support required for developing additional context needed to support the requirements;

8. The candidate approach should make every effort to maximise design capability.

## 3.9 Summary

Chapter three began by describing the requirements elicitation process examining the complexity of stakeholders that can be involved on projects. For DAS, AMs are at least partially compliant with the majority of characteristics for a desirable RE approach as defined in HCS. However, some shortcomings here suggest that further support for ASP is needed. After investigating the frequency of challenges reported in RE, stakeholder management, understanding and communication issues require further attention. A critique of existing approaches to RE, also draws attention to a series of pertinent limitations, and this presents a difficult challenge for integration with AMs in practice. Upon examining existing elicitation techniques and expanding further on these, three techniques; brainstorming, scenario analysis and prototyping can be described as user based, are iterative and collaborative and focus on both current and future business needs. This suggests that these techniques have the potential to be modified for a novel or adapted approach to RE.

AMs are favourable since they accommodate change taking an iterative and incremental approach to developing requirements. Particularly XP provides the most guidance and appears to be the most flexible with the least amount of rigor applied to the early stages of development. However, customer involvement is problematic when multiple stakeholders must be involved. In order to develop an evolutionary approach, flexibility and adaptation is important. Upon examining the challenges and factors for success, a set of requirements for a flexible evolutionary approach are derived.

# Chapter 4  Exploratory Case Study

## 4.1 Overview

Chapter 4 presents the initial exploratory case study undertaken. This began with an investigation into the roles and challenges for an agile team where the author acted as a participant-observer on an agile project.  This is followed by a series of interviews conducted with practitioners to develop a deeper understanding for how requirements are elicited in industry. The findings from these two studies inform the development of the proposed solution presented later in chapters 5 and 6 respectively.

## 4.2 Evaluation of Roles and Challenges for an Agile Team

To develop a deeper understanding for agile software development, the author played the role of participant-observer in an agile project conducted in an academic setting. This opportunity provided first-hand experience on an agile development project including the difficulties encountered by an agile team. The study was conducted with a team of four final year computing students using Scrum as their development approach. Prior to the commencement of the project the team had previous knowledge of AMs, particularly Scrum.

The problem to be addressed, involved consideration of a timetabling system, examined over a six week period which took place on a part time basis over six two hour sessions. Observations were recorded after each working session. During the project the team were situated in a large room with a table in the centre and tools such as the whiteboard, flipcharts, marker pens and post it notes were available. The role of the customer representative and Product Owner (PO) was played by a member of staff and the role of the Scrum Master was played by the author.

At the end of the project the team were also asked to explain the status of the project to an independent reviewer. There are a number of reasons in a live project where it may be necessary to provide an *on the spot* explanation for the project status to date. For instance, a new member unexpectedly assigned to the team may require an update, a senior figure from the target domain may request an overview of the current status to assess progress, or a new stakeholder may take over the role of the customer on projects. Considering that Scrum generates additional artefacts that assist in the visualisation of the project status, this project provided an opportunity to assess how the presence of such artefacts may assist the team in creating an overview of the project, understanding this clearly and conveying progress to date to an outside stakeholder. The purpose of the independent review was therefore to evaluate the teams understanding of the project and their ability to communicate this clearly using the artefacts that had been developed.

### 4.2.1 Direct Observations

The team studied the problem background and initially, a brief discussion took place with a customer representative available. One particular difficulty that was observed was the lack of focal point for the discussion. Despite various potential users being suggested by the PO, the focus was very narrow on the user that most closely matched the developers themselves. The group then commenced writing user stories, however, the customer representative was not consulted during story writing and the sprint plan did not include the customers input. For instance, the team occasionally sought clarification for general questions from the customer, however, during sprint planning, prioritization of the actual stories written did not involve the customer. This indicated that the team had first assumed what stories should be written and second, the order in which stories should be developed. As development progressed whole group communication was only observed during the daily stand up meetings.

During the third session further problems emerged as communication breakdown occurred. Although two team members consistently worked together, the remaining two operated more independently and during one short stand up meeting it became apparent that some stories already developed had in fact been duplicated, here, time had been wasted by separate team members unnecessarily developing the same functionality. Although reasonable progress was made throughout the project, communication between team members did not improve as for the remainder of the project, the team continued to work separately. This indicated that communication problems had not been fully resolved since a more collaborative effort did not develop between the team members after this point.

### 4.2.2 Customer Experience

One problem observed was that the developers ignored the customer representative, instead making assumptions about the problem based on their own experience. This in turn led to user stories that were written from a technical perspective representing the *system* rather than the *business problem*. Despite a customer proxy being available this customer's involvement during the prioritization was minimal. As target users were not clearly defined, consideration for their requirements in prioritization decisions were absent.

### 4.2.3 Independent Review

At the end of the project a short review was conducted where the team were asked to explain the project to an independent person who had no previous involvement or knowledge about the status of the project. This took approximately 15 minutes. Specific questions asked related to: *the project background, target domain users, process followed, how the problem background was understood, project progress, problems faced, plans for progression* and *changes from the initial plan*.

The team used the Scrum artefacts with the user stories created which were displayed on the wall. In particular the project was described by making reference to the sprint backlog and remaining stories which had not yet been completed were visible in the product backlog. Initially the group appeared confident in explaining the project however this dissipated when they were asked to explain the problem to be addressed. This appeared laboured as they had difficulty providing a clear explanation and frequently reverted to using technical terminology which had been discouraged.

A lack of focus was also observed here for the overall goal of the project and user stories were based upon system rather than customer needs. A mismatch in the terminology between the reviewer and the team members suggested that a common language was also missing. When the team were asked which stories represented user needs, the question was not clearly answered and they claimed that *they* were also the potential users for the system. Without the presence of a problem overview only a development perspective of the problem background could be observed.

### 4.2.4 Summary

In summary, participant observation on this project presented an opportunity to develop a greater understanding into the roles and challenges for an agile team. This project suggests that difficulties can emerge remaining focused when an overall project goal or high level objective is not clearly established from the outset. Here, a focus tilted in the direction of the team resulted in developing requirements reflecting the technical rather than the business nature of the problem. This had occurred after story writing and prioritization did not directly involve the customer representative. Also, a common language had not been established between team members for communication throughout the project. This can also contribute to difficulty providing a clear and coherent explanation of the project status to an independent person. Communication issues can emerge not only between team members but also between the customer representative and the team.

This suggests that despite the fact that Scrum supports the generation of additional artefacts that aim to visualise the high level perspective of current progress, this may not necessarily improve (a) *understanding between members (including the customer)*, (b) *support for the development of a collective goal*, or (c) *the communication of progress to date to an unexpected stakeholder*. Also, despite the fact that simple tools had been utilized, *a common language* between members did not appear to have developed.

## 4.3 Industry Interviews

Based upon a review of the literature as presented in chapter 3, and as part of the first and second objectives, this case explores *the process of eliciting requirements* as the single unit of analysis across a number of organisations from the perspectives of nine industry practitioners. As such a series of interviews were conducted to develop a deeper understanding for requirements elicitation in practice, and in particular, the factors affecting this process from a communication perspective. For the purposes of confidentiality, each organisation including participants interviewed were given pseudonyms. The specific interview protocol followed is explained in further detail in section 2.8.2.1. The following sections present a summary of the main findings that emerged.

## 4.4 Main Findings

Alongside the tools and techniques used to elicit requirements, a number of additional activities relating to stakeholder management were important during the process of eliciting requirements on projects. This is presented in the following sections.

### 4.4.1 Tools and Techniques

One unexpected finding showed that currently only a single participant employed a dedicated COTS requirements tool. All other tools utilized are those that support *communication of requirements* between stakeholders on projects. Specifically two companies had developed in-house tools but these are not described by participants as requirements tools, and one is described as *"effectively a communication portal"*. Here, features developed for in-house tools cater more for specific situational needs.

Overall, across all interviews a number of collaborative interactive tools and techniques were used to elicit requirements. Stakeholder management involves identification, access to, engagement and subsequent involvement of relevant stakeholders on projects. Figure 10 shows the set of commonly used tools and techniques on the left column. The top right row indicates the list of participant organisations and an 'x' in each column shows which tools and techniques had been employed across all interviews. Collaborative tools and techniques such as *storyboarding*, *mock up scenarios*, *brainstorming* and the *whiteboard* are most commonly used among the smaller organisations. Informal meetings are regularly employed by all organisations, two support this by conducting formal meetings to clarify and review requirements and workshops including JAD further indicate that group interaction techniques support elicitation in practice.

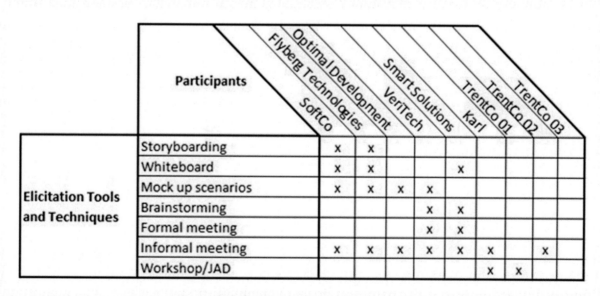

| Elicitation Tools and Techniques | Participants | SoftCo | Flyberg Technologies | Optimal Development | VeriTech | SmartSolutions | Karl | TrentCo 01 | TrentCo 02 | TrentCo 03 |
|---|---|---|---|---|---|---|---|---|---|---|
| | Storyboarding | x | x | | | | | | | |
| | Whiteboard | x | x | | | x | | | | |
| | Mock up scenarios | x | x | x | x | | | | | |
| | Brainstorming | | | | x | x | | | | |
| | Formal meeting | | | | x | x | | | | |
| | Informal meeting | x | x | x | x | x | x | | x | |
| | Workshop/JAD | | | | | | | x | x | |

*Figure 10 Elicitation tools and techniques*

## 4.4.2 Stakeholder Management

An additional set of activities appeared to surround stakeholder management. Figure 11 shows on the left column, the set of commonly practiced stakeholder management activities that assist in successfully communicating requirements. The top right row indicates the list of organisations and an 'x' in each column shows which activities had been employed across all interviews.

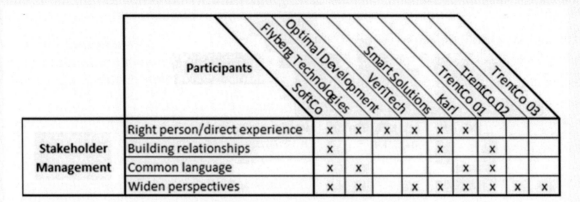

| Participants | | Flybers Technologies SoftCo | Optimal Development | Smart Solutions VeriTech | Smart Solutions | Karl | TrentCo 01 | TrentCo 02 | TrentCo 03 |
|---|---|---|---|---|---|---|---|---|---|
| **Stakeholder Management** | Right person/direct experience | x | x | x | x | x | x | | | |
| | Building relationships | x | | | | x | | x | | |
| | Common language | x | x | | | | x | x | | |
| | Widen perspectives | x | x | | | x | x | x | x | x |

*Figure 11 Stakeholder management activities*

Three participants asserted that specific abilities are required for successful customer representation. This includes trust, flexibility, regular feedback and a good communicator. However, a challenge here is that it is not known in advance which qualities representatives possess therefore software organisations cannot be assured if the project is likely to succeed until after the representative has become involved. This suggests that requirements development would benefit from this need being explicitly conveyed to a given target domain from the outset.

In the remaining cases where particular qualities for the customer profile were not explicitly stated, practitioners referred to the importance of the customer representative having *direct experience* with the requirement to be addressed for the purposes of successfully communicating the necessary problem context to developers.

In the large organisations, stakeholder management was more structured indicating that engineering requirements by including stakeholders with specific areas of expertise at different stages during the development cycle can provide high level validation of potential requirements. Support needed for a rotating stakeholder group was evident since the priorities of a diverse set of perspectives become relevant at different stages during development.

Another activity involves building long term relationships with business stakeholders as an important part of elicitation since requirements had been successfully communicated between stakeholders given this condition. Also, four participants confirmed that using a common language to communicate requirements is important during elicitation.

It is also important where narrow perspectives exist to develop a wider more representative view of a given requirement. This necessitates suitable stakeholders with diverse viewpoints assembling during elicitation for a short period of time. In order to establish a collective perspective and to identify and resolve potential conflict, this initial stage should be conducted in an informal dynamic manner.

### 4.4.2.1 Communication between roles

Figure 12 illustrates an example of the diverse stakeholder roles that emerged throughout this study. Of particular interest is that different roles are relevant to the requirements during inception, development and post deployment. During inception a broad range of roles crossing different disciplines can be involved. After inception internal and external teams with equally diverse roles interact as the project proceeds to implementation. Early adopters can also interact with the teams at this point. When the project has been delivered another diverse range of roles can be involved when new requirements or change requests have been identified in the target domain environment.

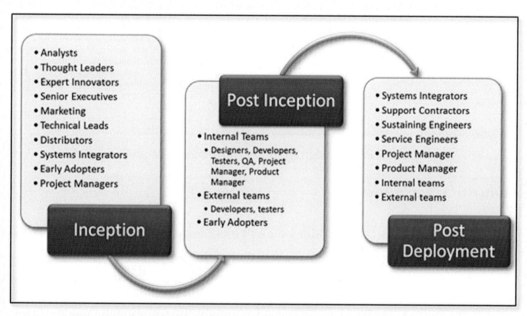

*Figure 12 Stakeholder roles relevant at different stages of a project*

Depending on the expected context of use, requirements may also need to be specified at different levels of granularity to be reused. This requires support for a collaborative approach from suitable or directly experienced representatives. As mentioned above, in the cases where narrow perspectives emerged this necessitated developing a wide or more broadened view of the requirements. A consequence of this was that priority shifted from stakeholders with narrow perspectives to involving more stakeholders than originally anticipated to develop a more collective view. An unpredictable factor here is that this only becomes apparent after early encounters with stakeholders. This suggests that the priorities of a diverse range of stakeholders require support to better manage multiple changing viewpoints of a given requirement.

As illustrated in Figure 13, four triggers could be observed where the priority of requirements along a time continuum shifts between different stakeholders during a project, these include:

the quality of stakeholders, resource availability, vertical scope of requirements and the project timeline. The following points elaborate on this.

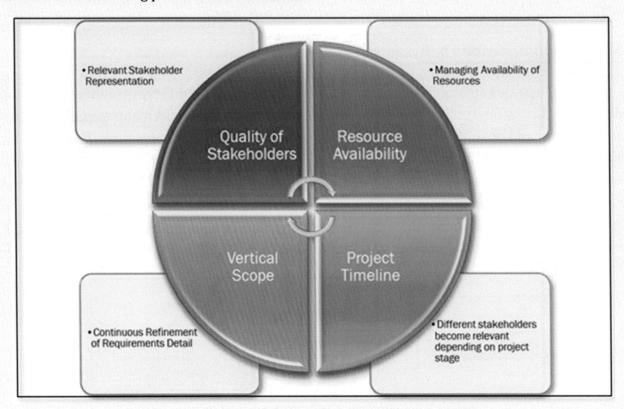

*Figure 13 Priority shift between stakeholders on projects*

### 4.4.2.2 Quality of stakeholders

The involvement of unsuitable stakeholders on a project is generally unforeseen. However, this is important since once it becomes apparent, this triggers priority to shift to other stakeholders. Solutions in practice to the situation of unsuitable stakeholders on projects are not formally documented and the process of identifying and resolving the situation of unsuitable stakeholders generally proceeds in an ad hoc informal manner. Since the potential qualities of stakeholders are not known prior to early encounters, this presents a problem that is clearly difficult to predict in advance.

### 4.4.2.3 Resource availability

The availability of resources is important where a relevant stakeholder is not accessible. In practice, when this problem becomes apparent, priority shifts to the next available resource. However, the next available stakeholder may not be suitable or could equally yield new requirements or even new stakeholders who need to be consulted. Another point here is that this subsequent stakeholder may be to some extent removed from the context of the requirement to be elicited. This presents a potential risk to the accuracy of requirements being elicited from this resource. Problems such as these continue to trigger priority to shift between available resources until the requirement has been refined to the appropriate level of detail for implementation.

### 4.4.2.4 Vertical scope

Early requirements are generally high level. However, when more detail about a requirement is needed, it could be for the purposes of exploration, clarification or to support reuse. Broadly defined high level requirements can obscure recognition of the appropriate level of detail needed for implementation. Consequently, requirements acquire depth as more relevant detail emerges. Here, this concept is referred to as *vertical scope*. However, in order to elicit the requirement to an appropriate level of depth, other stakeholders often need to be consulted, and subsequently, new requirements can emerge from this. This triggers priority to shift to stakeholders who provide more specific detail as it is needed. This is also relevant when requirements need to be specified at different levels of granularity to support multiple potential target audiences.

### 4.4.2.5 Project timeline

As the project timeline progresses, different stakeholders can become more relevant depending on the stage the project is at. For instance, for the purposes of elicitation, priority begins with relevant stakeholders in the target domain who initially assert requirements. However, during the latter stages, more technical requirements detail is gradually acquired. This triggers a shift in priority to designer stakeholders who become more relevant during design, developer stakeholders who become more relevant during implementation, testers who become more relevant during testing and so on.

Overall, and on a wider scale, whether stakeholder priority shift occurs due to the quality of stakeholders, resource availability, vertical scope or project timeline, factors that contribute to each shift in priority are initially unknown hence equally difficult to pre-empt. Each of the four contributing factors that trigger the shift are subsequently affected by a series of volatile inputs not formally documented, measured or channelled during requirements elicitation. This suggests that the process of shifting priority between relevant stakeholders during requirements development overall, takes the form of an informal ad hoc process.

The industry study suggests that each path through the enactment of the process of successfully communicating requirements occurs in a unique and unpredictable manner. For instance, the case study presented here illustrates that the successful communication of requirements depends on a number of contributing factors that do not appear at the outset to follow any particular pattern, for example:

- The extent to which a stakeholder is considered appropriately qualified to provide accurate and relevant requirements detail is initially unknown prior to early encounters with a development team. However, this problem dissipates as strong team-customer relationships gradually build overtime;

- The extent to which the appropriate requirements resources can be identified and made available for ongoing involvement throughout projects is also unclear. Certain unexpected constraints for instance, with regard the availability of resources must be managed as they dynamically emerge;

- The depth of requirements in terms of how much detail will be needed for implementation is clearly not known in advance. However, this gradually emerges with continuous refinement;

- As the project timeline proceeds different roles including members of the development team may unexpectedly require more specific detail to be sought from the original stakeholders. Again this presents a volatile factor since exactly which detail will be required and from whom, is not known in advance.

In all of the above cases, priority in terms of the type of resource and the specific requirements detail needed, constantly shifts between available resources. However, considering that this was only recognisable in hindsight, a problem for each project, is that the order of this shift between relevant resources is not known in advance of development, and as such it remains difficult to pre-empt and manage this as projects proceed.

One consequence of this is that each instance of the process of *successfully communicating requirements* in practice involves a series of volatile factors as inputs. These inputs present the opposite of what is needed to develop and improve requirements process using predictive instrumentation. Instead it appears to be important to utilize emergent instrumentation to enable a lightweight yet structured approach to support the evolution of requirements as they appear to emerge overtime. Overall, this unpredictable shift in priority suggests that balancing the priorities of a rotating stakeholder group needs support and direction from the outset. It is also clearly evident that the process of elicitation in practice is indeed affected by a set of human related factors that require additional support to be resolved for a mutually beneficial outcome.

### 4.4.3 Discussion

In relation to stakeholder management activities detailed in 4.4.2, customer representatives must possess particular key skills and/or direct experience for communication to succeed during elicitation. Discovering genuine stakeholders surrounded the idea of relevant stakeholder representation where developer stakeholders were trying to distinguish between theoretical and genuine stakeholders (one has direct experience in the problem domain, the other has not). This also included ideas behind the concept of the 'right' stakeholder which is supportive in part of Boehm and Turners CRACK qualities needed from customer representatives for successful communication on projects. Here, the term 'right' can be viewed as situationally specific meaning it is context-dependent and as such, the term cannot be universally defined.

The extent to which customers possess the skills and qualities desired, cannot be predetermined in advance of the commencement of projects. In fact, this is entirely subjective since such skills and abilities may be *unique* for multiple diverse stakeholders involved in each situation. While this rather volatile factor concerning the skill base of stakeholders is initially unknown, its presence nevertheless is key to effectively communicating requirements. It can therefore be stated that the criteria contingent upon successful communication of requirements in practice to prevail, are in fact, amethodical. This point is also supportive the work of Elliot-Sim *et al.* (2008) who identify *"good communication"* as an amethodical property in RE.

Building long term relationships with stakeholders can also be considered entirely subjective since it is not known in advance how this can be successfully achieved. As pointed out by one expert practitioner, RE *"is a personality-driven activity"* and as such it crosses over into the socio-cultural aspect of requirements elicitation. The need for, alongside the extent to which long term relationships are established is initially unknown, it can therefore be stated that the criteria contingent upon successfully building long term relationships over time are in fact, amethodical.

The challenge of narrow perspectives on projects is also inherently complex; for example when narrow perspectives are detected, more specific questions must be answered, such as: how do we know this? which stakeholders have these?, how narrow are they?, what other stakeholders and/or sources are relevant to contact in order to widen perspectives? will other stakeholders need to be involved from this stage on? will new unexpected requirements emerge from this? and how will this affect the overall business goal? Informal process used in practice to detect and resolve narrow perspectives is indicative of the presence of one or more amethodical systems development characteristics. Further, a successful solution to this problem in practice is to broaden perspectives which occurs both in an informal dynamic manner, and outside of the normal development schedule. This suggests the criteria contingent upon effectively detecting and solving the challenge of narrow perspectives on projects in practice, are in fact, amethodical.

Finally, the notion of a rotating stakeholder group also defies rationalist logic in that; it illuminates a process of continuous refinement in cases where further requirements detail is needed for development. Priority between stakeholders and indeed other resources then constantly shifts in order to gain access to the appropriate detail required. This shift in priority between available resources to refine further detail, occurs in an ad hoc informal manner. As such, the consequences in that; the potential for a myriad of new requirements and/or new stakeholders to become involved is heightened. Problems that emerge from this explosion of unexpected information are also managed in an informal ad hoc manner throughout development.

This continuous shift in priority between relevant resources, occurs overall in an informal dynamic manner, and outside of the project schedule. This suggests that the set of additional stakeholder management activities identified in this study can be described as an amethodical exemplar responding to emergent systems development needs. This confirms previous research in this area; that it is indeed necessary *"to provide amethodical software practitioners tools and process models that support improvisation and provide the resources to innovate, while still using a software process"* (Gallardo-Valencia and Elliot-Sim et al. 2008).

One consistent theme emerging throughout the industry study was *obtaining relevant information from relevant sources.* Relevant is not a term that can be universally defined but building on McGee

Lennon's (2008) suggestion that an approach is situation dependent, relevance is a situationally dependent term because the meaning of relevance does not exist in isolation from its context. Here, relevance is a variable since from situation to situation the meaning of the term differs for each target domain. The degree to which existing information is relevant according to the current state of affairs is not measured by existing requirements techniques methodologies or approaches.

According to the ideas behind amethodical systems development, both methodical and amethodical views or interpretations of some idea, specific piece of text, or in this context representation of a requirement need to be simultaneously present. Truex *et al.* (1999) warn against favouring one view over the other claiming instead that since the meaning of terms is a volatile variable, any solution needs to facilitate the continuous overturning of this meaning to detect both methodical and amethodical attributes of a problem being expressed (Truex *et al.* 1999).

A solution may be found by linking OST investigations to the initial elicitation stage of projects. For example, OST encourages the emergence of collaborative and committed representatives from a group of participating stakeholders, giving them the authority to take responsibility to resolve existing problems. This may provide additional support for the identification of appropriate or relevant stakeholders immediately prior to and during inception.

Conflict identification is encouraged to emerge as early as possible and OST creates a forum to develop clear understandings and mutual resolution between stakeholders. Limited access to stakeholders may also be considerably discouraged for elicitation since OST deliberately seeks to attract those with relevant abilities and expertise to resolve problems. This makes the explicit claim that those *directly experienced* with the problem and *genuinely interested* in resolving it, are valued and must be present from the outset.

In summary, a suitable structure is therefore required to support:

- Participatory elicitation between multiple diverse stakeholder groups;

- Early identification and resolution of conflict;

- Management of multiple changing stakeholder priorities;

- Identification and access to the appropriate stakeholders;

- Understanding and communication through the development of a common language;

- The development of a representative perspective of requirements to be addressed.

## 4.5 Summary

This chapter presented the exploratory case study which began with evaluating the roles and challenges for an agile team, observations showed limited interaction between the customer and the development team. The customer although physically present was mostly isolated from the project and developers implemented stories from a technical perspective rather than according to business value set out by the customer. The team had difficulty explaining the project to an independent reviewer using the Scrum artefacts with user stories alone. A common language did not appear to have developed between members and the project status was explained from a technical rather than a business perspective.

This was followed by the second part of the exploratory study which conducted a series of interviews with industry practitioners providing further insights into how requirements are elicited in practice. This confirmed that support is needed for an interactive effort during elicitation and also for the role of the customer in practice. Also it is necessary to develop a collective viewpoint and balance priorities shifting between multiple diverse stakeholders on projects. Overall the set of stakeholder management activities conducted to successfully communicate requirements in practice were identified as predominantly amethodical. This suggests that a suitable structure must also consider the capability to detect amethodical problem space attributes affecting the communication of requirements during the problem definition stage.

# Chapter 5 Open Space Technology (OST)

## 5.1 Overview

As part of the proposed solution, this chapter presents a brief history and background of OST including the main components, specific activities and roles involved in using the interaction technique. The broader context in which OST has been previously employed is also discussed and this includes where the interaction technique has been used and subsequently recommended in software development in particular. A fictional OST scenario is then presented to illustrate how the approach might be applied to a given problem space.

## 5.2 OST History and Background

OST was first developed by Harrison Owen in the 1980's as a result of his experience organising a large conference in which it was later discovered that the most beneficial interactions between participants had taken place during the *coffee breaks* of the event. The intentions behind developing OST as an interaction technique were to reproduce what is termed *"the level of synergy"* dynamically created in informal settings and to combine this with effectively achieving the goal of central importance to participants (Owen 2008).

OST is best suited when the following five conditions (Corrigan 2012) are considered to be true:

1.  A real *business issue* is required which refers to some problem where there is a genuine need to reassess the context of the situation and develop a new solution. Hence, ideal situations might include entirely new ways to approach an existing real world problem. Equally this can result in supporting the development of innovative solutions;

2.  *A great deal of complexity* exists. For instance, complexity in situations where considerable difficulty exists in understanding the problem background and moving toward a solution that requires participative collaboration from those concerned;

3.  *Diversity in participants* is needed in OST to enable many relevant viewpoints to emerge and integrate around a common problem. This helps to develop a broader more representative perspective of both the problem context and the solution space. Assembling participants from a variety of different backgrounds, experiences, skills and abilities has shown that many different viewpoints can contribute to better understanding and subsequently a more fully informed solution can be developed;

4.  Another key component is the presence of *passion* which includes *conflict*. With passion participants are genuinely interested in the issue to be resolved. As differing viewpoints

emerge conflict is expected to occur but unlike typical meeting approaches, OST takes advantage of conflict as an opportunity to air important issues potentially obstructing productivity between groups. This is achieved by embracing conflict through a process of collaborative group negotiations and creating empathy between viewpoints;

5. OST performs most effectively when situations of genuine *urgency* exist in terms of the available timeframe to solve complex issues. For instance, this might include a currently overdue work schedule where quick decisions are required. This last point is also relevant to software engineering since schedule overrun can present a genuine risk factor and complex problems typically need to be resolved both quickly and effectively throughout development.

### 5.2.1 Four principles and one law

Four principles and a single law must be adhered to for effective OST interactions to prevail (Herman 2013). The principles are:

1.  Whoever comes are the right people;

In the context of business domains this principle maps well where a goal of strategic importance must be achieved and it is necessary to assemble multiple diverse perspectives to contribute toward a solution. In line with the concept of voluntary self-organisation, the first principle accepts that the participants, by attending an OST meeting, have expressed a genuine interest in addressing the main objective. Thus, it is assumed that those present are the relevant people needed to contribute a comprehensive perspective for examining the problem context and developing a suitable solution (Herman and Corrigan 2002). This is relevant to software engineering since missing stakeholders who can contribute significantly to the problem, can be included. Those who have not yet been identified as important stakeholders for solving specific problems are also encouraged to emerge as early as possible in the development process.

2.  Whatever happens is the only thing that could have happened;

Innovative solutions to problems are often derived through unique paths of investigation (Holman 2010). By giving participants permission to proceed in an intuitive manner, they are directed toward taking responsibility for how a given situation might be collectively perceived, understood and improved. As such this principle encourages participants to embark upon uniquely fresh paths toward solving problematic situations (Herman and Corrigan 2002). This is advantageous since the contribution made in terms of knowledge transferred between participants develops a well-informed and valued set of improvements as outputs. The principle conveys that participants are encouraged to clearly value what they have achieved rather than becoming unnecessarily distracted by asking if it could have been done better in other ways (Owen 2008).

3.  Whenever it starts, is the right time;

Useful problem solving activities do not begin automatically after setting a fixed time to begin, instead they occur in a unique, dynamic and unstructured fashion (Holman 2010). Rather than focusing participants on starting according to the convention of structured time, participants should instead perceive the start time as when they have begun to engage in effective discussions (Herman and Corrigan 2002). This is particularly important for software development where the time available for stakeholders to contribute to the project must be more efficiently and effectively managed.

4. When it's over, it's over.

Similarly, the last principle states when it's over it's over; and this diverts participant focus from giving greater importance to a fixed time slot in favour of empowering participants to cease activities only when the problem has been fully examined to the appropriate level of depth desired (Holman 2010).

In conjunction with the four principles, OST defines a single law which is considered critical to successful interactions between the relevant participants. This is known as the law of mobility which states that:

*"If you find yourself in a situation where you are not contributing or learning, then move to somewhere where you can"*

During OST, this law permits participants to move in an ad hoc manner between focused discussions depending on which topics are of specific interest to them and where their expertise lie. The law of mobility can be recognised as an important mechanism for achieving a continuous flow of dynamic interactions between interested participants. This is clear since it explicitly and publicly states that for every interaction, active participation is strongly encouraged.

It is acknowledged that although the above principles may be perceived as simple, strict adherence to them is strongly recommended (Herman 2002), as this behaves as an important mechanism to continuously redirect participants toward focusing on the *problem context*.

### 5.2.2 OST invitation

In general, prior to the commencement of an OST investigation, participants are invited to attend. Initially, the broader objective is organised in advance, this is included in the invitation which should be kept simple consisting of:

1. The theme: ten words or less capturing the main objective of the meeting;

2. The background or rationale to the problem being investigated;

3. Logistics including the location, start and end of events;

4. The promises which are:

- Every issue of concern to anybody present will have been raised, if they took responsibility for doing that;

- All issues will have received full discussion, to the extent desired;

- A full report of issues and discussions will be available for all participants;

- Priorities will be set and action plans will be made.

## 5.2.3 Physical aspects of OST

An important part in the use of OST relates to how the participants are physically positioned during the interaction. For instance, it is considered adversarial to seat participants in squares, opposite each other or in rows typical to a classroom like setting. Instead it is recommended that participants are seated in a circular fashion in order to create *a circle of open communication* since this discourages the propagation of any potential power relations that may exist between participants during OST.

It is recognised that separate sections of the meeting venue known as *break out areas* are needed for smaller sub groups to conduct focused discussions and improve concerns of specific interest to themselves later on. Another separate section of the venue is recommended for laptops and printers which can be used to produce a report consisting of the OST proceedings.

An important part of OST is the use of *the wall*. For instance, the main objective is encapsulated as a *theme* and placed on the wall in a position visible to all participants. The role of the theme serves as a constant reminder to help keep participants focused around the issue of central importance. The theme is always posed in the form of a question which deliberately provokes the ideas of participants in contributing towards solving the problem. Here, the aim of the theme is to attract expertise inviting contributions towards a viable outcome (Owen 2008), (Herman 2002).

Additionally, the wall is divided into two subsections known as the *marketplace* and the *bulletin board*. The marketplace is the section used to post the topics of the agenda known as *concerns*. Once concerns have been voiced and explored, the bulletin board provides a separate section of the wall used to post flip chart sheets containing improvements proposed in relation to each topic or concern raised. Improvements are subsequently prioritized by the participants to indicate which are the most important to proceed with in terms of an action plan for change.

The decision about how long OST should take also depends on the purposes for which the participants intend to use the approach. For instance, OST has been successfully conducted over shorter periods such as a single day or a few hours. The shortest time-frame in one case reports where an OST investigation held in an education setting, successfully completed within a 55 minute time slot (Owen 2008). Therefore agreeing on the timeframe to conduct OST depends on the issue under investigation, the number of participants and the time available to conduct the session. In cases where increased conflict and complexity exists, it is recommended that OST should be conducted over a three day period since more in-depth discussions may be needed for a practical plan for improvement to be developed.

In order to maintain mutual respect for the differences in cultures between a diverse set of participants, it is recommended that OST does not become interrupted by fixing time schedules for all participants to break for refreshments such as coffee or meals. This is also relevant for the maintaining the dynamic flow of important discussions which may become disturbed by the requirements of universally scheduled break times. Instead, participants should be encouraged to take *"natural breaks"* encouraging *"voluntary self-organisation"* around this need (Owen 2008).

OST differs from the traditional group meeting format in that it communicates to participants that the objective is to collaboratively develop mutually beneficial solutions to a common problem as a primary outcome. An important part of achieving this is the concept of *"being authentically present",* which discourages a passive attendance favouring a more proactive and participative approach toward problem solving (Owen 2008).

A key difference between OST and other group interaction techniques such as JAD, focus groups and formal meetings, is that OST does not dictate the format in which topics are expressed, explored or how improvements should be presented. Instead participants are collectively encouraged to use a *common language* to ensure that the focus remains on the problem context keeping presentation as simple as possible. On the other hand this is equally advantageous for participants who require content to be structured in a specific manner since the level of formality required is decided by the participants themselves. The agenda in terms of the topics to be discussed is also generated dynamically by the participants present at the start of, and not prior to the commencement of an OST investigation.

## 5.3 OST Activities

Four important tasks involved in the OST process can be observed. Since each task has a relationship with the outputs generated from the previous task, a general sequence in which the tasks occur can be discerned. These are summarised in Figure 14 as follows:

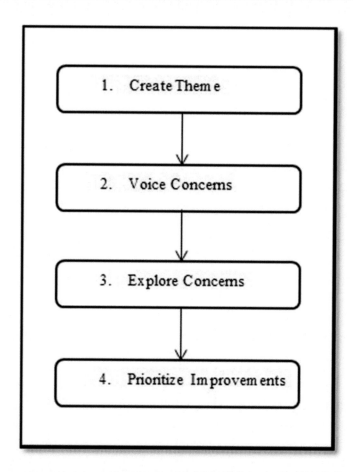

*Figure 14 Steps in OST*

The first task is to *create a theme* which broadly captures the overall objective that participants must achieve as the outcome of the OST investigation. The theme is described as *"the simplest possible statement with the largest possible purpose"* (Herman 2006). This is usually developed in advance of the OST investigation and based upon the theme, the relevant participants *voice concerns* specific to their area of expertise. Here, concerns relevant to participants directly experiencing problems, which relate to the theme, can be raised. These are publically displayed on the *marketplace* section of the wall.

Participants including those who have not explicitly raised concerns then have an opportunity to sign up for a more focused discussion to address concerns. Collectively the list of concerns represents the set of topics on the agenda which have been dynamically created by the participants. Interested participants represent the list of stakeholders who are relevant to the discussion for specific concerns. The third task involves these relevant participants, namely those who have signed up for particular concerns, dividing into subgroups to *explore concerns* by conducting focused discussions for each topic raised. During these focused discussions participants suggest how the topic could be resolved and collaboratively make improvements on each concern. Improvements made are then publically displayed on the bulletin board section of the wall and whole group collaboration is then required to *prioritize improvements* indicating the order in which each improvement will be implemented.

## 5.4 OST Roles

Other components include the definition of a set of roles; it is important to note that the only role that is assigned in advance of the OST meeting is the role of the facilitator. All other roles are dynamically self-assigned by participants during and not prior to OST.

### 5.4.1 Facilitator

At the start of an OST investigation the facilitator conducts the opening speech which consists of welcoming participants and explaining the process of OST. Here, the role of the facilitator involves *opening space* for participants to develop ideas that explore the theme to an appropriate level of depth needed. It has been recommended that in order to avoid a potentially biased, predefined or directed outcome, the facilitator should be an independent person with no particular stake in the outcome of the OST event.

The facilitator also ensures that the signage is placed appropriately around the venue. This includes placing the theme, the four principles and the law of mobility publicly and visibly to all participants present. The facilitator is also responsible for cordoning off a number of break out areas used for the smaller more focused group meetings to take place later on. Primarily, the role of the facilitator involves opening and ending daily sessions, and encouraging participants to continue to self-organise around the main theme to be resolved.

### 5.4.2 Convenor

The role of the convenor is assigned to participants who raise concerns about the theme to be addressed. Convenors assert concerns using A4 sheets of paper and pens. Each concern is then posted on the marketplace section of the wall. Participants who become convenors automatically elect themselves as committed to taking responsibility for the concern. This includes later conducting a smaller more focused discussion which will consist of only interested parties who will address the concern and offer potential improvements. The list of concerns posted on the marketplace collectively denotes topics of the agenda dynamically generated by the participants themselves.

### 5.4.3 Scribe

During the more focused discussions the role of the scribe is assigned which involves quickly documenting the key points being made by participants during the exploration of specific concerns. Often the convenor may assume the role of the scribe, this task is important for recording key points during discussions and also notes taken from all scribes develop later into a document forming the proceedings of the meeting which is subsequently available for each participant at the end of the OST session.

### 5.4.4 Participants

Outside of the specific roles defined above, the remaining participants consist of those who have some stake in the outcome of the OST investigation. In business domains for instance, this could consist of differing levels of user groups or those who interact with a process being re-engineered. Participants involved have a specific interest and are considered to have experiences, skills and abilities needed to contribute towards improving the situation of concern in a more fully informed manner.

## 5.5 Application of OST

OST has been applied internationally across both for profit and not for profit organisations. The technique has been extensively used across a broad range of community based initiatives for developing innovative solutions to address long term complex socio-cultural problems including the prioritization and subsequent development of organised plans for improvement (Herman 2003). OST has also been used to achieve convergence for complex and sensitive political issues between opposing groups in combative situations (Herman 2003), (Owen 2008).

The approach has been used by national, regional and municipal governments to include existing local knowledge in the development of political strategies, with the benefits of a participative contribution from citizens (O'Connor and Cooper 2005).  OST has also been employed for the purposes of strategic direction setting and the renewal of organisational structure in educational systems such as the US National Education Association (Owen 2008). Other examples include reorganisation of strategies for inner city schools in the U.S where a new agenda informed by community wide participation has been implemented (Herman 2003).

In business domains OST has been employed for product design and strategic planning (Herman and Corrigan 2002). Most notably for Boeing the technique addressed access to necessary resources for effective product design during the development of pressurized airplane doors (Gleiberman 2009). This required the expertise of numerous geographically dispersed stakeholder groups spanning multiple disciplines, a task that was achieved using OST.

Larry Peterson, founder of the Open Space Institute of Canada reports on the success of a series of OST investigations for a number of Canadian corporations. In particular, the approach transformed decision making processes for a large financial institution based in Montreal (Peterson 2009).  AT&T are reported to have reduced ten months of design and planning into a single OST investigation which involved combining the expertise of twenty five multiple diverse contractors, conducted over a two day period (Herman 2003).

### 5.5.1 OST in software development

Tartaglia and Ramnath (2005) provide an experience report detailing success in using OST in software development to resolve cross-team development issues. The development effort involved ten teams working on a project divided into eighteen iterations.

Originally, in using plan-driven development, structured communication was strong between lead business analysts, programming leads and test leads. However, communication channels between the business analysts, programmers and testers actually conducting the work had been generally weak. Time elapsed creating a delay between decisions made and the decisions subsequently being relayed to the roles involved in completing the tasks. Problems emerged due to a lack of direct communication between these roles (Tartaglia and Ramnath 2005). This led to the development of better support for *"the concept of self-managed teams"* (Tartaglia and Ramnath 2005).

One solution proposed was to perform a Scrum of Scrums (SOS), however, this took much longer than initially expected and a key problem was that detailed information needed was still missing. Instead, a series of OST investigations were conducted which successfully resolved cross team issues being encountered.  The authors believe that the success was achieved because the OST investigations specifically attracted interested parties, a mechanism which addressed the critical inclusion of roles that had a direct relationship with the issues being encountered.

While this experience report may be limited to within a single organisation, Tartaglia and Ramnath (2005) have demonstrated that OST can be used to dynamically resolve cross team issues in software development. However, the authors do not elaborate on how OST could be linked to any specific software development method.

The Seattle Area Software Quality Assurance Group (SASQAG 2006) highlighted that human interaction makes up almost 90% of time spent on software projects. With this in mind they have successfully used OST to improve their organisations service to members, and specifically recommend the approach for meetings, creating agendas, requirements elicitation, process improvement and stakeholder involvements during software development.

In using OST as a method to share domain knowledge, Dingsøyr and Bjørnsson (2005) highlight the potential of OST stating *"neither developers nor their customers know exactly what information is critical".* They recommend its use in *first* customer encounters suggesting this as a means to find *common ground* for stakeholders understanding software development and likewise developer understanding of the target domain. Although the authors have argued for the use of OST and have proposed future research in this specific area, no further indication is given as to how this might be achieved.

Herman (2013) reports on a situation where XP was used during an OST investigation which took place in 2002 to determine business needs for bespoke software required. In this case, 75% of participants attending had no prior experience with the programming language being used. This had significantly improved during the OST investigation after non-technical stakeholders participated in the XP practice of pair programming during the event. This took place during six iterations, taking 1.5 hours each, over a nine hour period in which stakeholders left the OST investigation with working software.

OST originator, Harrison Owen reports on another situation where a set of diverse stakeholders conducted an OST investigation in which six software products were *"sketched out"*, during the session. In this case five of the software products had later been successfully deployed (Herman 2013). Further, Larry Peterson has used OST for the development and testing of concepts which included defining and clarifying requirements for software systems (Herman 2013).

The agile community recently began widely adopting OST as an effective means for conducting conferences globally (Agile Open 2013). Unlike the traditional conference format, activities are loosely structured around broader themes of central importance and participants dynamically conduct their own sessions focusing on the topics they are most interested in. Using a less formal conference structure has enabled participants to focus more closely on issues specifically relevant to themselves. The difference between OST and the traditional conference approach is that discussions are not restricted to a set of topics prescribed in advance of the event, instead OST enables relevant issues for discussion to dynamically emerge according to the needs of participants as the conference proceeds. Altering the conference format in this manner has presented unique opportunities for exchanging knowledge between a variety of differing levels of participant expertise.

## 5.6 Example of a Fictional OST investigation

This section presents a fictional example of an OST investigation used here to demonstrate how the technique could be applied and to illustrate the typical artefacts produced. For the purposes of background context the general scenario used is summarised as follows:

*Developers at Software Company InnoTech have been experiencing difficulties resolving the cause of reported defects since no clear link exists between the requirements and higher level business context. The company have researched many popular traceability tools and although a top of the range tool was previously chosen, a number of bottlenecks still exist in achieving upward traceability from defects to their associated functional requirements and the higher level business processes associated with these. To help resolve the situation, InnoTech are holding an OST meeting with stakeholders in the company to determine how upward traceability could be improved.*

In relation to the above scenario, the main OST steps are now explained:

### 5.6.1 Step 1 - Create a Theme

Figure 15 shows a hypothetical theme used here to illustrate how OST might address this situation:

*Tackling Traceability?*

*Figure 15 Theme*

## 5.6.2 Step 2 - Voice Concerns

The stakeholders study the theme and brainstorm general concerns each of which must be directly related to the above theme. Convenors voice concerns by writing them down, signing their initials on the concern and posting this on the marketplace. Once all concerns have been raised, other stakeholders interested in specific concerns indicate so by signing their initials on the concern under the convenors initials as shown in Figure 16. The first concern raised here is *"Addressing problems with existing tools?"*. For the purposes of illustration, only a single concern is used here, however, typically a number of concerns can emerge and are documented in a similar manner.

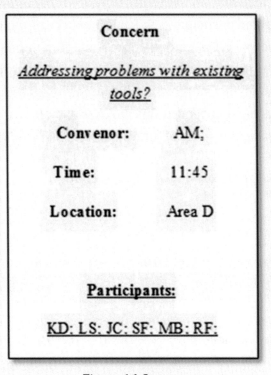

*Figure 16 Concern*

## 5.6.3 Step 3 - Explore Concerns

Smaller groups consisting of the interested participants then conduct a more focused discussion on the topic of concern. Here stakeholders relevant to the particular concern occupy the break out areas provided where each concern is then further explored. In the context of the given theme, the above concern: *"addressing problems with existing tools"* might break down into a number of different parts during this more focused discussion.

During the focused discussion at step 3 participants interact contributing their expertise to the specific topic. The convenor initiates the discussion and the scribe documents the steps taken by the group as the exploration phase proceeds. At step 3, simple tools are used to quickly document key points that emerge surrounding the context of the topic to be addressed. This is summarised as a diagram in Figure 17 showing an example of some points that could be made with this concern explored in more detail.

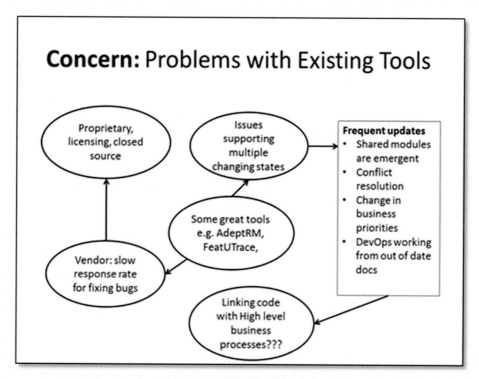

*Figure 17 Explore concerns*

Once concerns have been sufficiently explored, participants then move towards developing potential improvements. Figure 18 shows an example of one improvement being made which in this case is to customize an in-house tool to resolve traceability issues. Once improvements have been made they are posted on the bulletin board and stakeholders then decide on the order of priority in terms of the action plan for change.

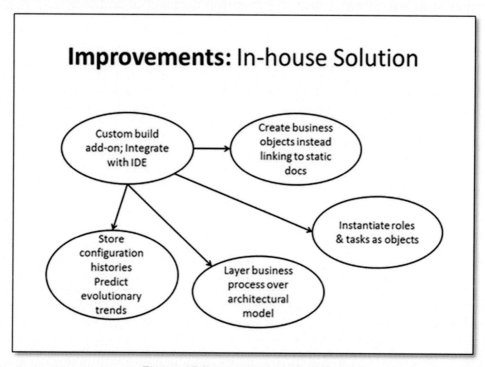

*Figure 18 Improvements identified*

### 5.6.4 Step 4 - Prioritize Improvements

Prioritized improvements represent the action plan for change and are posted on the bulletin board as the output of the original concern raised. The list of prioritized improvements is indicated in numerical order as shown in Figure 19.

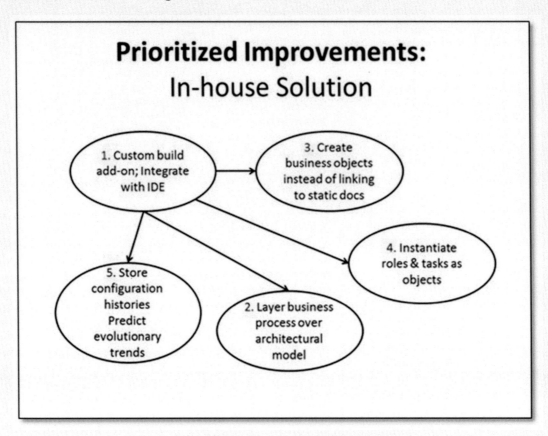

*Figure 19 Improvements prioritized*

Text based scenarios can also be produced during OST to provide additional understanding of the diagrams sketched out, the following scenario presents a walkthrough of the list of improvements in their order of priority:

*One proposed improvement is to custom build an add-on to integrate with the development environment currently being used. This will involve creating a new business process layer to sit over the architectural model. Business objects can then be dynamically generated instead of linking to previously static representations of documentation. To achieve this, roles and tasks as part of business process will need to be instantiated as dynamic objects which link the business process to existing requirements since a clear link must be visible between functional requirements and the business process associated with them. Inconsistencies between business and functional requirements must be automatically visible and developers can access the business process layer at any time. Changes made to business processes will be flagged to developers who interact with that business process and changes integrated will also be persistently stored in order to develop a history of previous configurations to predict trends.*

Table 11 shows a summary of the hypothetical OST investigation presented here. Typically the key outcomes of each step would contribute towards the book of proceedings issued to each participant at the end of the OST event.

*Table 11 Four OST steps and context of outputs produced*

| Step | Output |
|---|---|
| 1. Create Theme | Tackling Traceability? |
| 2. Voice Concerns | Addressing problems with existing tools |
| 3. Explore Concerns | **Problems identified**<br><br>• Other great tools exist – AdeptRM and FeatUtrace but..<br><br>• Vendor has slow response rate for fixing bugs<br><br>• Proprietary tool – licensing closed source<br><br>• Issues exist in supporting current changing states across all vendors<br><br>• Frequent updates caused by the integration of shared modules which are emergent – code gets updated documentation does not<br><br>• When conflict is resolved changes don't reflect in documentation<br><br>• Developers are working from out of date documentation<br><br>• Changing business priorities<br><br>**Improvements Identified**<br><br>• Custom build a new add-on to integrate with IDE<br><br>• Create business objects instead of linking to static documentation<br><br>• Instantiate roles and tasks as objects<br><br>• Create a business layer over the architectural model<br><br>• Store configuration history to predict evolutionary trends |
| 4. Prioritize improvements | 1. Custom build new add-on to integrate with IDE<br><br>2. Create business layer over architectural model<br><br>3. Create business objects instead of linking to static documentation<br><br>4. Instantiate roles and tasks as objects<br><br>5. Store configuration history to predict evolutionary trends |

## 5.7 Summary

Chapter 5 described how the OST group interaction technique works in detail. This began with a focus on the history and background including the general set of rules recommended, the activities involved and specific roles employed in implementing the approach. The context in which OST has been used in general was also discussed including where the approach has been previously implemented in software development contexts. A fictional OST investigation was then presented and this illustrates a walkthrough of the steps involved in OST with the artefacts produced as outputs of a typical OST investigation.

# Chapter 6 Linking OST and XP

## 6.1 Overview

Chapter 6 explores a set of discernible similarities between the OST interaction technique and AMs. This begins with a focus on the links between the broader agile philosophy and OST. Then OST is evaluated for its potential to support the development of agile models as artefacts used as inputs for development. Section 6.3 presents the extent to which the XP values, principles and practices further comply with the OST technique. Finally, the OpenXP framework introduces how both these approaches can be linked through the development of Usage Scenarios.

## 6.2 OST and the Agile Philosophy

The agile philosophy promotes a set of principles. Five principles in particular stand out as directly comparable with OST, these are described in the following points.

First, AMs state that *"Our highest priority is to satisfy the customer through early and continuous delivery of valuable software"* (Ambler 2009c). In achieving this principle it is stated that rather than designing everything upfront, *"an evolutionary approach to development appears to work much better"* (Ambler 2009c). Since OST encourages root cause analysis of existing problems and based upon this, solutions collaboratively emerge, it therefore embraces an evolutionary approach to problem solving which is entirely consistent with this statement.

Secondly, *"Business people and developers need to work together daily throughout the project"* (Ambler 2009c). Practicing ASP and the adoption of inclusive tools and techniques are imperative to successfully realizing this principle. One prerequisite for success in OST is the necessity for diverse participants to proactively engage in solving issues of common interest. One important point here is that OST supports the use of a common language in bridging a set of diverse backgrounds and the use of simple universal tools enables inclusion between stakeholders spanning multiple differing disciplines. It could therefore be stated that OST is consistent with this second agile principle.

The third principle states: *"Build projects around motivated individuals, give them the environment and support they need and trust them to get the job done"* (Ambler 2009c). Under this principle, it is stated that people need to be *"willing to work together collaboratively"* Ambler (2009c). Rather than specifically prescribing what individuals ought to do, OST strongly emphasises placing trust in participants to *"resolve the issues for themselves"* (Owen 1995). OST is consistent with the agile statement since self-organisation is continuously encouraged during interactions and participants must be interested, committed and motivated to successfully achieve the common objective.

Fourth, *"The most efficient and effective method of conveying information to and within a development team is face-to-face conversation"* Ambler (2009c). A collaborative hands-on interaction is strongly encouraged between OST participants in expressing concerns and exploring potential improvements. OST is consistent with the above statement since face-to-face communication is equally considered a valuable method of conveying information between participants during interactions.

Fifth, *"The best architectures, requirements and designs emerge from self-organising teams"* Ambler (2009c). One of the key components of OST is that participants continue to voluntarily self-organise around a common issue to be resolved. As concerns are explored, the root cause of issues is encouraged to surface and solutions emerge in a collaborative manner. Participants also have specific background expertise in the problem domain and are encouraged to proactively self-organise around problems relating to themselves, on a voluntary basis. These points indicate a strong potential match between OST and this particular principle.

Other similarities between the agile philosophy and OST should also be noted. For agile development the visibility of requirements and tasks, is clearly emphasised through the use of tangible artefacts, simple tools and the storyboard or the wall to communicate, manage and report progress. For instance, in OST, the wall is divided into the marketplace, a section of the wall used to post concerns using A4 sheets of paper and a second section, the bulletin board, is occupied by improvements made to concerns using flip chart sheets of paper. In agile development the storyboard or wall is used to display index cards or post-it notes containing user stories.

Another important point is that both approaches manipulate the positioning of artefacts which represents motion through different stages of progression when moving towards a solution. Additionally, both recognise the importance of full collaboration between relevant stakeholders in developing a mutually beneficial outcome. These similarities suggest that these two approaches have the potential to integrate well.

### 6.2.1 Criteria for developing agile models

Ambler (2002) defines seven characteristics to determine whether or not a model can be considered to be agile. These are summarised in the following points.

First, any agile model should fulfil the purpose for which it was created. Here, agile models can be used for the purposes of communication with stakeholders, understanding of a problem or to provide detail needed for implementation.

Second, agile models must be understandable for the *intended target audience.* In order to maximize understandability an agile model should be communicated in terms that make sense to the stakeholders intended to use the model. Here, terms such as language and notation used should be considered.

Third, agile models should be sufficiently accurate. This is determined by the audience intending to use the model, and sufficient accuracy depends on the degree to which the model addresses or fulfils the purpose for which it was drawn. Here, agile models do not need to be meticulously accurate, they *"just need to be accurate enough"* (Ambler 2002).

Fourth, agile models should be sufficiently consistent. This characteristic points out that inconsistencies between models used to represent requirements can often be tolerated provided that the model continues to remain useful for the purposes of which it was intended. Again this is determined by the target audience.

Fifth, agile models are sufficiently detailed. An agile model should include detail that is relevant to the particular audience intended to use it. The question of whether a model is sufficient is determined by the intended target audience.

Sixth, agile models provide positive value. Agile models must in the first instance be beneficial to project stakeholders, here agile models that are considered useful provide positive value to the development effort.

Seventh, agile models are as simple as possible. Ambler (2002) encourages the use of simple models that provide clarity and understanding, keeping models as simple as possible helps to improve communication between project stakeholders.

Clearly, the degree to which agile models consist of the above characteristics is best determined by the audience for which the agile models intend to address. In this context and particularly relevant to Agile Model Driven Development (AMDD), OST participants are permitted to decide whether the artefacts produced during OST are: informative, understandable, sufficiently accurate, consistent, detailed and whether or not they provide positive value for the intended purpose. Further, in linking OST with AMs another key connector lies in the fact that OST privileges the use of simple tools and techniques including the use of common language which once more is determined by the audience for which the purpose of the artefacts intend to address. This suggests that it may be possible for stakeholders to produce agile models as the output from OST investigations.

## 6.3 OST vs. XP values, principles and practices

This section examines the extent to which OST complies with XP practice specifically in the areas of Requirements Analysis and Planning, Team and Human Factors and Software Design. XP is governed by five values, fourteen principles and twenty four practices (Beck and Andres 2005).

### 6.3.1 OST vs. XP Values

The first of the five values emphasises the importance of *communication* between stakeholders, the team and also between teams on software projects. Here, it is recommended that communication be maximised to reduce problems that arise during projects. Since OST maximises open communication between participants, the interaction technique is consistent with what this first value aims to achieve.

The second value suggests *simplicity* be exercised to reduce complexity and increase autonomy in the solutions undergoing development. OST complies here since the approach also recognises the need for simplicity in terms of the tools and techniques used to communicate, explore and improve business concerns.

*Feedback* as a metric for progress is considered the third value and an important mechanism for fostering successful communication between relevant stakeholders. OST values instant face-to-face feedback from the participants present during interactions. The interaction technique therefore complies with the value of feedback as defined by XP.

Alongside communication, simplicity and feedback, *courage* is the fourth value added, this value aims to build developer confidence when important decisions need to be made. OST does not explicitly make a statement about the term courage, however, a continuous encouragement around voluntary self-organisation is key in terms of helping participants to make decisions independently.

The fifth value is *respect* which states that the previous four values cannot be mutually beneficial without added respect between relevant stakeholders who are working on, contributing to or affected by a solution under development. Although OST does not explicitly make any statement about respect, it can be assumed that respect is valued in OST since mutually beneficial decisions are equally as important to achieve in OST.

The above points suggest that all five of the XP values are closely aligned with the values of OST, this indicates an amenable combination between the two approaches.

## 6.3.2 OST vs. XP Principles

As shown in Table 12, OST is directly comparable with four of the XP principles. The first column in Table 12 lists the particular XP principles and the second column shows the extent to which OST complies with each. The similarities between these principles and OST are then described in further detail.

*Table 12 Compliancy mapping between XP principles and OST*

| XP | OST |
|---|---|
| Mutual Benefit | ✓ |
| Diversity | ✓ |
| Opportunity | ✓ |
| Accepted Responsibility | ✓ |

### 6.3.2.1 Mutual benefit

It is important that requirements developed are first and foremost *mutually beneficial* to all stakeholders involved. This principle is instrumental in developing successful solutions and subsequently building long term stable relationships between software teams and stakeholders from the target domain. OST complies with this principle since the approach favours developing mutually beneficial solutions for all stakeholders with a common issue of concern. Here, OST could help to extend the principle of mutual benefit from XP into the business domain.

### 6.3.2.2 Opportunity

The principle of opportunity suggests that problems should be perceived as opportunities for change. From this positive perspective Beck and Andres (2005) explain that for each problem, opportunities exist for learning and further development. In OST, existing problems are also treated as opportunities for change. A key outcome of OST is that change as a result of the investigation is expected to occur. In particular, by raising concerns OST participants are encouraged to embrace change by examining existing problems with their current situation and investigating problems to the appropriate level of depth is not only required, but strongly supported by OST. This suggests that the principle of opportunity in XP could be supported and further extended into the business domain through a link with OST.

### 6.3.2.3 Diversity

The principle of diversity should be embraced as an important part of team dynamics. Conflict is described as inevitable and it is not considered beneficial to assemble groups that consist of stakeholders possessing similar skills, rather, diversity in the knowledge base of the stakeholders is preferred since a variety of opinions and ideas help to incorporate a wider view, this contributes positively to the development of a well-informed solution. This is a particularly important element since *"cultural diversity is beneficial for promoting creativity and innovation"* in software development (Jain 2012). A condition for success in OST is that participants come from a variety of diverse backgrounds, consisting of many different skills, experiences and abilities. OST embraces conflict by creating the setting in which conflict will most likely emerge as early as possible during elicitation. OST is fully compatible with the principle of diversity since it is specifically recommended in situations where a diverse group of participants are involved and the presence of conflict including passion is embraced during OST investigations.

### 6.3.2.4 Accepted responsibility

The principle of accepted responsibility states: *"responsibility cannot be assigned, it can only be accepted"* (Beck and Andres 2005). If for instance a developer accepts responsibility for a user story, s/he declares this by signing initials on the story card. The developer also accepts responsibility for the design, development and testing of that user story (Beck and Andres 2005). Similarly, in

OST, convenors automatically accept responsibility for issues they have raised rather than having the responsibility assigned. Further, this also includes accepting responsibility for convening a more focused meeting consisting of other interested participants who will contribute towards developing improvements on the issue raised. Similarly to XP, in OST convenors also sign their initials on concerns to declare responsibility and later the remaining interested participants sign their initials declaring interest in collaborating towards the solution. These similarities suggest that OST could potentially bridge the principle of accepted responsibility from XP into the business domain.

### 6.3.3 OST vs. XP Practices

Alongside values and principles, XP also defines a set of 24 practices. Table 13 shows that similarities exist between six of the XP practices and OST. Practices are numbered along the left column, each practice is listed in the centre column and OST compliance is indicated by a tick in the far left hand column. This is then explained in further detail.

*Table 13 Compliancy mapping between XP practices and OST*

| XP Practices | | OST |
|---|---|:---:|
| **Requirements Analysis and Planning** | | |
| 1 | User Stories | ✓ |
| 5 | Real Customer Involvement | ✓ |
| **Team and Human Factors** | | |
| 11 | Sit Together | ✓ |
| 12 | Whole Team | ✓ |
| 13 | Informative Workspace | ✓ |
| **Design** | | |
| 18 | Root Cause Analysis | ✓ |

### 6.3.3.1 Requirements analysis and planning

Requirements describing functionality should be written as user stories. Similarly to user stories OST fosters the storytelling mode for raising concerns and developing improvements. With a link between OST and XP a high level requirement written as a concern is later broken down into user stories and subsequent tasks. This provides upper level context from which user stories are then drawn. Linking the two approaches enables a single common language to be used via storytelling for communicating high level concerns, transforming these into scenarios as improvements and then writing user stories.

Real customer involvement is necessary so that stakeholders who are affected by a solution participate in quarterly and weekly planning activities. For OST to be successful, genuinely interested participants take part. In this context real customers have a genuine interest in the success of a software project and a link with OST provides a forum for interested stakeholders or indeed a team of relevant yet diverse customer representatives to actively participate during elicitation.

### 6.3.3.2 Team and human factors

In order to maximise communication, teams should *"sit together and work in an open space"* (Beck and Andres 2005). OST complies with this principle since interactions between interested participants occur *in Open Space*. Also the physical positioning of participants in OST maximises open communication between those present.

Whole team implies that the team should be comprised of the individuals with the skills and perspectives needed to develop a successful solution. OST complies with this principle since after concerns have been raised smaller more focused meetings are convened between a refined group of *interested stakeholders* with related experiences who bring a variety of perspectives to contribute toward resolving concerns. Diversity in skills and backgrounds is also expected to inform a successful solution.

Informative workspace refers to working in a setting where artefacts such as posters are used to inform the team about the project status, progression and tasks yet to be performed. OST is clearly compliant with this principle since contextual artefacts are positioned in delegated sections of the wall. Similarly to the wall in XP, the positioning of OST artefacts posted on the wall has the potential to communicate progression between the theme, concerns and business improvements, prior to writing stories. A link between OST and XP aims to produce tangible artefacts that provide additional informative context for stories being developed. Physical artefacts created and the links between each can also be visualised and traced during development.

### 6.3.3.3 Software design

It is recommended that root cause analysis be exercised when defects have been isolated, some form of contingency plan should be in place to tackle recurrence of the same issues where the root cause has already been identified. It should be noted that defects in this context are viewed as either new requirements or changes to existing requirements. OST encourages participants to resolve concerns by exploring the full context of problems before developing improvements. This involves continuing to investigate the source of a problem until interested participants are satisfied that the sufficient amount of effort has been paid to resolving the issue. In the context of defect analysis, defects could be raised as concerns to attract the relevant expertise to examine the issues to the appropriate level of depth needed. A link between OST and XP would therefore have the potential to support root cause analysis of isolated defects throughout projects.

Considering the above points, in summary, OST is fully compliant with the five XP values. Also the approach can be considered compliant with four of the XP principles and under the areas of requirements analysis and planning, team and human factors and design, OST also complies with six of the XP practices. Two are corollary practices while four are primary practices.

## 6.4 Introduction to the OpenXP Framework

As shown in Figure 20, the OpenXP Framework has been developed to offer a conceptual structure for linking OST, a group interaction technique with XP, a highly flexible yet subtly structured AM. Problem understanding is achieved and associated models produced through the OST analysis which forms the basis for using the XP development method. However, since neither OST nor XP provides recommendations on techniques to explore specific features these two phases are linked by the development of usage scenarios for each of the agreed improvements. Scenarios are important as the linking activity since the output in terms of improvements produced by OST can be interpreted as a set of scenarios that provide input for creating user stories in XP. Also, prior to developing user stories, interested OST participants have prioritized high level business improvement scenarios for development in advance of the commencement of XP.

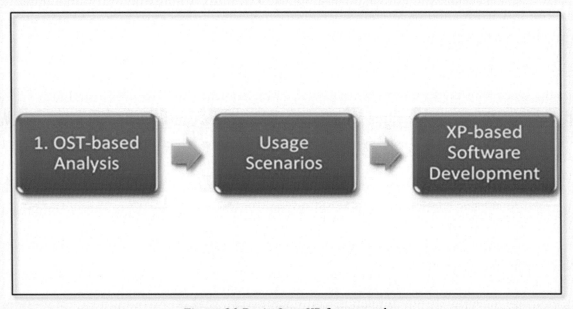

*Figure 20 Basic OpenXP framework*

Table 14 lists the steps in the OpenXP framework, this is presented in a sequential manner for clarity. The first column presents nine process steps across three phases. The first phase, steps 1 to 4, covers the *OST analysis*, while the third phase, steps 6 to 9, covers the *XP activities* associated with the development of user stories and iteration planning. Connecting these two activities is the *link phase* which explores scenarios of use for the business improvement that has been ranked the highest priority. In effect this dictates a *release* of software and agile development can proceed in a more focused manner. The second column summarises the *purpose* of each step, while the expected outputs are indicated in column three.

*Table 14 Outputs of each step using the OpenXP framework*

| Step | Purpose | Output |
|---|---|---|
| **Phase One: OST-based Analysis** | | |
| **OST 1:** Create theme | Provide the centre focus, the objective for the meeting | One sentence meeting agenda posed in the form of a question |
| **OST 2:** Voice concerns | Elicit requirements as concerns directly relating to theme | High level requirements raised as concerns surrounding the theme |
| **OST 3:** Explore concerns | Describe, elaborate and explore requirements collaboratively and identify appropriate improvements | High level requirements more comprehensively examined and a set of potential improvements identified |
| **OST 4:** Prioritize improvements | Organise business improvements based upon priorities | Prioritized set of high level business improvements |
| **Phase Two: Linking Activity** | | |
| **Link 5:** Develop scenarios | Establish more refined detail for the highest priority improvement | Potential usage scenarios (Flexible format – can use multiple modes of expression) |
| **Phase Three: XP-based Software Development** | | |
| **XP 6:** Create user stories | Create more detailed requirements from personalised scenarios | Lower level requirements |
| **XP 7:** Prioritize user stories | Organise the order in which stories will be completed | Prioritized set of user stories |
| **XP 8:** Plan iteration | Organise prioritized stories into iterations | Planned iterations of stories to be implemented |
| **XP 9:** Implement stories | Write code to develop stories | Working software |

The following points explain each of the steps as shown in Table 14 in further detail. Phase one consists of the OST analysis which involves four steps:

## Step 1: OST – Create Theme

The first step involves creating the theme which provides the centre focus for the meeting. This captures the overall objective of the meeting through a single sentence, which is purposefully composed in the form of a question to encourage discussion. In relation to software development the theme here is intended to capture the essence of the business problem and to show more clearly what the software solution must address.

## Step 2: OST - Voice Concerns

All stakeholders present focus on the central theme and then voice concerns directly relating to this broader overall objective. The output is that each concern at this stage can be perceived as a high level business requirement where some plan of action is needed to address the objective. All interested stakeholders sign up to partake in a more focused meeting to discuss a high level requirement of mutual interest.

## Step 3: OST – Explore Concerns

During step 3 concerns that have been raised by stakeholders are explored. This involves separate subgroups forming which consist of only the interested stakeholders who meet to further explore high level business concerns as requirements. Here stakeholders gather into more focused groups to describe and elaborate on high level requirements. One benefit of including this step is to facilitate the emergence of additional related requirements. The output is a set of improvements which often include flipchart sheets containing high level business requirements more comprehensively examined. Since stakeholders must use a common language, the format can be rough and sketchy and all interested stakeholders establish a collaborative understanding for the business concerns raised. The interested stakeholders collaborate in making improvements to the business requirements examined. The output here is that flipcharts are drawn up containing potential improvements informed by experienced stakeholders.

## Step 4: OST– Prioritize Improvements

Step 4 involves organising business improvements according to the priority assigned by the stakeholders present. This step produces a subset of high level requirements prioritized according to business value. This is equally important if stakeholders realise at this point that some business concerns may need further investigation before a software solution should be considered. This step aims to encourage decisions to be made early from a business perspective with regard to whether or not business value is perceived in the improvements identified during this step. The output for this step produces a prioritized set of improvements representing potential high level business requirements that have been explored in further detail.

## Phase two: Step 5: Linking Activity – Develop Scenarios

Phase two consists of the linking activity which involves developing scenarios. For step 5, the original subgroups then reconvene to develop detailed scenarios based upon the highest priority improvement. The format of scenarios is flexible, for example, outputs could be text-based, elaborate diagrams, video clips, a sequence of photos, or comic book drawings. During step 5 multiple modes of expression can be used to promote the use of a common language between stakeholders. This is important in reducing any learning curve that can be introduced when using a new technique. And crucially, stakeholders remain focused on organising and resolving problem space content rather than becoming distracted with how this should be presented.

## Step 6: XP – Create User Stories

Step 6 involves writing user stories based upon the scenarios drawn up. It is anticipated that creating user stories after scenarios have been developed may help developers to remain focused on writing stories that are specifically related to the scenarios produced as the output of OST. The aim of scenarios here is to capture a broader or higher level perspective of requirements and creating stories directly relating to the scenarios intends to elicit more detailed lower level requirements.

## Step 7: XP – Prioritize User Stories

After user stories have been created it is necessary to organise which functionality will be implemented first. In general, the customer representative decides the order in which stories are expected to be completed which results in a prioritized set of user stories. The team then develop the stories in the prioritized order set out by the customer representative.

## Step 8: XP - Plan Iteration

During iteration planning the team use the prioritized set of user stories organised from the previous step to divide the programming tasks for the project up into a number of iterations.

## Step 9: XP - Implement Stories

During step 9 for implementation, developers begin by focusing on the first planned iteration. User stories are taken down from the wall chart and developed to produce working software. Figure 21 illustrates the nine steps in the OpenXP framework.

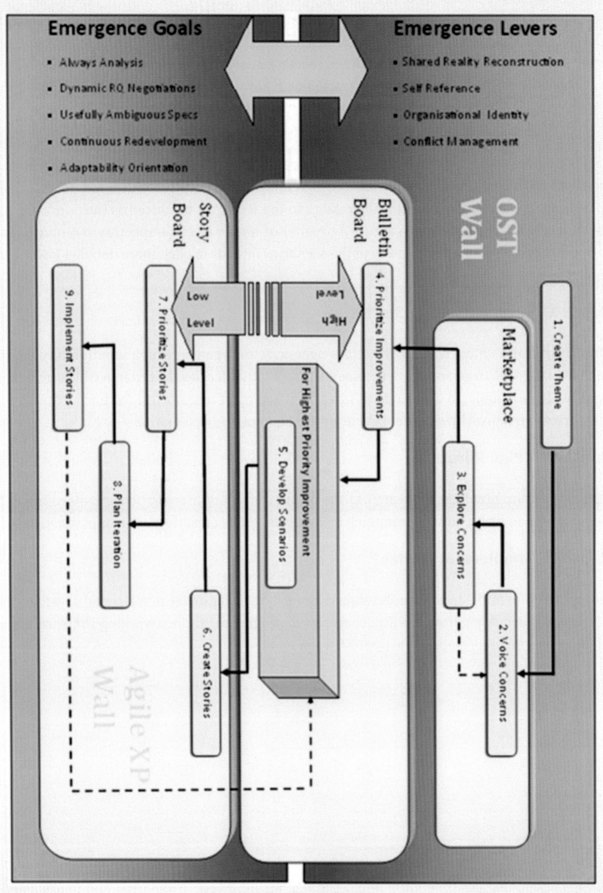

*Figure 21 The OpenXP framework*

## 6.5 Interaction between OpenXP steps

The OpenXP steps one to nine appear to occur in sequence as shown in Figure 21 however, some iteration between these steps is anticipated. This is indicated by the dotted line in Figure 21 which shows at least two points at which iteration is expected. For instance, during the exploration of concerns at step 3 it is quite possible that new concerns may arise during these more focused discussions as the intention here is to encourage participants as experts in the problem domain to source the root cause of issues to be improved. This could easily illuminate related concerns that may need to be separately voiced by participants. During exploration it may emerge that a concern has a wider scope than initially expected and in this case, the concern could be broken down further into smaller parts. For this reason, a feedback loop is included from step 3 back to step 2 as shown in Figure 21 to accommodate situations where this may arise.

The second point at which iteration is expected is between step 9 and step 5. Here, after stories have been implemented, developers can return to step 5 to develop scenarios for the next highest priority improvement. Since high level priority is linked to business value which may regularly change new scenarios may need to be developed from the concerns raised in accordance with this. Here, a feedback loop is included to enable new scenarios to be developed when a change in priority occurs. This is indicated by the dotted line where step 9 returns to step 5 as shown in Figure 21.

## 6.6 Underpinning Emergent Systems Development

Earlier on, the concept of emergent systems development was discussed with particular relevance to its role for competitive and dynamically changing business domains. This illustrated that in order to effectively manage consistent change, innovative business organisations now need to put in place practical support for the levers that stimulate emergence alongside the goals that such emergent organisations must strive toward achieving.

Focusing solely on the three levers first, OST alone can be described as an approach that supports *shared reality reconstruction, self-reference and organisational identity* and particularly in relation to managing conflict, the *dialectics of organisational autopoiesis*. For example, the focused discussions which commence at step 3 enable interested stakeholders to dynamically generate a *shared mental model* of the situation to be addressed. In doing so, stakeholders are encouraged to make reference not only to this shared mental model but also to previous versions of the business organisation in terms of learning from, and incorporating how problems had been historically solved in the past. This subsequently informs the development of a set of business improvements as a specific outcome. Lastly the process by which dynamic domains emerge necessarily involves embracing a healthy degree of conflict over consensus which is supported by OST and XP from the outset.

Moving on to the goals for emergent domains, XP can be described as a development approach that supports the specific goal set that must be achieved. For example, XP supports a state of *continuous analysis, dynamic requirements negotiations, incomplete but usefully ambiguous specifications, a continuous redevelopment perspective* and *adaptability orientation.* This is evident since the XP development method expects to continuously refine requirements throughout development. Dynamic requirements negotiation is supported by ongoing face-to-face communications with the customer representative. It is also very clear that XP favours incomplete but usefully ambiguous specifications, this is strongly supported by the overarching perspective of the agile philosophy on customer collaboration and individuals and interactions.

XP also expects that business needs evolve in line with constant competition over time and as such the software projects that underpin DAS need to be approached from a perspective of continuous redevelopment. Finally, adaptability orientation can also be described as a goal that XP embraces since change to all aspects of development including the underlying system architecture are expected to occur. For example, XP encourages regular refactoring, short builds consisting of fully tested working software and only artefacts (including code) that prove useful are kept and maintained overtime. In combining both OST and XP, the OpenXP framework has been designed with special consideration for the need to underpin the levers and goals needed to successfully develop emergent software systems in complex business domains.

## 6.7 Introduction to the confirmatory case studies

In line with the research question set out in section 2.2.1, two confirmatory case studies were conducted in order to test whether the OpenXP framework could improve the facilitation of agile requirements elicitation. These case studies specifically address the third aim as listed in section 2.2.2 and the fourth objective set out in section 2.2.3.

For both confirmatory case studies, the focus remained on the process of eliciting requirements as the unit of analysis. As a result of the literature review and the exploratory study the set of propositions that emerged are as follows:

1.  Activities conducted prior to phase three would not be difficult for developers to understand and would not introduce a steep learning curve;

2.  Developers would use the framework steps as described;

3.  Activities conducted prior to phase three would assist the team in understanding the problem background;

4.  Artefacts generated prior to phase three can produce agile models;

5.  Artefacts generated prior to phase three would provide additional context for communicating the project status to an outside stakeholder.

The first confirmatory case study focuses on testing the first three propositions while the second confirmatory case study tests the fourth and fifth. The second proposition is also retested in the second confirmatory study conducted.

The research setting for the first and second confirmatory case studies involved two groups of final year computing students. The first confirmatory study involved fourteen participants while the second confirmatory study overall involved ten.

For each case study, the student groups were divided into two teams. One team followed XP-only while the other team followed the OpenXP framework. Both teams were given the same scenario summarising the problem background and during development each team also had direct access to a customer representative. The role of the customer representative was played by a member of staff and for the OpenXP teams; an independent member of staff performed the role of the OST facilitator.

Prior to the commencement of the project both groups had previous knowledge of AMs, particularly XP, and were also familiar with various requirements elicitation techniques. Throughout each case study observations were regularly recorded during each session and afterwards questionnaires were used to collect data to obtain feedback from the participants. Particularly for the second confirmatory case study, interviews were also used to obtain additional feedback from the participants.

For the first confirmatory study, both teams were required to address the same problem: *"A Student Registration System"*, which was to be implemented over an eight hour timeframe spread across four separate sessions. For the second confirmatory study, both teams were also required to address the same problem *"A Taxing Challenge"* which was to be developed within an eight hour timeframe spread across four separate sessions.

At the beginning of each case study the OST process was explained to the OpenXP participants and the appropriate OST signage was posted on the wall. This included the theme, the four principles, the law of mobility and two separate sections of the wall denoted the marketplace and the bulletin board. The OpenXP teams were encouraged to sit in a circle with A4 sheets of paper and pens placed in the centre of the circle. With consideration for the problem background, the theme for each project sought to encapsulate the main objective to be achieved and this was decided in advance of each case study. The theme was then placed in a position on the wall visible to all OpenXP team members. The themes for both confirmatory studies were defined as follows:

1. *"To explore an efficient registration solution to satisfy multiple stakeholder perspectives?"*

2. *"How can we develop an efficient and easy to use tax collection system within a three week timeframe?"*

For each case study, at the start of the first session the facilitator explained the OST process to the OpenXP teams. This included the four principles and the law of mobility which were written on large flipchart sheets and posted on the wall around the room. The facilitator focused the group on the theme of the project which was also placed in a position visible to all members. The division on the wall separating sections allocated to the marketplace and the bulletin board were also explained.

The Open XP teams were seated in a circular fashion with pens, sheets of paper and masking tape in the centre of the circle. Once the facilitator had announced the theme, individual group members were encouraged to study the theme and come to the centre of the circle and use the blank A4 sheets of paper and pens provided to write down any concerns they had which directly related to the theme. The facilitator also explained that once concerns were raised, they should be voiced to the group and then placed on the marketplace section of the wall.

The facilitator also explained that members who raise a concern automatically become convenors who accept responsibility for holding a more focused meeting addressing the concern. Additionally, it was explained that each convenor should then arrange a time and place to convene a more focused discussion to explore and develop improvements on specific concerns raised, where other group members could partake in contributing a viewpoint. These case studies are presented in detail in chapters 7 and 8 respectively.

## 6.8 Summary

Chapter 6 described the broader connections between the agile philosophy and OST indicating that OST has the potential to support five of the principles from the agile philosophy. In addition to this the artefacts produced as the outputs of OST investigations have the potential to support the seven criteria for determining whether a model produced can be considered agile, as defined by Ambler (2002).

Similarities between OST and the XP values, principles and practices indicate that OST complies with all of the XP values and four of the XP principles. In the areas of requirements analysis and planning, team and human factors and software design, OST is compliant with six XP practices. In summary, correlations between OST and the agile development method suggest through clear similarities, an amenable combination. The proposed solution, the OpenXP framework was then presented detailing the steps involved in implementing the linked approach. Finally, the two confirmatory case studies as detailed in chapters 7 and 8 were introduced.

# Chapter 7 Confirmatory Case Study One

## 7.1 Overview

Chapter 7 presents the first confirmatory case study conducted to test the performance of the OpenXP framework. For brevity sake, only the main findings are discussed in detail with respect to the propositions defined at the beginning of this case study. More extensive detail on the specific artefacts generated by both teams alongside the in-depth direct observations recorded, and the analysis of responses from the questionnaires can be found in Walsh (2014). The case study background and the set of propositions that direct this study are first detailed in section 7.2. The main findings are then discussed in contrast with the original propositions set out at the start.

## 7.2 Case Study background and Propositions

The aim of this case study was first to determine whether or not it would be practical to combine OST with XP and secondly to evaluate whether a link between the two approaches had an effect on both the team and the project. With this in mind one objective of this case study was to gain a better understanding of the consequences of adding OST to the initial stages of XP development.

As such, this case study has focused on first determining the difficulty required for developers to understand and use OST, as this would provide an indication about the learning curve that might be expected for developers in using the framework. This case also aimed to determine whether developers using an agile approach, would strictly adhere to the nine framework steps as described. The last focal point was to establish by the project end, whether conducting an OST investigation would assist the team in understanding the problem background.

### 7.2.1 Unit of Analysis

In line with the exploratory case study detailed in chapter 4, the unit of analysis for the first confirmatory study remained fixed on the process of how requirements are elicited. As such a set of propositions are predicted in advance. These are listed as follows.

### 7.2.2 Propositions

1.  Activities conducted prior to phase three would not be difficult for developers to understand and would not introduce a steep learning curve;

2.  Developers would use the framework steps as described;

3. Activities conducted prior to phase three would assist the team in understanding the problem background.

To address these propositions some specific questions that require attention include:

i.    *How difficult is it for developers to understand and use OST?*

ii.   *Would the developers use the steps as described?*

iii.  *Would performing OST assist the team in understanding the problem background?*

## 7.2.3 Problem Background

This study was conducted in an academic setting and the project involved the development of a student registration system. Table 15 shows a description of the problem background provided to each team. Fourteen final year computing students were divided into two teams. The first team followed XP exclusively while the second team followed the OpenXP framework.

*Table 15 Problem background*

---

Currently concerns have been expressed about the student registration facilities provided by the Metropolitan and District Institute of Technology (MADIT). In general, problems have emerged when different categories of students have attempted to register. To date students, academic staff, management and department administrators have expressed concerns about the facilities.

Particular problems include: checking whether students are eligible to register with the institute. Also, personal details may not have changed for Returning (non-first year) students, yet they are still required to complete the same first year form. For students required to repeat exams, results are published very close to registration date. Repeating students are often treated in the same way as first year students without checking if they are already eligible for registration.

Erasmus students must enrol on a course but this may not exactly match the requirements of their own college, one problem here is selecting modules from different courses and years. For Post-Graduate students, no distinction is made between taught and research students, one difference here is that term times are different.

Mature students often transfer directly to 2nd year. Also – students have expressed a problem that they cannot be fully registered at the institute if they have not received a decision on grants or fees assistance. Likewise grants and fees assistance is not awarded by the various bodies (e.g. county councils, Vocational Education Committee (VECs) unless the student has been fully registered.

---

## 7.3 Main Findings

This section presents the main findings that emerged from the first confirmatory case study. Clear differences between the performance of both teams are first presented, the specific questions probed for each of the three propositions set out at the start are then discussed in depth.

### 7.3.1 Customer involvement and self-organisation

One observation was that the XP-only team did not regularly reflect on stories developed or work yet to be completed during sessions two, three and four and problems emerged with whole team collaboration and developing a collective understanding. In contrast, the OpenXP team reviewed progress more collaboratively having engaged in regular communication spending short periods of time at the beginning of each session reviewing progress at the wall. In this case, the OpenXP framework appeared to better facilitate a collaborative development effort since the evidence suggests that the OpenXP team self-organised around progress updates and interaction throughout the project could be described as dynamic. The customer representative was regularly involved and team-customer communication was effectively facilitated.

### 7.3.2 Producing a quick and usable design

Another difference between the performance of both teams was in the time spent investigating the problem background before stories were written. Extra time was needed to implement OST activities and the XP-only team had moved at a quicker pace since they had spent 45 minutes with the customer representative prior to writing stories. Initially, this was 30 minutes ahead of the OpenXP team. However, OpenXP recuperated on time lost later during design. At the end of the project, it transpired that 30 minutes had been wasted during design since the design produced by the XP-only team was not usable. In contrast to the design activities conducted by OpenXP, no time was wasted as this team produced a usable design. This appeared evident after the design artefact (class diagram) produced had been used during coding and no evidence suggested that any communication problems or difficulties on decision making with regard to design had been experienced by the OpenXP team. The XP-only team spent 95 minutes on a larger less focused architectural design whereas the OpenXP team were more focused having spent 65 minutes conducting the same activities.

### 7.3.3 Managing scope

The XP-only team had also experienced scope creep which did not occur for the OpenXP team. In contrast, consistent reference had been made to the scenario diagram (detailed later in section 7.3.7) during story writing which focused on a single aspect of the problem domain in-depth first. The scenario diagram had also been used to assist with the clarification of scope.

### 7.3.4 Early detection of overlapping requirements

For the XP-only team, during implementation, overlapping requirements emerged after five user stories unnecessarily included aspects of the same feature to login, whereas, OpenXP had not experienced this problem and direct observations showed that this team had detected an overlapping ambiguous requirement, prior to creating user stories.

### 7.3.5 Developing a common understanding

The OpenXP team consistently referred to the artefacts during implementation. The initial OST meeting did create an environment where viewpoints could be easily exchanged. This appeared to have helped the team to form a common understanding of the project. In contrast, the XP-only team seemed to take a more plan-driven approach with a large initial design whereas the OpenXP team appeared to be more focused on and better understand the whole problem.

### 7.3.6 Proposition One

This section now discusses the first proposition which focused on addressing the following question:

    i.     *How difficult is it for developers to understand and use OST?*

OST had been explained to the OpenXP team in advance of the commencement of the project. With steps 2 and 3, commencing at a slow pace initially and since only one concern had been raised this indicates that the team had not been fully confident with the OpenXP approach initially. This could be due to two reasons: first, none of the participants had previous experience using OST, and second, the nature of OST requires that participants self-organise accepting responsibility for issues regarding a common theme to be addressed. Self-organisation requires taking the initiative and it is not unusual for participants who have not previously practiced the approach to feel apprehensive about doing so since this requires a different more proactive approach to problem solving. This appears plausible since the team were initially brought out of their comfort zone but gradually contributed to a more interactive discussion as step 3 progressed. This indicates that OST may have provided the right amount of encouragement for the team to feel comfortable with a new approach taking their own initiative to self-organise and contribute multiple viewpoints.

OST requires that simple tools be used. The team in general may have been previously familiar with these since no difficulty was observed in using the tools. For instance, flipchart sheets, pens, masking tape and A4 sheets were used and in terms of the content produced, freeform sketch like drawings encouraged outputs generated to be simple and straightforward which appears to have helped the team to remain focused on solving the problem and rather than becoming distracted by having a specific format in which this should be expressed or presented. This suggests that the team experienced little or no learning curve in implementing OST, also, no difficulty in communication was observed with this team which suggests that a common language between members of the group had formed. The four principles and one law also appeared to seamlessly integrate into background of the project.

### 7.3.7 Proposition Two

The second proposition outlined at the start focused on addressing this next question:

> ii.      *Would the developers use the steps as described?*

The first step in OpenXP involves creating a theme to capture the overall objective of a project. In general this is decided in advance and as such it is not possible for participants to deviate from the first step. For the second step, one participant voiced a concern which was examined by all participants later at step 3. Initially it was not expected that the group would begin discussing the problem background prior to voicing concerns. In general, for OST alone, no such discussion takes place as participants study the theme, any background information to the problem they are presented with however, no discussion is expected in OST until step 3. In this case a short discussion had commenced prior to voicing concerns which had not been expected to occur. However, time spent on this was not considered a waste since it appeared as though the short discussion that took place here had helped the team to focus on *what concerns should be raised* for step 2. For the process of actually voicing concerns, it was evident that this occurred as expected since the convenor adhered to the steps for using the tools provided, vocalising the concern and posting this on the marketplace accordingly. The first concern raised was *"what are the differences between these student categories?"*

For the third step, exploring concerns commenced as expected since the scribe role was assumed by the convenor and the remaining participants collectively took responsibility for addressing the issue raised. Elicitation was participative with members of the group exchanging different opinions. The exploration phase revealed that misunderstandings could be clarified prior to the commencement of XP activities when differences between the Mature Student and Post Leaving Cert (PLC) categories eventually merged as a result of the collaborative discussions that took place during this step. This prevented the high level requirements specific to these student types from overlapping.

For step four, improvements were prioritized in a straightforward manner where consensus had been reached about the prioritization of the improvements made without much deliberation. This too had been participative since contributions appeared to be balanced involving all team members and consensus was reached in a collaborative manner indicating that this step had occurred as expected. This is also interesting since prioritizing improvements resulted in only *one aspect* of the system being focused on for scenario development in the fifth step.

Step five involved developing scenarios for the highest priority improvement and in this case one student category had been selected for specific focus. The scenario diagram represented a freeform drawing which could be described as *rough and sketchy*. For example, the diagram produced was similar to a thought bubble where stickmen characters were drawn at the centre followed by a rough sketch of a laptop characterising a typical student registering through the Central Applications Office (CAO) route. This was very similar to a brainstorming session and the key points documented on the diagram related to the various avenues of entry that could be pursued by this student type. Each point made was then connected by drawing arrows from the student character linking to all possible routes a CAO student might take to enter the Institute. Connections were also drawn from the bubble showing dependencies between successful registration and grant status, whether fees had been paid or not and if so what method for example giro or cash could be used to make a payment.

During scenario development self-organisation had been successfully encouraged with all members offering equal contributions. This also became evident after one participant took the initiative to write a text-based version of the scenario diagram. Although the scenario in narrative form was not explicitly referred to for the remainder of the project, it was clear that this had resolved misunderstandings at the time that it was created suggesting that it had been used for the purposes of clarification. This had improved the OpenXP teams understanding of the first prioritized business scenario.

For step 6 creating user stories commenced as expected with the team moving into story writing after the scenario had been drawn in the previous step. Observations also indicated that user stories were solely based upon the scenario diagram since this artefact was the main focal point for the discussion around the creation of stories. This was clear since this artefact remained on the flipchart stand as the team sat in a semi-circle consistently referring to the diagram for story writing during step 6.

Steps 7 and 8 occurred as expected with stories prioritized and added to the plan for the first iteration. Although during iteration planning the team began to discuss more detailed aspects of the stories which resulted in a decision that the first prioritized story would need to be developed before any other stories in the iteration plan.

As a result of discussions regarding design, all team members became focused on a single story which required whole team collaboration to establish a design for the data model. Finer detail emerged after a class diagram was produced which indicated that another set of more technical stories relating to the development of the first prioritized story were needed. Iteration was observed here where the team during this step returned to step 6 creating new stories that emerged from the design. Steps 7, 8 and 9 subsequently commenced as expected as these stories were then prioritized, assigned to iterations and implementation continued.

Later a second clear iteration through the XP steps could be observed where another story involving UI design caused the team to return to step 6 where another set of technical stories emerged. Subsequent steps proceeded as expected with new stories prioritized, organised into the iteration plan and the team then moved into implementation. One point to make here is that stories of a technical nature emerged after elicitation with the customer representative; these had been reprioritized over the stories initially prioritized for development by the customer representative.

In summary, with the exception of a discussion which took place between steps 1 and 2, the team had adhered to the 9 steps in the framework as expected. This unexpected discussion which occurred during steps 1 and 2 does not appear to have had a negative impact on the implementation of the remaining steps as described. Instead, with the exception of a few minutes delay, this slight deviation caused an issue to be raised which was of common concern since the whole group had opted to address this later during the third step. Also, after this point, the group grew more confident self-organising around tasks without prompt or further delay which indicates that a link with the OST technique may have gradually encouraged the team to adapt to using their own initiative and this continued for the remainder of the project.

### 7.3.8 Proposition Three

The third proposition outlined at the start of the chapter focused on addressing this last question:

> iii.      *Would performing OST assist the team in understanding the problem background?*

The third question sought to determine whether OST would assist the team in understanding the problem background. In particular, feedback from the questionnaires indicates that conducting an exploration phase with the customer representative had clarified requirements suggesting that the team had been able to develop a clear comprehension of the problem space to be addressed. Multiple viewpoints were exchanged during negotiations which helped to clarify misunderstandings between participants. Introducing prioritization of high level improvements appears to have also benefitted the team in deciding which requirements were the most important for developing one aspect of the system.

The high level concern related to a broader overview of the requirements and developing the scenario diagram had helped the team to visualise a wider perspective of the problem before moving into story writing. It was also expressed that user stories had been easier to write based upon the scenario diagram generated. For one aspect of the system, the scenario had increased understanding for the team. Another interesting point was that unanticipated complexity involved in the first prioritized story had been revealed after the scenario had been developed. This indicates that the team developed a good understanding of what was required in implementing this aspect of the system earlier on.

The class diagram later produced on a separate flipchart was also moved from the bulletin board to a position closer to the workstation which indicates that the artefact had been useful during implementation, also another team member had photographed this artefact which further supports this statement. The scenario diagram produced as the output of OST represented a broad view of the issues to be addressed for the main student category whereas the user stories drawn from this were perceived by participants as the details needed to implement this broader view. Here, OST facilitated the elicitation of broader high level business concerns where the team were able to focus on one aspect of the system in-depth which appears to have benefited XP activities such as story writing at step 6 later on. This is evident since the feedback suggests that team had a better understanding of the requirements as a result of using OST. Overlapping requirements had also been detected in the scenario before user stories were created.

The effort required for developers to understand and use OST appears minimal since although the group were initially apprehensive this had dissipated as step 3 progressed. Also, the team moved through the steps after this point without any problems which suggests that it had not been difficult for the team to implement the approach. Further, it had been initially anticipated that the time needed to implement OST might impose a delay on normal XP activities. This initially proved true since the XP-only team began writing stories 30 minutes ahead of the OpenXP team. However, as the project progressed it emerged that OpenXP completed design activities 30 minutes in advance of the XP only team. Upon the analysis of user stories created, observations and feedback from the questionnaires it became clear that 30 minutes had been wasted during design for the XP-only team since this team were still struggling to reach agreement about the UI design by the end of the fourth session. This indicates that using OST may have benefitted the OpenXP team as design activities appeared to be effective since no evidence exists to suggest that any time had been wasted for this team. Also on this point negotiations appeared amicable since no issues had been experienced reaching consensus with regard to decisions needed about the design of the solution for the OpenXP team.

It is worth noting that although the XP-only team had a design artefact, rather than using the flipchart sheets, this had been drawn on the whiteboard and photographed which was not openly visible to all team members throughout development. In contrast, the OpenXP team created an informative workspace since the artefacts generated were placed on the marketplace and bulletin board visible to all team members and one design artefact was moved closer to the workstation during pair programming. Also, the team continued to use the blank flipchart sheets for the design during XP activities which may have been encouraged by having initially used these tools during the first two phases.

Prioritization of high level improvements appears to have helped the OpenXP team to focus the implementation of a single aspect of the system in greater depth and the complexity of the project had emerged from the artefacts generated as a result of utilizing the interaction technique prior to moving into XP activities. On the question of whether or not OST assisted the team in understanding the problem background, overall this could be described as positive.

## 7.4 Summary

In summary, the findings presented here confirm that the OpenXP framework was beneficial for exploring requirements with the customer prior to writing stories; clarifying misunderstandings amongst the group; prioritizing requirements and writing user stories. This case study suggests that the OpenXP team benefitted from having developed a collaborative understanding of the problem domain prior to moving into XP activities. With reference to the propositions defined at the start, these have been confirmed indicating that developers did not experience difficulty understanding and using OST, the steps were used as described and overall, the evidence presented here suggests that the linked approach assisted the OpenXP team in understanding the problem background.

# Chapter 8 Confirmatory Case Study Two

## 8.1 Overview

Chapter 8 presents the second confirmatory case study conducted to test the performance of the OpenXP framework. Again, for brevity sake, only the main findings are discussed in detail with respect to the propositions defined at the beginning of this case study. A more extensive account of the specific models created by both teams alongside the in-depth direct observations recorded, and the analysis of responses from the questionnaires and interviews conducted, can be found in Walsh (2014). The problem background and the set of propositions that direct this case study are first detailed in section 8.2. A discussion then contrasts the main findings with the original propositions set out at the start of this final confirmatory study.

## 8.2 Case Study Background and Propositions

The aim of this case study was to conduct a second evaluation of the OpenXP framework and to expand further on the results of the previous confirmatory case study. Of particular interest is whether this case confirms the previous case that linking OST with XP could be considered a practical approach to agile software development. This involved developing a more comprehensive understanding for the consequences of adding OST to the initial stages of XP. To achieve this it was important to examine whether a link between the two approaches had an effect on the team and the project.

As such, this case is specifically focused on first determining once more whether developers using an agile approach would strictly adhere to the nine framework steps as described. This was achieved by determining whether this second proposition from the previous case could be confirmed or not. Secondly, with consideration for the specific criteria for determining whether a model could be considered agile as detailed in section 6.2.1, the fourth proposition was tested in this case for the first time. This sought to determine if any of the artefacts produced prior to phase three could be considered *agile models*. This proposition is tested with feedback collected from a series of individual interviews conducted with the OpenXP team members at the project end.

With reference to the difficulties experienced for an agile team in explaining the project status to an independent person, as detailed in section 4.2, the fifth proposition, predicted that the artefacts generated prior to phase three would improve the communication of project status to an unexpected person. Therefore, it should be noted that the methodology for this case slightly differs at this point from the confirmatory case conducted in the previous chapter. For instance, in order to test this particular proposition, halfway through the project both teams gained a new member. This proposition then focused on whether both teams could effectively communicate the project background to the new member, and subsequently the extent to which both additional members could seamlessly integrate with each development team for the remainder of the project.

## 8.2.1 Unit of Analysis

In line with the exploratory case study detailed in chapter 4, and the first confirmatory study detailed in chapter 7, the unit of analysis for the second confirmatory study also remained fixed with continued focus on the process of how requirements are elicited. As such a set of propositions are predicted in advance. These are listed as follows.

## 8.2.2 Propositions

1.  Developers would use the framework steps as described;

2.  Artefacts generated prior to phase three can produce agile models;

3.  Artefacts generated prior to phase three would provide additional context for communicating the project status to an outside stakeholder.

In addressing these propositions, some specific questions that required attention included:

i.    *Would the developers use the steps as described?*

ii.   *Could the models created prior to phase three be considered agile models?*

iii.  *Would using OpenXP assist developers in explaining progress to date to a project stakeholder who unexpectedly joins the project late?*

## 8.2.3 Problem Background

Table 16 shows the problem background for the taxing challenge presented to both the OpenXP and XP-only teams at the start of the project.

*Table 16 Problem background*

---

**"A Taxing Challenge"**

The Republic of Takedoughiville urgently needs to establish a service for its Revenue collection. The head of its Inland Revenue, Mr. Imadeamess Ullpay, has provided you with the following information. *"We need an efficient Tax Collection system that is easy to use … and we need it in 3 weeks."* However, a clerk in the revenue office has realized that you might need some more detail. He has said that the system should permit the entry of personal details which could be retrieved and organised at a later date. Also, to begin, he has provided some information on *personal tax allowances, tax bands* and *health contributions*.

---

In addition to the problem background further information was provided indicating the details of personal tax credits to be applied, tax rates and bands and the rate for Pay Related Social Insurance (PRSI) and health contributions.

## 8.3 Main Findings

This section presents the main findings that emerged from the second confirmatory case study. First, the key differences between the performance of both teams are presented, and the specific questions probed for each of the three propositions set out at the start, are then discussed in depth.

### 8.3.1 Differences in the timeframe to complete tasks

Initially it took 75 minutes longer for OpenXP to conduct OST activities prior to phase three which supported the possibility that the additional activities may impose a time delay for an OpenXP team. However, a comparison of the timeframes between both teams for story writing alone shows that the OpenXP team had completed this task in 60 minutes while the XP-only team took 110 minutes to conduct the same task. This indicates that the OpenXP team completed story writing approximately 50 minutes in advance of the XP-only team.

During session two, the difference in the timeframe to complete story writing between the two teams including the discussions held, appeared to balance out with a total of 180 minutes for XP-only while this took 175 minutes for OpenXP. This shows that despite the 75 minutes extra time needed to conduct initial OST activities in session one, OpenXP moved ahead having finished writing stories and tasks 5 minutes in advance of the XP-only team by the end of the second session.

### 8.3.2 Customer involvement

The OpenXP team had successfully involved the customer representative whereas the XP-only team had created initial stories without explicitly involving the customer representative. In contrast, it is possible that a greater level of involvement may have been encouraged by inviting team-customer participation using the interaction technique in advance. This may have supported a more participative elicitation process for the OpenXP team.

### 8.3.3 Demonstration

For the XP-only team, a number of stories relating to the actual task of calculating tax had not been completed, as a result, this team were unable to demonstrate that this functionality was complete by the project end. In contrast, the OpenXP team demonstrated a fully working prototype, developed in line with user stories created, and within the timeframe allocated for the project.

### 8.3.4 Streamlining OpenXP

During session two, as implementation began at step 9, it was noticed that some existing stories needed to be broken down further into tasks. When problems emerged here, an unexpected observation was that the OpenXP team returned to OST to raise a further set of concerns with the customer representative. An extra feedback loop was clearly observed during the second session after the OpenXP team unexpectedly returned to phase one in the framework (OST: Step 2) to raise the new set of three concerns which emerged after implementation began. It had originally been expected that OST activities would only occur prior to and as a feeding activity for the XP process through the development of scenarios. However, this case shows that the team continued to use OST after XP activities commenced to support the situation where problems encountered particularly in relation to the complexity of stories, needed to be quickly resolved, and without hindering normal XP activities. This has demonstrated that during implementation, concerns can also be raised if complexities emerge during the development of prioritized stories. Since this occurred after implementation began, it is necessary to document this additional feedback loop between step 9 from implementation back to step 2 in the framework.

Overall, this suggests that four feedback loops are needed to reflect iteration that has occurred here. Figure 22 shows the refinements made to the framework as a result of conducting OpenXP in this specific development context.

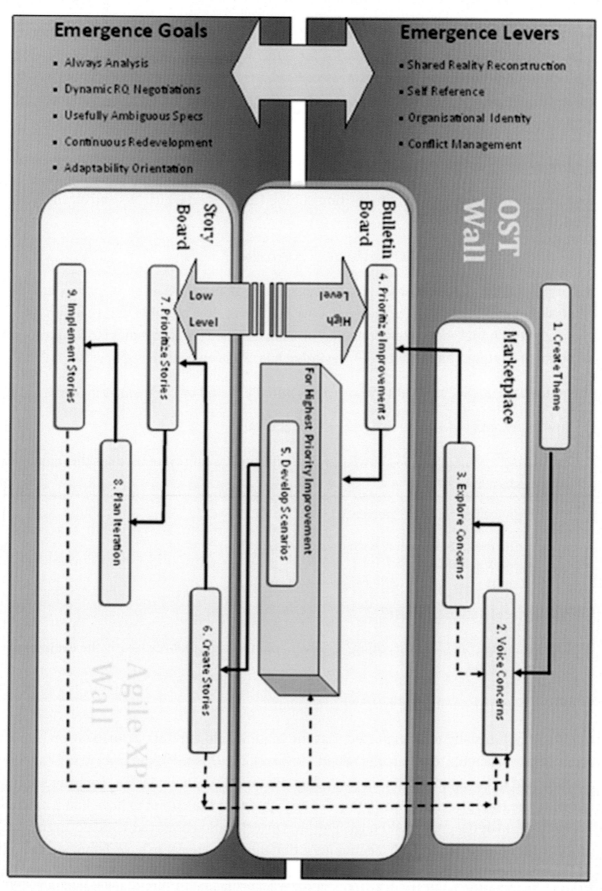

*Figure 22 OpenXP revised model*

As shown in Figure 22, during both story writing and implementation, developers can return to step 2 if concerns need to be resolved during these steps. During implementation developers can also return to step 5 to develop new scenarios for i) the next highest priority improvement and ii) to accommodate situations where business value changes causing business improvements to become reprioritized. For step 3 concerns can also be raised if they arise during the exploration of an existing more complex concern.

### 8.3.6 Proposition One

This section now discusses the first proposition outlined at the start which focused on addressing the following question:

> i.    *Would the developers use the steps as described?*

On this first question, an unexpected short discussion took place between steps one and two, but discussions in OST do not normally begin until step three. It is possible that (similarly to the previous case) this initial short interaction may also have helped the whole team to focus on *what concerns should be raised*, and as such this deviation has not been considered a waste.

Step 2 commenced as expected with five concerns initially raised by the team as follows:

1. How many data types need to be stored in database?

2. Easy to use?.. what previous knowledge of computing/taxing systems, does the main users of the system have?

    a. Novice (very little experience)

    b. Intermediate (familiar with computers/tax)

    c. Expert (has used a wide range of systems)

3. What type of database to use?

4. Do we need to consider everything? E.g. event of marriage, divorce, death, the event of who will be an adult?

5. Which platform should the system be based on?

Clearly it had not initially been expected that the team would conduct prioritization prior to developing improvements for concerns raised. However, the OpenXP team prioritized concerns before they had been explored in this case. This demonstrates a deviation from the steps as described in the framework, however, this did not appear at the outset to have had a negative impact on the team or the project. Although high level prioritization occurred, it did not occur in the sequence expected. One point worth mentioning is that this does appear to have demonstrated self-organisation amongst the team at a very early stage in the project, since the reason for prioritizing concerns was to ensure that all members could be present for the focused discussions for each of the concerns raised. It should also be noted that prioritization would be expected to occur naturally in using OST alone since participants are encouraged to self-organise around resolving conflicting issues such as all participants opting to attend concurrent sessions (Owen 2008), a problem which must be managed by the participants themselves in OST. Another possible reason for the whole team opting to prioritize early in order to discuss concerns separately, may relate to the size of the participating group. Typically in large OST investigations, running focused discussions concurrently is practical and efficient. For this case study the group was very small (initially 4 members) and quite focused on a specific goal to address a number of concerns that were commonly related to all the participants present.

Step 3 commenced as expected with a number of concerns explored. The scribe roles were effectively assumed and the remaining participants collectively took responsibility for addressing each of issues raised. Elicitation could also be described as participative with all members of the group collaboratively involved.

Step 4 was skipped as prioritization had unexpectedly occurred prior to step 3 in this case. A further deviation of the steps was observed after the OpenXP team did not create a separate scenario artefact for step 5. However, this is not considered to be problematic in this case since the team still used the improvements produced as outputs from OST to provide additional context for writing user stories at step 6. This could be explained by the fact that the concerns raised during this project were very focused asking specific questions which did not require a significant amount of exploration. It appears as though the improvements contained details that were at the appropriate level of depth needed and developing further scenarios was not necessary for writing stories in the context of this case.  Steps 7, 8 and 9 occurred as expected where the team organised the user stories according to their order of priority, added these to the iteration plan and proceeded with implementation.

While clear deviations in the steps as described could be observed, there is no evidence to suggest that this had a negative impact on the team or the project. This suggests that regardless of this deviation, the OpenXP team still benefited from using the framework and the outcome for the project itself was positive considering that this team were able to produce a fully functional prototype by the end of the fourth session.

## 8.3.7 Proposition Two

The second proposition outlined at the beginning of this chapter focused on addressing this next question:

> ii.    *Could the models created as outputs from OST be considered agile models?*

Interviews conducted with the OpenXP team focused closely on determining whether the models produced as outputs from OST could be considered agile models. According to the participants the response received here was generally positive on this point.

In determining whether a model can be considered agile, Ambler (2002) includes terms such as 'sufficiently detailed', 'understandable' and 'accurate' for the purposes of intended use, also the artefacts must provide positive value. These questions rely on a given participants opinion of what exactly constitutes terms such as 'sufficiently accurate, detailed, or what exactly the term value refers to'. For instance, a term such as *sufficient* is a criterion only measurable by a given participants opinion of what the term should mean which is also bound to the situation or the context under which the models are actually used. This can only ever be determined by the participants' opinions of what constitutes Amblers (2002) terms.

As such, the interviews confirmed that the models produced in OpenXP had provided positive value, fulfilled the purposes for which they were created, were sufficiently understandable, consistent, and detailed. Each member on the OpenXP team also strongly agreed that overall the models generated during OST could be described as simple. Having received an overall positive response from the OpenXP participants, this suggests that the models created prior to phase three in the framework could all be described as agile models according to the seven criteria as defined by Ambler (2002).

### 8.3.8 Proposition Three

The third proposition outlined at the beginning of the chapter focused on addressing this final question:

> iii. *Would using OpenXP assist developers in explaining progress to date to a project stake-holder who unexpectedly joins the project late?*

Immediately prior to session 3, each team gained a new member. Before session three commenced, both teams were unaware that a new member would be joining the project. The OpenXP team used the wall to illustrate a map of the project to the new member. For instance, the team were able to provide a straightforward explanation of progress made in the project to date. OpenXP began by explaining the user stories on the wall chart including a colour coded scheme and the significance of a set of sticky discs used for prioritization. This developed into a fluid explanation as the bulletin board was also used to explain the wider context of the stories written. The team stepped backwards here, first from stories and tasks, then to the bulletin board and reference was also made to the marketplace to explain that this section of the wall had been used to raise issues that needed to be resolved during the project. The four principles and the law of mobility were also referred to by separate team member as the group stood around the wall. This took approximately five minutes and the new team member did not have any difficulty integrating directly with the team.

This is comparable to the XP-only team since the new member for this team required an explanation which feedback from the interviews later confirmed, had taken 30 minutes initially. Later in the project one hour had been wasted after it became clear that the new member had incorrectly implemented one of the user stories. Further delays ensued as this problem then had to be rectified alongside two other members of the team which took a further 30 minutes. This brought the total time needed to bring the new member up to speed to 2 hours.

During the interviews, one participant elaborated that the new member on the XP-only team had not fully understood the requirements which only emerged later during implementation. For the XP-only team, this suggests that the initial explanation provided using the stories and the wall chart alone, did not necessarily communicate a clear and coherent account of progress made to date. With consideration for the difficulties experienced later during implementation, this also suggests that the new member had not effectively integrated onto the project. Overall the OpenXP team explained the project coherently and in a much shorter time period of 5 minutes and since the new team member integrated onto the project without problems or introducing a schedule delay, this suggests that the OpenXP team were able to communicate progress to date more effectively which resulted in the new team member subsequently integrating well into the project.

## 8.4 Summary

In summary chapter 8 presented the second confirmatory case study which began with a set of propositions defined at the start. The results then presented the logic linking back to these original propositions. Overall, for the XP-only team, problems emerged in understanding the problem domain, determining user needs, breaking down and estimating tasks, making decisions, resolving misunderstandings and stories had been difficult to create without developing a clear understanding of the problem space in advance. In contrast, the OpenXP framework had provided support for raising and visualising concerns emerging early on in the project. The focused discussions had assisted in clarifying misunderstandings and the improvements made had supported the team in reaching a commonly agreed understanding.

An unexpected finding also emerged since it had not been expected that the team would return to OST after development began. Here, technical issues emerged and the team self-organised without prompt, raising an additional set of three concerns which were then resolved using the group interaction technique. Stories subsequently emerged from these concerns after more focused discussions were held to resolve them. This illustrates the potential for OST to be streamlined alongside XP activities for the purposes of resolving unexpected concerns that may arise after phase three has commenced. In light of this finding, an additional revised version was then documented illustrating the unexpected feedback loops that emerged from the enactment of the OpenXP framework for this particular development setting.

Finally, the first proposition was disconfirmed since the developers did not use the steps in the framework as described. However, this does not appear to have had an adverse effect on the project or the team since a fully functional prototype was still developed on schedule and within scope. The second proposition was confirmed which suggested that the artefacts produced as outputs from OST could be described as agile models. The third proposition was also confirmed indicating that the OpenXP framework assisted developers in explaining progress to date to a stakeholder who unexpectedly joined the project late.

# Chapter 9 Expert Evaluation

## 9.1 Overview

In order to validate the OpenXP framework two independent expert reviews were conducted. The three phases of the OpenXP framework were explained and the artefacts generated during both confirmatory case studies were displayed on the wall. Feedback was elicited through focused interviews (the interview guide is discussed earlier in section 2.8.2) This chapter presents a summary of the feedback received from each reviewer.

## 9.2 Interview 1

The first interview was conducted with Ms Silvana McMahon, a software quality assurance engineer and certified senior test analyst. Ms McMahon's role includes full software development lifecycle exposure with specialist experience in business analysis and communicating requirements between roles for defect management including regression testing and system testing. She has co-ordinated distributed teams on both large and small projects in the development of bespoke transaction systems, interactive voice recognition, switch telephony systems and web-based applications for the financial sector. In the context of this research, Ms McMahon has first-hand experience managing multiple diverse stakeholders, including conflict identification and resolution and risk based prioritization of functional business requirements across a wide range of end user perspectives.

### 9.2.1 Requirements depth

The theme was described as a good starting point for software projects and Ms McMahon agreed that the specific themes developed formed the centre focus for both confirmatory case studies. However, once focused discussions begin, detail more specific to the problem context would emerge and she felt that at this point, *"the theme would become largely irrelevant"*. Silvana emphasised that for projects with greater complexity, concerns are likely to be much broader relating to the wider aspects of a given business problem. Her opinion was that *"a lot more concerns"* might emerge during step 2. After studying the physical artefacts generated during the two confirmatory case studies, Silvana perceived *"a straight forward definite connection"* between the concerns raised, improvements made and the user stories that had been drawn from these. This suggests that a logical path between high level and low level requirements detail was visible.

### 9.2.2 Identifying high level business requirements as concerns

Silvana asserted that voicing concerns was *"essential"* for identifying high level business requirements. In her experience it regularly transpired that high level requirements had not been identified earlier in the development process. This had a negative impact on *"more than just the individual project"*, the problem continued to proliferate *"impacting business as a whole".* She emphasised the importance of recognizing high level requirements as soon as possible to successfully integrate changes *"in a smooth fashion, to ensure business continuity".* In her opinion, this could be achieved through *"informal interaction"* between stakeholders and addressing potential issues in advance.

### 9.2.3 Benefits of the focused discussions

Ms McMahon described the more focused discussions as *"very important"* asserting that one of the key issues in a complex problem space is the involvement of a variety of stakeholders. Being able to address each need in a balanced appropriate manner requires the right amount of exploration in advance. She pointed out that without input from multiple stakeholders whose perspectives vary, it is not possible *"to get a full perspective of any problem".* In her opinion *"the concern is never ever going to be isolated"* to a specific product or stage in a lifecycle and *"actually being able to discuss concerns is invaluable".* Silvana believed that the full impact involved for implementing improvements for concerns could also be investigated during the more focused discussions.

She elaborated further that the focused discussions could help stakeholders to reach agreement after negotiations about cost benefit analysis asserting that it was important that *"the perceived benefit was actually beneficial"* for the business. Her opinion was that if these types of concerns are raised as early as possible, a more representative perspective of the full impact of a proposed change could be discussed during the focused meetings. Another point made was that the more focused discussions would have the capacity to detect and better manage the impact of a change in business direction, earlier on in projects. She predicted that the OpenXP framework would benefit collaborative discussions needed between groups of stakeholder representatives specifically for performing root cause analysis in the identification and resolution of system defects.

### 9.2.4 Iteration between the OpenXP steps

Ms McMahon had regularly experienced situations where, after potential issues were first raised, it later transpired that this *"was never ever the full set of concerns".* She recalled multiple occasions when unanticipated problems with requirements had emerged at a later stage which needed regular negotiations. For this reason she strongly agreed that stakeholders would benefit from being able to voice other potential concerns that may emerge during the focused discussions.

In her experience requirements were not well-defined unless they could be tested, which clearly indicated that *"something was wrong"* with the requirement as originally specified, and this resulted in revisiting stakeholders for further refinement of the necessary detail. With regard to this the expert strongly agreed that stakeholders would benefit from being able to voice other potential concerns that may emerge during story writing, pointing out that this was *"definitely needed"*.

Ms McMahon advised that particularly for testing complex scenarios, constraints can unexpectedly prevent all potential scenarios from being fully tested and it is necessary to be in a position where requirements most closely aligned to the currently perceived business value, can be reprioritized. She advised that prioritization is an iterative process and for this reason she suggested that stakeholders would also benefit from being able to voice concerns that emerge during the prioritization of user stories. In her experience, usage scenarios had been particularly beneficial for ensuring that requirements were appropriately prioritized. Considering this Silvana suggested that stakeholders would also benefit from being able to raise concerns during scenario development, to accommodate new contexts of use emerging.

### 9.2.5 Benefits of the two-step approach to prioritization

In general, the two-step approach to prioritization of business improvements and user stories was welcomed since *"a tension exists"* between what the customer requires and *"what is possible to deliver from a development perspective"*. On this point, she distinguished between two types of prioritization from her experience, one from a customer point of view, and the other from a technical point of view. Business stakeholders prioritized requirements according to business criticality where the same set of requirements were also prioritized by the development team depending on the level of technical complexity involved. For this reason, she advised that the additional feedback loop from prioritization of stories back to voicing concerns would initiate important discussions where collaboration is needed to appropriately align both the business and technical aspects for each individual requirement during prioritization.

### 9.2.6 Scenarios as the linking activity

Ms McMahon described phase two, scenario-based development as *"a very direct link"* between OST and XP. For instance, improvements identified as the outputs of OST could be interpreted as scenarios since they represented potential usage scenarios of the high level business context of requirements. She emphasised the importance of determining all possible routes that could be pursued in relation to how a given requirement might be used. Silvana asserted that scenarios provide additional context particularly for the purposes of deriving *acceptance test criteria* for requirements. She continued stating that user stories would be easier to write based on the scenarios created and *"getting the right user stories"* could be assured through usage scenarios as the mode of expression for linking OST with XP.

### 9.2.7 Application of the OpenXP framework

Silvana had first-hand experience coordinating regular communications with multiple diverse stakeholders which she described as informal processes that had grown organically *"out of that need to satisfy business requirements"*. She described OpenXP as *"so much more valid"* since it would succeed in facilitating such processes if the framework were to be applied in practice. Upon studying OpenXP as a complete software process, Silvana replied: *"I don't think it is just useful, I think it is essential".*

In summary, Ms McMahon elaborated that OpenXP would encourage both business stakeholders to consider the technical perspective and developers to consider the business perspective of requirements. In relation to how the framework might perform in practice, her opinion was that prioritization would occur based upon *"all of the concerns of all of the various stakeholders"* across both business and technology domains which would support the delivery of correct user stories and test cases with the appropriate order of priority assigned to each requirement. For instance, she pointed out that concerns raised could be related to business criticality and the actual development of requirements including testing. Overall, her opinion was that the OpenXP framework does not *"just hit a business issue, it hits an entire graft of issues throughout the lifecycle of a change made".*

## 9.3 Interview 2

The second interview was conducted with Mr Neil Clynch, a senior software engineer currently developing bespoke application software in the area of medical device research. Mr Clynch has experienced implementing plan-driven development methods in accordance with the ISO 12207 international standard for systems and software engineering lifecycle processes. He has also worked extensively with the practical implementation of a number of AMs in industry and is proficient in Agile Model Driven Development (AMDD), Scrum, XP, Test-Driven Development and refactoring.

Neil has first-hand experience introducing agile development techniques in the design and development of mobile media solutions, he has delivered both stand alone and end-to-end enterprise web based applications. Neil's role has included requirements elicitation, functional specification design, development, testing and support. Neil was also involved the development of bespoke business intelligence software for the ministry of finance in an Irish state government project. Additionally, Mr Clynch is an internationally published author having contributed to the field of software engineering through the development of SADAAM, a software agent development methodology utilizing AMs to facilitate the development and implementation of multi-agent systems.

### 9.3.1 Requirements depth

Neil strongly agreed that raising concerns was beneficial for identifying high level business requirements as soon as possible during projects. One point made here was that stakeholders need to *"commit as early as possible to their own requirements"* and identifying high level concerns would assist stakeholders with both the prioritization of requirements and informed decision making, *"the earlier this is achieved, the better".*

Neil asserted that the specific themes developed for both confirmatory case studies had provided the centre focus for what needed to be achieved describing this as *"quite straight forward".* He asserted that the concerns raised in both case studies had a direct relationship with the themes describing the content of these artefacts as *"important information needed to fulfil the requirements".* In Neil's opinion the artefacts produced between steps 1 and 6 for the first confirmatory case study, specifically represented the wider business perspective of the student registration problem. He could see a logical link between the concerns raised, and the scenarios developed as business improvements asserting that at step 6 more detailed lower level requirements had emerged from this previously developed context. With regard to the artefacts produced in this case study, Neil described this project as having *"a nice flow"* where high level business concerns linked with the lower level detail needed for implementing the requirements.

### 9.3.2 Benefits of the focused discussions

Neil strongly agreed that the framework would support more focused discussions which are regularly needed. He viewed this initial investigation as useful for the purposes of negotiating and clarifying high level business requirements. In the case where multiple focused discussions simultaneously take place, Neil advised that in general while business problems could differ the technical solutions could be very similar and in this case it would be wise to situate a stakeholder with technical expertise in each focused discussion to ensure that the technical aspects of concerns receive the appropriate amount of attention during the initial investigation.

In general his opinion was that approaching high level concerns from multiple software team roles would be beneficial for getting an overall and representative perspective during the focused discussions. Neil had regularly experienced situations where finer details including test criteria were generally unforeseen only emerging after *"you get deeper into development".* With regard to this his opinion was that obtaining the appropriate level of detail needed for requirements as soon as possible is considerably beneficial. In particular, Neil felt that the OpenXP framework was relevant to the scope of *testing requirements.* The expert explained that when stakeholders specify requirements too broadly *"it is hard to establish the appropriate tests"* and with OpenXP, the more focused discussions support the developer perspective in establishing test criteria upfront.

### 9.3.3 Developing additional context through scenarios

Neil took particular interest in the first confirmatory case study where one aspect of the student registration system was discussed and improved at high level and stories elicited consisted of detailed requirements for this singular aspect of the system. It was clear that the highest priority usage scenario received in-depth focus rather than broadly developing all aspects of the system at once and in his opinion, this was very useful. He asserted that if this project had been developed in an industry setting, prioritizing high level scenarios first and eliciting stories needed for this singular aspect would expose further dependencies in other scenarios yet to be developed. In the event of this occurring existing dependencies could be revealed earlier by using the OpenXP framework. In general taking an iterative approach to the development of prioritized scenarios was welcomed. Mr Clynch asserted that producing scenarios with the relevant stakeholders would *"give the development team enough information to progress"* with the highest priority business requirements first. He strongly agreed that user stories would be easier to identify based upon the scenarios produced.

### 9.3.4 Iteration between the OpenXP steps

Neil strongly agreed that stakeholders should be able to voice concerns during the focused discussions in order to accommodate any important issues that might emerge during this initial investigation. Further, he strongly recommended that stakeholders should also be able to voice concerns if necessary during scenario development. This he felt was very important for accommodating the likelihood that with increased complexity, multiple scenarios would yield new concerns during scenario development at step 5. These could be quickly identified and resolved using OpenXP.

Mr Clynch agreed that it should be possible for stakeholders to voice concerns during story writing pointing out that *"quite often details can be missed"*, a problem that could be identified and quickly rectified using OpenXP.   The expert supported the necessity for voicing concerns during implementation. However, since this may occur during development, he felt that addressing concerns may need to be supported with online collaborative forums in cases where the relevant stakeholders are not directly available.

### 9.3.5 Issues for developers

Upon studying the technical concerns raised for confirmatory case study three, where the OpenXP team returned to OST to voice technical concerns, Neil expressed concerns about how many meetings would be required and also whether the relevant stakeholders could be present for each meeting needed. Here, he voiced that difficulties could be experienced in practice with getting stakeholders to *"commit to meeting at certain times"*. From the development perspective, Mr Clynch stressed on the importance of also having a stakeholder with technical expertise present during initial investigations advising that *"nine times out of ten you have to go back"* to the stakeholders to clarify requirements detail. Neil suggested that given such circumstances, the use of collaborative online forums such as Skype and shared workspaces such as wikis where existing artefacts could be asynchronously reviewed by the relevant stakeholders. The expert also warned that the appropriate business stakeholder representatives, particularly those who are in a position to regularly meet, should be specifically sought.

### 9.3.6 Traceability of the artefacts produced

Neil advised that clear decisions are needed to demonstrate when agreement on requirements has been reached. With regard to this he stressed the importance of formally acknowledging key points from the outcomes of the initial investigations.  One suggestion here was that it would be beneficial if stories could be more explicitly linked upward with their associated usage scenarios, business improvements and the original concerns raised. Considering this he suggested that explicitly numbering the artefacts would help to discern clear links between associated artefacts gradually generated during each step. This in turn would provide a bidirectional trace between the tangible artefacts produced.

### 9.3.7 Application of the OpenXP framework

In Neil's experience *"it is easier for stakeholders to give you a broad scope"*, however, finer detail is needed to specify requirements to the appropriate level of depth needed. In his opinion OpenXP avoids the situation of stakeholders remaining too broad in their description of requirements. The expert recalled first-hand experiences where general high level expected functionality can already be known in advance. In his opinion, presenting a set of envisaged high level requirements in conjunction with the theme would further direct stakeholders toward deriving detailed requirements from the outset.

From Neil's experience *"it is very important"* to begin a software project by identifying the potential problems and opportunities that currently exist in a given domain. He asserted that *"the earlier this is established, the better"*, advising that as development begins issues inevitably emerge that need to be resolved and feedback is needed to clarify specific detail as projects progress. Here, *"getting the customer to decide"* what is required *"from the initial outset"* would be valuable in order to *"be clear and concise about requirements"* as early as possible. Neil felt that OpenXP offered *"a good way to get stakeholders to think along this direction".*

In summary, Neil understood the first two phases of the framework as the business perspective of the problem being addressed in advance. The expert voiced that in using AMs *"you don't really start to think about the detail until you go to sit down"* to develop stories and it would be useful to develop additional context in advance. He felt that this early interaction would contribute toward building a good relationship with business stakeholders from the start. His opinion was that the framework would focus stakeholders on the detail needed first. With OpenXP he recognised that refinement is achieved earlier stating that the framework will *"force the stakeholder"* to more fully examine the business need and to *"narrow down the scope to the point where you can actually write a detailed requirement".*

## 9.4 Summary

Chapter 9 presented the analysis of feedback from two expert evaluations conducted to validate the OpenXP framework. In general both interviews suggest that the framework received a positive response overall. A number of valuable expert opinions were offered and suggestions were made indicating further improvements that may benefit the use of the framework for application in practice.

# Chapter 10 Putting it all Together

## 10.1 Overview

Chapter 10 concentrates on the wider perspective of the OpenXP solution focusing on how the broader features of the framework fit together. Alongside the steps 1-9 which have been described, explained and tested in previous chapters, this solution also encompasses four distinct facets. These involve: *Stakeholder Coordination*, *Business and IT Alignment*, *Effective Communication* and *Adaptability Integration*. As shown in Figure 23, each facet consists of one or more strategic functions which are then described in detail. Five specific lean principles that have been applied are also discussed showing where each is addressed using OpenXP. The chapter then concludes with a look at agile business analysis today and how this role can now be further supported for OpenXP teams.

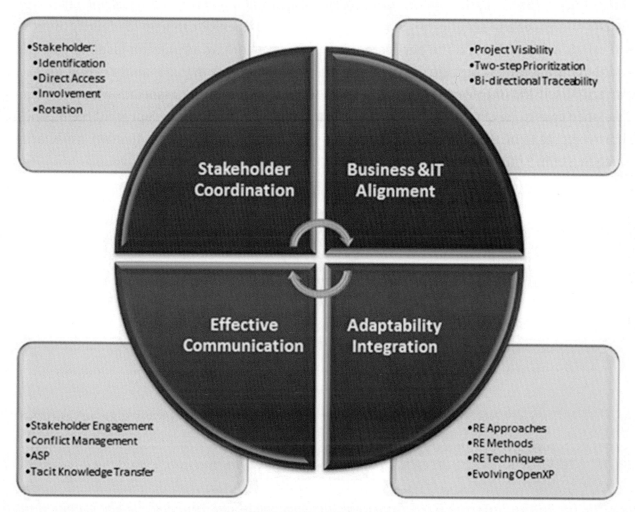

*Figure 23 The four OpenXP facets*

## 10.2 Stakeholder Coordination

The Stakeholder Coordination facet is primarily responsible for the identification, access, involvement and rotation of stakeholders on projects. Chapter 5 explained the components of the OST interaction technique and specific role definitions which included the role of the convenor. Due to the phase one activities that commence in the OpenXP framework, convenors are automatically considered to be *Collaborative*, *Authorised*, *Committed* and since they have identified and developed improvements to the business problem, they are also considered to a certain extent, *Knowledgeable* and *Representative* business customers. One clear advantage to encouraging these CRACK characteristics to emerge from the convenors of OST focused discussions is that phase two and three activities can now commence with the additional benefits of involving stakeholders consisting of the set of key skills, experience and abilities required for a successful software development effort, as defined by Boehm and Turner (2003).

### 10.2.1 Member Associations

Stakeholders who partake in the focused discussions can also be structured using the stakeholder onion model. The benefits here include that this structure can be adapted to specific target domain audiences and significantly, applying this model in OpenXP, can help to identify the roles and relationships between the participants who are affected by a common issue of concern. Additionally another advantage to organising stakeholder groups in this manner is that for each concern raised and improved through a focused discussion, a member association has now been developed consisting of relevant stakeholders that have been identified to represent the business improvements to be made. Figure 24 illustrates the formation of a Level 0 member association consisting of five initial stakeholders with one acting as the convenor for this group.

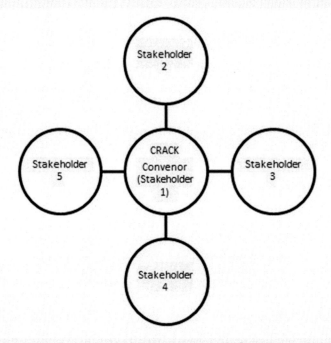

*Figure 24 Level 0 member association based upon focused discussion participants*

## 10.2.2 Customer Involvement

Considering that the same member association has been involved from the start, in identifying and exploring concerns, transforming these into a set of prioritized business improvement scenarios and then co-writing user stories jointly with the help of developers, it can therefore be stated that each convenor is representative of at least one business concern raised, together with its corresponding set of prioritized improvements recommended. As such the convenors from each member association (responsible for conducting each focused discussion) could later become involved with the development team on a more regular basis by adopting the role of the customer. Figure 25 shows how customer involvement with the development team can now be structured to include the CRACK convenor from each member association to clarify specific requirements, generate feedback and to gradually refine the necessary requirements detail to the appropriate level of depth needed for implementation.

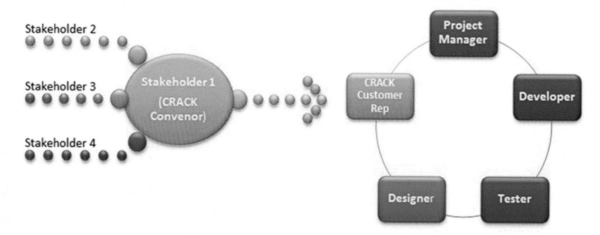

*Figure 25 Structured customer involvement during OpenXP development*

### 10.2.2.1 Addressing Limited Access

One other point on the value of such dynamically generated member associations is that there now exists a number of alternative stakeholders related to the business improvements who could be consulted in the event of limited access to the convenor. Similarly, if the convenor is required to provide information to the development team about some aspect to which he/she is not fully sure about, then the remaining stakeholders in the existing member association can be consulted to contribute toward refining the specific detail required. This in turn ensures that the improvement being implemented consists at all times of a decision making process that is fully informed by the expertise from the relevant stakeholders identified by each member association.

### 10.2.3 Larger Stakeholder Groups

It is also important to manage situations in which ultimately large groups of stakeholders may comprise the participants present during phase one's OST investigation. In this case it may not be practical to have a large group involved with the development team during implementation.

Essentially, a contingency plan is needed to mitigate the negative effects of this situation on any given development effort. As such, it is possible with the OpenXP framework to dynamically form broader level member associations consisting of CRACK customer teams to address this issue.

*A CRACK customer team can be defined as a team of all the convenors who represent the set of prioritized business improvements under a single theme of common significance*

Here, CRACK customer teams can dynamically form and engage regularly for the purposes of ensuring that the broader project vision remains closely aligned primarily to the production of business value, as the project proceeds through to completion. Figure 26 shows the formation of a Level 1 CRACK customer team consisting of five main stakeholders with the team convenor situated in the centre.

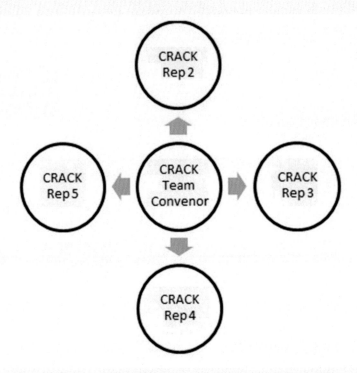

*Figure 26 Level 1 CRACK customer team representation*

Let us consider an example; that five by five member associations dynamically emerge through the focused discussions (step 3) during phase one activities for a given problem investigation, and this results in a total number of 25 stakeholders being collectively included. Rather than directly involving all these stakeholders on a development team, each member association formed through the focused discussions could be classified as *related* to a specific aspect of the problem, its concern, improvements and user stories generated. This means that business stakeholders including convenors identified by their member association *only* need to be involved later during development when feedback or some detail relating to their own business improvements requires clarification from the team. Figure 27 shows that by assembling customer teams in this manner we can separate, yet fully involve CRACK representatives (at different levels) during development, *when and only where* their feedback is specifically relevant to a single aspect of the business improvement to be implemented.

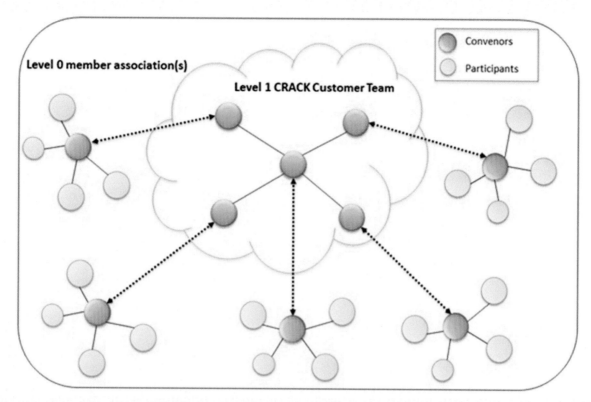

*Figure 27 CRACK representation with larger stakeholder groups*

A distinct advantage of coordinating stakeholders in this manner is that CRACK customer teams on the broader level would be responsible for contributing toward systematic checkpoints providing *reflective improvement* of the business concept. This measure ensures that regular and consistent feedback cycles from the wider business perspective are continuously built into the communication process throughout development.

## 10.2.4 Rotating Stakeholder Groups

As presented earlier in Chapter 4, industry practitioners found it challenging to manage the changing priorities of a rotating stakeholder group. OpenXP addresses this by accepting from the outset that stakeholders who form member associations dynamically, are at liberty to flexibly rotate. For instance, the law of mobility requires that OpenXP participants can move between groups in cases where they feel they are either not learning or contributing during the focused discussions at step 3. In this case stakeholders are encouraged to self-organise by either posting a new concern or by joining an alternative discussion. OpenXP does not expect the stakeholder group to remain fixed and as such this more flexible approach anticipates a healthy degree of rotation to amplify learning between groups. A sensible amount of rotation between groups is recognised and embraced as an important part of a collective learning process for stakeholders involved in the problem definition stage. Figure 28 illustrates how business and development team roles can interact where larger groups become involved using OpenXP. The blue dotted arrows indicate rotation between stakeholders on member associations and between developers on the XP teams. The red dotted arrows signify bidirectional communication including rotation between the convenors on member associations, CRACK customer teams, and their subsequent involvement on the XP teams later during development.

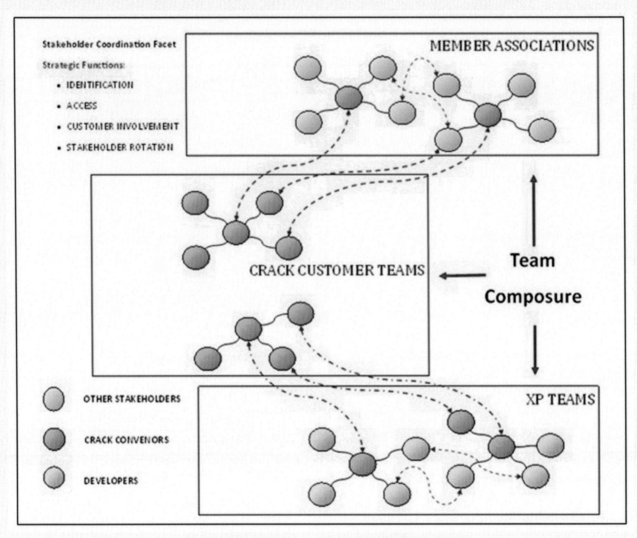

*Figure 28 Stakeholder coordination with OpenXP*

## 10.4.5 Informal Social Networks (ISNs)

As mentioned earlier in chapter 3, the formal organisation chart used for stakeholder identification in business domains tends to characterise the normal and typically expected behaviours where rules, regulations and/or procedures for work activities are explicitly stated within organisations (Jablin and Putnam 2001). Informal organisational networks consist of *"human interactions which usually develop spontaneously in response to unexpected circumstances"* (Jaffee 2001), (Robbins *et al.* 2001). For rapidly changing competitive business domains, it is necessary to be able to respond quickly and this *"requires multidirectional communication flows"* operating *"at a much wider bandwidth than depicted by organisational charts"* (Ali 2011). It is therefore crucially important during requirements elicitation in competitive business environments to be cognizant of potential for ISNs. However, as previously mentioned, a key challenge is that, although they clearly exist, due to the informal nature of ISNs, they are difficult to detect, model and visualise.

As an evolutionary approach, OpenXP recognises the value of informal dynamic communication and as such the framework positively exploits the potential benefits of ISNs as early as possible during elicitation. For example, communication structure at the start is purposefully relaxed to support and encourage the emergence of dynamically generated member associations, each of which consists of set of informally established roles and relationships (these could be automatically identified by the BA). Interaction between stakeholders then proceeds in an informal, collaborative and inclusive manner during the focused discussions. The framework thus harnesses the value of ISNs in the context of identifying additional roles and relationships between these during elicitation. This measure aims to foster the benefits of ISNs and to act as a supplement to the set of recognised roles and relationships established through existing known perhaps more readily available sources, such as the formal organisation chart.

## 10.3 Business and IT Alignment

One crucial goal in achieving business and IT alignment overall is to make sure that the perceived benefit of software developed, is *actually* beneficial for the business. This section describes how the business and IT alignment facet implements three strategic functions, namely; the *two-step approach to prioritization*, *bi-directional traceability* between tangible artefacts produced and how a greater degree of *project visibility* overall can be achieved through the dynamic generation of higher level business context.

### 10.3.1 Two-step Approach to Prioritization

In XP development alone the earliest stage at which prioritization is conducted is after user stories have been created when the customer representative prioritizes each story for development. While this organises the order in which requirements will be developed, it does not provide a link between prioritized requirements and the higher level business context to which these requirements are related. This can present developers with a lack of provision of contextual detail needed for requirements during implementation. This can also create further difficulty for achieving upward traceability for the requirements developed at a later stage.

With consideration for this problem, OpenXP has introduced a two-step approach to the prioritization of business valued improvements to be made. In phase one business improvements are developed as the outcome of specific concerns explored. The first step then involves *high level prioritization* where each business improvement is organised for development by the relevant stakeholders present. This measure ensures that only previously identified units of business value are later implemented as part of the software solution. Once business improvements have been prioritized, usage scenarios for the highest priority improvement are developed. User stories are subsequently drawn from the scenarios. The second step then conducts *low level prioritization* as part of the XP development process that normally takes place. Taking this two-step approach ensures that both the business and technical aspects for each requirement are appropriately aligned before development proceeds.

## 10.3.2 Project Visibility

As a by-product, OpenXP necessarily generates an explicit link between upper level business context and lower level technical detail needed for requirements development. Dynamically generated business artefacts can be hierarchically arranged creating additional context and upward visibility for developers. For instance, the problem to be investigated goes through a process of transformation from the theme to related concerns into a prioritized set of improvement scenarios which are then used to inform story creation and development.

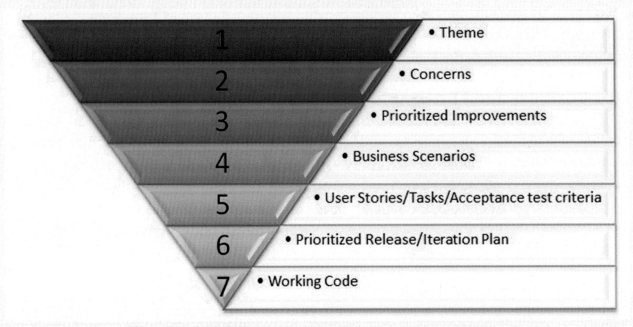

*Figure 29 OpenXP layers representing upper level business context*

Particularly for traceability, vertical scope (as defined in Chapter 4) is relevant here since requirements acquire depth as more specific detail emerges. As shown in Figure 29, each row illustrating the artefacts produced as the outputs from each step in the framework can be broadly structured into a set of hierarchically organised layers. This arrangement creates an upward trace between the artefacts produced from working code (in the technical domain) to the prioritized set of improvement scenarios with related concerns and theme(s) (in the business domain). Developers can then trace upwards by linking the artefacts through each layer in order to access higher level business context associated with each requirement.

## 10.3.3 Bidirectional Traceability

*Figure 30 Traceability between the artefacts produced on each layer*

As shown in Figure 30, through the production of a set of logically linked artefacts, a bi-directional trace can be achieved between the set of tangible artefacts created. In this manner the framework provides a greater degree of project visibility overall. OpenXP therefore advocates developing a depth first approach to investigating the vertical scope of requirements throughout elicitation. In turn the two-step approach to prioritization can be further supported by being able to physically link, hence, visualise the extent to which business and technical requirements align accordingly as development proceeds. This helps stakeholders involved to develop and maintain a shared mental model of the overall project goal as both the business and technical perspectives of a requirement can be viewed simultaneously. For software portfolios, both release planning and iteration planning may also be better informed since dependencies that emerge between artefacts produced across different layers can also be visualised on the wall.

## 10.4 Effective Communication

One critical goal in developing successful software solutions is that requirements are effectively communicated between developers and other stakeholders on projects. This section describes in detail how effective communication can be achieved using OpenXP. The strategic functions of this facet involve *engaging stakeholders* and *managing conflict*. This includes active participation, self-organisation, implicit knowledge transfer and developing a common language for communication on OpenXP teams.

### 10.4.1 Engaging Stakeholder Groups

A major concern for RE in dynamically changing business environments has been successfully engaging multiple diverse stakeholder groups. This is achieved using OpenXP where the focused discussions commence. Successful interactions between relevant representatives are however, necessarily contingent upon the following additional factors:

#### 10.4.1.1 Active Stakeholder Participation (ASP)

AMs recommend ASP, a highly participative and iterative approach to requirements development (Ambler 2002). However, significant problems have been reported in achieving this on projects in practice (Wang *et al.* 2008), (Mohammadi *et al.* 2009), (Hoda *et al.* 2010b). OpenXP is designed to improve communication and understanding by supporting ASP during agile requirements elicitation. This is achieved by supporting the role of the customer in the areas of decision making, conflict negotiation and multiple diverse stakeholder collaboration. This framework was designed to create an appropriate support structure to improve communication and understanding and to encourage a more proactive engagement during team-customer interactions.

#### 10.4.1.2 Self-organisation

By creating a link between OST and XP, OpenXP continuously encourages voluntary self-organisation considering this key in terms of helping stakeholders to make decisions independently. However, self-organisation requires taking the initiative and as the case studies presented earlier (Chapter 7, 8) have shown, it is not unusual for participants who have not previously practiced the approach to feel apprehensive about doing so since this requires a different more proactive approach to problem solving. However, regardless of this slow start, clear signs of self-organisation gradually emerged and a collaborative approach eventually developed during the focussed discussions at step 3. With respect to the self-organising aspect of this, OpenXP effectively facilitated the transition between an initially passive toward a more proactive and participatory elicitation process. This was also achieved at the earliest possible point during in phase one activities in the framework. As such, OpenXP can be described as a framework that has focused on developing a suitable *user inclusion* strategy to support ongoing *ASP* during team-customer interactions, this considers further direction needed in terms of the additional leap required to proactively encourage *self-organisation* including the role of customer representatives on teams.

### *10.4.1.3 Tacit Knowledge Transfer*

In order to effectively communicate tacit subject matter expertise between relevant business and technical development roles, it is first necessary to support the cross-fertilization of a wide variety of ideas between multiple diverse stakeholder groups involved on complex software projects. However, implicit knowledge transfer between diverse relevant representatives requires a collaborative environment with the development of a common language to promote mutual understanding during face-to-face communication. The following points elaborate on how OpenXP achieves this.

### *10.4.1.4 Developing a Common Language*

The OpenXP framework has taken advantage of several benefits of the use of face-to-face communication via simple tools during stakeholder interactions:

- Simple tools help to focus stakeholders on examining problem space content rather than becoming distracted by how the content should be structured. The context of the problem is initially privileged over deciding how the content produced should be organised. This is important especially where the full context of a problem is not yet fully understood;

- Simple tools promote communication on a level that all stakeholders are likely to understand. The important thing here is not to introduce a novel or adapted approach with a steep learning curve since this could prevent stakeholders from participating in the technique or marginalise potentially important contributions to problem understanding from being offered;

- Alongside examining the problem space and promoting communication, simple tools also support the development of a common language between participating stakeholders. Stakeholders assembling for the focused discussions are at liberty to use their intuition. Described later in section 10.5, this includes reusing existing known approaches and techniques (or useful parts of these) they may already be familiar with as a group. For instance, if a given group of stakeholders in a focused discussion were familiar with the use of storyboarding, card sorting or laddering, there is nothing to suggest that such techniques could not be used during exploration or while developing improvements to concerns. OpenXP automatically empowers stakeholders to use techniques for solving problems that they are familiar with themselves.

### 10.4.2 Embracing Conflict

A key prerequisite for success in OST, is that passion including the potential for conflict is present. The XP development method alone also supports embracing conflict which is expected to naturally arise due to the diverse range of stakeholders that can be involved. By creating an explicit link between these two approaches (underpinned by emergent systems development (section 3.6.2)),

OpenXP extends additional support for conflict to emerge as early as possible during projects. Further, the focused discussions in OpenXP are closely aligned with Cohen (2010)'s research on the topic of argumentation. From this perspective, a successful discussion in conflicting situations requires developing effective arguments that communicate a set of valid points in order to make a given argument believable. However, to achieve this, certain conditions are required. For instance, of the 3 models of argumentation, Cohen (2010) states that while the *"argument as war"* metaphor is unfortunately the most dominant, it is also the most unhelpful approach that exists. As such the author asserts that in order to avoid this approach, it is necessary to create the conditions for successful argumentation to prevail, this in turn produces a mutually beneficial outcome during discussions.

As shown in Figure 31, embracing conflict necessitates consideration for four important elements that are involved for the process of effective argumentation to succeed. That is; for successful balanced and objective argumentation to prevail, it is necessary to *effectively facilitate deliberation, negotiation, compromise* and *collaboration* between those involved.

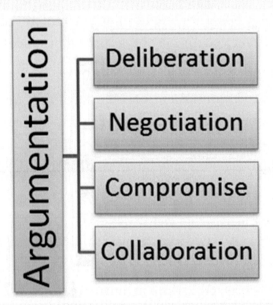

*Figure 31 Objective conflict management (Adapted from Cohen 2010)*

The focused discussions in OpenXP support the model for effectively communicating conflict as defined by Cohen (2010). First, time and space is explicitly created for stakeholders to consciously *deliberate* over important points relevant to the exploration and development of improvements for issues of common concern to all stakeholders present. *Negotiation* is clearly an important element in this process. When stakeholders assert their perspective of a given concern, others present are encouraged to empathise with this. This supports the development of an appropriate *compromise* aimed at addressing all important elements of a potentially conflicting view. Conflict is perceived as an opportunity to embrace and positively nurture different potential alternatives where such differences are considered valuable and may pave new perhaps even innovative approaches to solving existing complex problems. As alternative views including conflicting perspectives gradually achieve compromise, a *collaborative* approach subsequently emerges in developing an appropriate resolution; this in turn supports the emergence of a viable and mutually beneficial solution for all stakeholders involved. OpenXP thus offers an appropriate support structure for successfully communicating conflicting perspectives in complex problem situations; this measure aims to directly support the objective evaluation and resolution of conflict as soon as possible on projects.

## 10.5 Adaptability Integration

Many different techniques and methodologies are used to support requirements activities in software development practice. However, the extent to which any particular approach is chosen depends primarily on the business problem to be solved. This is also influenced by the imperatives and constraints often peculiar to specific situational circumstances. Indeed, practitioners may combine a selection of techniques or even parts of existing methodologies considered useful for eliciting requirements in a given domain. The choice of which approach to adopt must therefore be a careful decision. Regardless of this, it is necessary that any combination is flexible in that it can be adjusted accordingly whilst still proving useful. This section therefore describes the strategic function of the adaptability integration facet which is focused on the potential for existing RE models, methodologies, approaches and elicitation techniques to be adapted for use within the OpenXP framework.

### 10.5.1 Integrating Interaction Evolution (IE)

The IE model developed by McBryan *et al.* (2008) was described earlier in section 3.2.1 as an approach with the potential to manage consistent levels of change for DAS. However a significant problem remained in establishing how interdisciplinary stakeholders in this complex multi-user environment could engage to devise effective solutions in a collaborative manner. OpenXP offers a potential solution to this problem. For example, for the first step in the IE model, *opportunities for change* could be identified in OpenXP by raising concerns. Focused discussions surround the investigation of problems with relevant representatives which takes place during phase one in the framework. This is very similar to steps two and three in IE where it is necessary to *reflect upon* and *judge all potential alternatives* to address a given change. However, it should be noted that this only works in IE if relevant diverse groups of healthcare representatives are involved, the stakeholder coordination facet in OpenXP has the potential to address this problem. Step three in IE involves *making an informed decision* which must be based upon the outcome of intensive discussion between relevant HCS representatives, while the fourth step is to *implement* the decision made. The focused discussions in OpenXP offer a collaborative working environment in which problems are fully explored before business improvement scenarios are prioritized for development. Crucially for IE this includes investigating the multiple possible paths that could lead to a solution. Therefore the activities required to implement IE for the HCS domain could be effectively supported using the OpenXP solution. For example; OpenXP creates a direct and potentially seamless link between the specific steps involved in the IE model, and the XP software development process.

## 10.5.2 Integrating Existing Methodologies

From a plan-driven perspective, the successful implementation of many approaches designed to address requirements activities, is to a certain extent contingent upon the completeness of the artefacts or models produced (A short discussion on this topic is presented in section 3.4). Examples of such methodologies might include SSM, model driven and/or goal based approaches to RE. However, when considered from an agile viewpoint, the various models and diagrams created as the outcome of using existing approaches do not need to be rigorously complete, instead they must:

1.  Fulfil the *purpose* for which they were created;

2.  Be *understandable* for the intended target audience;

3.  Be *sufficiently accurate*;

4.  Be *sufficiently consistent*;

5.  Be *sufficiently detailed*;

6.  Provide *positive value*;

7.  Be *simple* as possible;

As long as the models produced as a result of using existing methods, can still be described as Agile Models according to the above seven criteria (defined by Ambler (2002)), OpenXP can offer support for the collaborative development of such artefacts, provided that they can be dynamically generated during phase one activities in the framework, and where this can be completed in an agile JIT manner. Given certain conditions, existing methodologies can therefore be adapted for use within the OpenXP framework. While in many cases it may not be desirable to adopt an entire methodology (Kurapati *et al.* 2012), certain elements of those methodologies considered useful could be implemented where appropriate to help to define the problem domain further. One suitable example that can be given here to illustrate this point is SSM.

As described in section 3.4.3, SSM consists of a seven stage process. It can be clearly observed that at a glance some of the activities in SSM are also similar to the activities that take place during the focused discussions in OpenXP. For instance once a problem in an ill-defined domain has been identified, the next step is to express the problem using rich pictures or diagrams. This is very similar to where concerns are being explored at step 3 in OpenXP. Likewise, the rich diagrammatic expression (step 2 for SSM), is then used to inform the development of a set of conceptual models (step 4 for SSM) to show what improvements can be made. Again this is very similar to making improvements as an outcome of the focused discussions in OpenXP. With both approaches the outcome is also to take action based upon specific improvements made. The approaches may differ however, depending on the level of detail required for developing clear and concise root definition of relevant system components in SSM. For instance, and in the context of using SSM in

OpenXP, the core activities of the system to be modeled do not need to be meticulously accurate or complete, since too much formality and/or detail needed to fully complete this step in SSM could destabilize productivity in OpenXP. Therefore, in order to adapt SSM for use within the OpenXP framework, it is important that any given root definition for the relevant system components is quickly established within a JIT manner.

Therefore, in cases where existing methodologies (or parts of these found useful) can be adapted, each approach can then benefit significantly from the additional advantages of being underpinned by an effective communications infrastructure with collaborative support for the involvement of a refined group of stakeholder representatives who are directly relevant to the problem to be solved.

### 10.5.3 Integrating Existing Elicitation Techniques

Similarly to the methodologies proposed to address requirements activities, existing elicitation techniques could also be modified for use in an agile context using OpenXP. Section 3.5 presented a classification of elicitation techniques. This sought to examine which techniques were iterative, collaborative, elicited both current and future needs and where these techniques focused on stakeholders as the main source of requirements. This categorisation revealed that brainstorming, scenarios and prototyping could be considered as techniques with the potential to be adapted for a novel approach to be developed in RE.

With reference to these three candidate techniques, the OpenXP framework has adapted these techniques by exploiting their benefits, reducing their limitations, and developing a support structure surrounding the application of these techniques. This is achieved by utilizing brainstorming while voicing concerns and during the focused discussions. During exploration, the problem definition and improvements made can also take the form of paper based prototypes and mock up scenarios. This takes advantage of the potential for prototyping as an iterative, collaborative, user based candidate technique that can also elicit both current and future needs. Depending on the nature of the problem to be investigated there is nothing to suggest that stakeholders could not opt to use a software prototype during the focused discussions as a means to examine existing problems. In fact, as detailed in section 5.5.1, Herman (2013) reports a situation where the requirements for a software solution were successfully agreed by prototyping a solution during an OST investigation.

Scenario development as an adaptable technique is also incorporated as the linking activity between XP and OST. OpenXP supports the perspective of the CREWS scenario classification framework (Rolland *et al.* 1998). For instance this recommends eliciting additional meta-information such as the form, purpose, contents and lifecycle of scenarios which can be used later to support the management of business scenarios produced. Particularly the form facet in the CREWS framework enables wide variety of scenarios to emerge using multiple modes of expression e.g. they can be text-based, rich freehand drawings, a series of photographs, scenes enacted in video clips or animated caricatures through techniques such as comic styles. Equally, from the development perspective, scenarios can emerge as UML diagrams, task models, personas, card sorts or laddering. The form in which scenarios will emerge is completely subjective since this depends entirely on the background experience brought in by the stakeholders present. As such, in using scenarios as the linking activity the OpenXP solution makes every effort to ensure that design possibilities are maximised as early as possible during elicitation. Primarily this measure supports a thorough initial investigation of the multiple possible paths that could lead to a solution. The difference with applying brainstorming, prototyping and scenario development techniques using the OpenXP framework, is that the relevant expertise are at the very least attracted, a dynamic informal interaction is supported, a common language with which to communicate is fostered, self-organisation is proactively encouraged and the development of a collective agreement for a mutually beneficial software solution is promoted. The OpenXP framework has therefore adapted how these techniques could be applied by incorporating them with the benefit of these additional advantages.

With specific relevance to collaborative group intensive techniques aimed at targeting early requirements activities, OpenXP can be described as a framework that addresses the known shortcomings of current group interaction techniques. This is achieved by explicitly recruiting stakeholders who have an interest in contributing to the resolution of the broader theme and concerns that emerge from this. The framework specifically favours heterogeneous groups at the problem definition stage and as such it can be described as an approach that supports multiple diverse perspectives on projects. OpenXP does not expect requirements to complete and supports continuous interaction throughout development, not just at the start of projects.

OpenXP practically guides stakeholders toward accepting responsibility for communication and negotiation of requirements throughout development. For example, the framework enables the facilitator to develop and maintain a dynamic atmosphere, and the law of mobility also provides a practical support mechanism embedded in the process specifically to prevent dominant group members from exerting too much control. OpenXP therefore encourages the genuine opinions of all relevant stakeholders to emerge in favour of reaching fully informed group decisions. This involves directing stakeholders to develop a balanced view representing the needs of those involved. In turn, this avoids biased decision making from prevailing among individuals and groups where conflict is positively embraced rather than being superficially addressed. Finally, this has the advantage of avoiding typical group interaction technique pitfalls such as the Abilene paradox (discussed earlier in 3.5.9) from developing during stakeholder interactions. Instead, it acknowledges and creates the precise conditions for effective communication upfront and stimulates a more proactive participation from stakeholders from the start.

### 10.5.4 Adapting OpenXP in practice

One goal that dynamically changing business environments must achieve is adaptability orientation. This is necessary in order to react flexibly to change in competitive business domains. This crucial aspect for emergent systems development is supported in OpenXP since practitioners are at liberty to drop, add or change the sequence in which the steps take place during implementation. For example and as evidenced by the case study findings presented in Chapter 8, developers may skip steps or change the sequence in which the steps take place, whilst still producing fully working software on schedule and within scope. The OpenXP framework may therefore evolve in practice *if and only if* in doing so, this adaptation in the steps taken, results in success for the both the project and the team.

### 10.5.5 Summary

In summary, this section explained how existing requirements methodologies and techniques can be used in conjunction with OpenXP implementations as long as they are conducted in an agile JIT manner. Generally, the artefacts produced as outputs from using any given approach must meet the seven criteria for determining when a model can be considered agile. Given these conditions, any existing method, approach or technique can be used to during the focused discussions in OpenXP to extend, refine and clarify the problem and to support the collaborative development of appropriate business improvements. Essentially the advantage of doing this is that stakeholders can be assured that many of the shortcomings of existing approaches can be successfully avoided. For instance, existing methodologies and techniques can be adapted for use in OpenXP with the benefits of a refined group of interested stakeholders being strategically coordinated, authentically present and actively involved in the process. The framework is also expected to evolve in practice in cases where particular changes incorporated have produced success for the team and the project.

## 10.6 Lean Principles Applied

This section examines where and how the OpenXP solution addresses a number of existing lean principles. These includes amplifying learning, empowering the team, building integrity into projects, making informed decisions and eliminating waste in the communication process.

### 10.6.2 Amplify Learning

Amplify learning is a lean principle that encourages tacit knowledge to be retained on software teams. Software development is recognised as a knowledge based activity and when learning is amplified, this supports the development of a collective knowledge base and in turn, this gradually improves the developers approach to problem solving over time. As previously elaborated in section 3.7.2, Hoda *et al.* (2010a) have shown that regular interaction between diverse cross-functional roles has the capacity to support development teams in learning from new domains, quickly becoming proficient in translating business terminology.

The OpenXP framework considers the importance of amplifying learning on teams with regard to this. This is achieved by supporting communication through the development of a common language with the use of simple tools during the focused discussions. In addition to this, OpenXP supports the cross-fertilization of ideas which in turn supports implicit knowledge transfer between multiple diverse stakeholder roles. However, it should be noted that support for this principle is *not* limited to roles only involved on the development team. Rather, OpenXP further extends this principle to include the business domain where learning is amplified between roles crossing both business and technology domains.

### 10.6.3 Empower the Team

This lean principle operates under the assumption that once software teams begin to develop tacit knowledge of subject matter expertise, the team should be empowered to implement necessary changes where a process (or part of a process) could be improved and where this results in delivering higher quality code to the business domain. One important aspect of team empowerment is that teams self-organise and that respect is also afforded to the competence of developers with regard to tasks that must be completed.

The OpenXP solution provides a suitable framework for teams to self-organise however, this is extended beyond the development team and into the business domain during elicitation. For example, phase one initiates voluntary self-organisation (with hands-on support) for business stakeholders who define the problem domain and identify appropriate improvements. This measure is expected to prepare business stakeholders in advance, for interaction with one or more self-organised XP development teams later on. This has the advantage that business stakeholders who form member associations or indeed broader CRACK customer teams, are permitted to empower themselves to make necessary changes where a process could be improved and where this too results in delivering higher quality business value to the domain.

### 10.6.4 Build Integrity In

Perceived integrity is relevant here since this refers to the *customers' perception* of business value produced. This is essentially measured by value that has been brought to the customer by the software solution delivered. OpenXP encourages integrity to be built in very early on from the start of projects. For example, the first two phases in the framework produce a collective vision of the overall project goal, this involves the consolidation of viewpoints from relevant business experts in the domain. By introducing these two important phases prior to commencing development, business stakeholders can be assured that the improvements to be made are driven primarily by business value perceived by themselves in advance. The second aspect of this principle is *conceptual integrity* which can benefit from the steps taken in OpenXP. For example, once perceived integrity is satisfied by the business domain this contributes to ensuring conceptual integrity in terms of how the architecture of the system develops and later integrates as a whole.

### 10.6.5 Informed Decisions

This lean principle asserts that decisions should be delayed until the last responsible moment, when as much information as possible is available. OpenXP applies this principle via the introduction of the first two phases in the framework. This requires that a considerable amount of upper level business context is dynamically generated by relevant business experts in advance of and for the purposes of developing a clear problem statement; thus assisting software development in the domain. As such, decisions about the requirements for the system are necessarily delayed until phase three activities commence. This has the additional benefit that user stories are only written based upon real business issues of concern that have been fully explored with a prioritized list of business improvement scenarios developed in advance. Also, the artefacts have been produced as a result dynamic informal focused discussions between relevant business stakeholders. Consequently, a measure such as this is advantageous since the stories created are necessarily more fully informed by the higher level business context dynamically generated prior to phase three.

### 10.6.5.1 Mitigating the risk of systematic bias

Section 3.3 made reference to a series of high profile software project failures which had been traced back to a set of systematic biases found in the management and decision making practices within organisations (Shore 2008). A consistent pattern among several of the examples in section 3.3 is that the biases have occurred as a result of a series of *narrow perspectives* continuing to prevail throughout the decision making process on software projects. One solution to the problem of narrow perspectives is to avoid being overly reliant on individual decision makers particularly during crucial requirements activities.

It would therefore appear logical that the potential for this problem to manifest could be significantly reduced if important decisions were instead encouraged to be made based upon a wider more representative view. This ensures that the decision making process only proceeds based upon the collective perspective of the relevant experts (including other relevant sources). Particularly in the context of requirements elicitation on complex projects, the OpenXP solution supports a gradual change in the organisational culture of individual decision-making in favour of a decision-making process that is instead more fully informed by a *"synthesis of expertise"* from all relevant sources in the domain.

### 10.6.6 Eliminating Waste

The successful identification access engagement and subsequent involvement of stakeholder groups crossing multiple diverse backgrounds is a major concern for RE in any ill-defined business domain. Effectively achieving this requires an entirely different approach when compared to the traditional approaches that have been historically used in the past.

With reference to the set of human-related factors that affect the communication of requirements between developers and other stakeholders as discussed in section 3.3, the challenges listed in Figure 7 could be described as types of waste that have been observed throughout the communication process during early RE activities. The existing defined RE approaches do not address the situation where project stakeholders (on the development team) lack implicit domain knowledge. This often becomes apparent in the latter stages of development where it is much more costly to rectify inaccurate or missing requirements found later in projects. This is important because waste is produced when this results in developers not fully understanding the requirements. Evidence from existing literature has shown that practical support has been consistently in demand for the effective management of potential conflict and this must be identified in the earliest possible stages of requirements development. For instance, when conflict emerges in the later stages of the project this introduces further risks in terms of cost and more time is needed to facilitate additional negotiations between the stakeholders who contribute toward finding a resolution. These points clearly demonstrate a number sources of waste occurring in the communication process during stakeholder interaction on software projects.

In addition to this, other types of waste include; when delays incur after the priorities of stakeholders unexpectedly change throughout development. The situation of stakeholders being unsure of what is needed and difficulty articulating requirements cause further delays in terms of the time frame available and the accuracy of requirements elicited. Due to the fact that these problems are not well managed, and can initiate significant schedule delays and unexpected rising costs, this introduces substantial risk in a project from the start. Essentially these issues represent types of waste that must be reduced (or ideally eliminated) in order to achieve more valuable interactions between business and technical stakeholders during the RE process. As shown in Table 17, OpenXP offers a practical solution to these specific challenges. The first column identifies a number for each challenge, column 2 lists the specific challenge and column 3 describes where OpenXP addresses each of the issues reported.

*Table 17 Broader RE Challenges Mapped to OpenXP Solutions*

| Existing RE Challenges | | OpenXP Solutions |
|---|---|---|
| 1 | Identification; Access; Engagement; Subsequent Involvement; Of Multiple Interdisciplinary Stakeholder Groups | • Interested stakeholders identify themselves early on;<br><br>• A collaborative environment is dynamically generated to support access and effective engagement of stakeholders;<br><br>• Subsequent involvement on projects throughout development is supported by coordinating stakeholders belonging to member associations who dynamically assemble during the first phase<br><br>• Multiple diverse stakeholder groups are a prerequisite for OpenXP to succeed; |
| 2 | Early Conflict Identification and Resolution | • OpenXP supports conflict identification and resolution since a healthy degree of conflict is required for the framework to succeed |
| 3 | Changing Requirements | • Underpinned by emergent systems development, changing requirements are regularly expected |
| 4 | Managing Changing Stakeholder Priorities | • The two-step approach to prioritization involves aligning both business and technical stakeholder priorities before development proceeds |
| 5 | Lack of Implicit Domain Knowledge | • Phase 1 activities develop a common language with simple tools and focus on co-creating business value between the domains |
| 6 | Stakeholders Unsure of what is needed | • Phase 1 activities are designed to support stakeholders in collaboratively defining the problem; This includes investigating multiple possible paths    that could lead to a solution |
| 7 | Difficulty Articulating Requirements | • OpenXP supports the development of a common language using simple tools to assist stakeholders in articulating and communicating requirements clearly |

In addition to this and with particular relevance to the more specific challenges for team-customer interaction in XP as reported in section 3.7.2.6, Table 18 shows that OpenXP addresses these challenges as follows: similar challenges have been grouped together for the purposes of convenience.

*Table 18 XP Challenges Mapped to OpenXP Solutions*

| | Customer Role Challenges | OpenXP Solutions |
|---|---|---|
| 1 | Cultural clash between business and technical stakeholders (Sharp and Robinson 2006) | Creates a collaborative environment upfront prior to involvement on projects |
| 2 | Low levels of customer participation (Wang *et al.* 2008),(Hoda *et al.* 2010b) | Motivates a higher level of proactive participation |
| 3 | Heavy burden placed on the customer (Wang *et al.* 2008) | Phase 1activities provide practical support to reduce any burden on the customer |
| 4 | Inadequate customer preparation (Wang *et al.* 2008) | Phase 1 activities prepare the customer in advance for adopting the role |
| 5 | Difficulty writing good quality stories (Wang *et al.* 2008) | Both technical and business stakeholders write user stories together |
| 6 | Time frame for feedback (Wang *et al.* 2008), Time constraints of the customer (Mohammadi *et al.* 2009) | Encourages direct face-to-face feedback initially and only targets specific stakeholder(s) from relevant member associations assembled in advance |
| 7 | Partial access to onsite customer (Mohammadi *et al.* 2009), (Cao L. and Ramesh 2008) | Member associations coordinate effective and efficient access to the customer role thus mitigating this risk |
| 8 | Customer disinterest in task not directly relevant to themselves (Mohammadi *et al.* 2009) | Significantly reduces this possibility by only targeting stakeholders to refine specific detail relevant to their own business improvements |
| 9 | Gap in terminology (Mohammadi *et al.* 2009), Gap in business and technical terminology (Hoda *et al.* 2010a) | Purposefully creates a common language and promotes simple tools to neutralize terminology prior to XP development activities |
| 10 | Reaching consensus (Cao L. and Ramesh 2008), False consensus (Fraser *et al.* 2010) | Circumvents false consensus by proactively supporting early identification of conflict with direct resolution through genuine consensus building |
| 11 | Intensive interaction needed at the start (Cao L. and Ramesh 2008) | Provides practical hands-on support for short but intensive team-customer interaction at the start |
| 12 | Customer role expands into teams of customer representatives (Martin *et al.* 2009a) | Convenors who form member associations develop into CRACK customer teams responsible for communicating between large diverse stakeholder groups involved |
| 13 | Maintaining diversity of opinion (Fraser *et al.* 2010) | Harnesses diversity of opinion as a prerequisite for success |
| 14 | Self-organisation on teams (Hoda *et al.* 2011) | Provides practical hands-on support for voluntary self-organisation to prevail |
| 15 | Prioritization (Racheva *et al.* 2010) | Introduces a two-step approach to the co-creation and prioritization of business valued software |
| 16 | Facilitation of face-to-face communication (Fraser *et al.* 2010) | Facilitates effective and efficient face-to-face communication |
| 17 | Sustaining trust (Fraser *et al.* 2010) | All inputs are considered valuable contributions to the problem definition stage This creates and sustains trust throughout development |

The first challenge in Table 18 draws attention to the potentially unanticipated risk of cultural clashes between roles crossing the business and technology domain. OpenXP specifically targets groups that consist of vastly diverse backgrounds and experiences. As such the approach can be described as one that not only supports, but favours cultural integration among groups that comprise a wide variety of interdisciplinary representatives.

Secondly, the risk of low levels of customer participation presents another challenge that is difficult to anticipate in advance of the commencement of projects. OpenXP addresses this issue during phase 1 activities. This is achieved by practically developing a collaborative working environment under which a high level of proactive participation occurs between stakeholders, prior to the commencement of XP activities in phase 3. For the third and fourth challenges: by explicitly conducting activities in a collaborative manner, phase 1 activities also aim to support and better prepare customer representatives thus reducing the heavy burden placed on the customer role. This also includes lack of customer involvement on projects which is addressed in the stakeholder coordination facet designed to create a user-inclusion strategy from the start. As the project progresses along a time continuum, continuous involvement is supported when CRACK customer representatives from the member associations directly coordinate with the development team.

The fifth challenge listed in Table 18 reports difficulty for stakeholders in writing good quality user stories. This problem is also targeted in OpenXP by ensuring that user stories are written with developers present to assist stakeholders with this task during step 6 (Phase three). Gradually over time it is expected that developers and stakeholders will improve on the quality of stories written together.

Challenge six shows that feedback can also be delayed due to the time constraints of customer representatives. Phase one activities encourage direct face-to-face feedback initially and then, only stakeholders from member associations are targeted when specific information is required in relation to their own business improvements. It is quite possible that the production of upper level business context (during the first two phases), may also reduce the frequency of contact since these artefacts will be available to assist developers during implementation. This takes into consideration the busy schedule of stakeholders as they are only contacted to clarify missing information or to refine existing detail for the requirements.

The seventh challenge in Table 18 asserts difficulties with partial access to onsite customers. This challenge is embraced by the OpenXP *stakeholder coordination facet* which is essentially responsible for developing stakeholder member associations (via the focused discussions) where each member relates to a specific business improvement. Limited access is mitigated because the convenor is involved throughout development as a CRACK customer rep on the XP team. Another measure that acts as a contingency plan in this respect is that for situations where the main CRACK rep is not available, it is also possible for developers to request feedback from the remaining stakeholders in the relevant member association. This process itself is also intricately related to the solution for the eighth challenge which refers to customer representatives experiencing disinterest in tasks not directly relating to themselves. This problem is mitigated in OpenXP because the stakeholder coordination facet in the framework only targets business stakeholders relevant to the improvements they own. The benefit of this is that the potential for waste is reduced when the limited timeframe that business stakeholders have is more *effectively and efficiently utilized* since they can be assured that they are no longer expected to be involved for tasks that do not specifically relate to their own business improvements on the project.

The ninth challenge emphasised the gap in terminology that must be bridged between the business and technology domain. OpenXP resolves this by purposefully supporting the creation of a common language favouring the use of simple tools in order to neutralize terminology for communication during stakeholder interactions. This discourages the use of any methods that involve a steep learning curve in favour of communicating from the outset, through a language that is common to all stakeholders present.

The tenth challenge raised in Table 18 is reaching consensus among diverse groups, this also includes avoiding false consensus from prevailing overall. The OpenXP solution solves this problem by creating the conditions under which conflict will most likely emerge as early as possible in the process. Conflict is embraced with the additional advantage of practical support for the development of genuine consensus between stakeholders. The exchange of multiple viewpoints between groups with respect to conflict is further supported by adopting Cohen (2010)s model designed for successful communication in situations where conflict is present. According to Cohen (2010), the four specific activities that are needed to achieve this necessarily involve deliberation, negotiation, compromise and collaboration. OpenXP embraces situations of conflict by supporting these activities during the focused discussions during phase one activities in the framework.

The eleventh challenge refers to difficulty surrounding intensive interaction needed between stakeholders at the start. OpenXP addresses this by providing practical support for short but intense team-customer interactions. A collaborative working environment is dynamically generated with a set of steps, tools and techniques included specifically to guide intensive interaction between stakeholders. In addition to this the role of the facilitator acts as a catalyst for directing effective interaction throughout the whole process.

The focus of challenge twelve is on the recent expansion from the customer role into multiple diverse stakeholder groups. A main prerequisite to the success of OpenXP as an evolutionary framework is that multiple diverse stakeholders are involved. OpenXP aims to eradicate this challenge by providing the appropriate working environment where the involvement of interdisciplinary groups can be very well managed causing the project to thrive given the presence of this condition. This aspect of the solution is also intricately relevant to the importance of maintaining diversity of opinion for challenge thirteen listed in Table 18. This can be assured since diversity of opinion must be maintained as it is required as a prerequisite for success in using OpenXP.

Self-organisation is reported under the fourteenth challenge in Table 18. OpenXP solves this problem by creating a working environment that encourages the voluntary self-organisation of stakeholders present. This is achieved through a practical support structure aiming to address this need prior to development activities in phase three. It is envisaged that after phase one activities complete, the foundations that have already been put in place for self-organisation will continue to support this practice as the project proceeds into the subsequent phases.

Challenge fifteen surrounds difficulty with prioritization since a joint effort is needed for business stakeholders to co-create business value with developers. OpenXP offers a two-step approach to prioritization. First business improvements are prioritized in advance by the relevant stakeholders, this ensures that prioritization consists of a joint effort from the business view early on. Secondly, stories are only created based on this previously identified business value. This step also involves a joint effort between business stakeholders and developers, prioritization of stories is then collectively conducted by the group.

Overall for the sixteenth challenge, face-to-face communication is the primary mode of interaction between stakeholders and developers in OpenXP. This is strongly supported as the most valuable means with which to communicate and provide direct feedback throughout development. Sustaining trust is also stressed as an important challenge to address in Table 18. Trust is recognised as an important aspect of successful communication this is also required for phase one activities to succeed. As such, the dynamic informal interactions conducted at the start place particular value on the inputs of all relevant viewpoints on a given concern to be resolved. OpenXP can therefore be described as an approach that aims to generate and sustain trust between stakeholders from the start.

In summary, this section looked at the broader RE challenges alongside the challenges that have been specifically identified for team-customer interactions in XP. With a specific focus on addressing these high risk pitfalls it becomes clear that by building a collaborative support structure around integrating diverse cultures, OpenXP has concentrated on reducing waste (in the communication process) produced by these challenges. This is achieved by creating a collaborative working environment under which many of these challenges can now be effectively embraced.

Finally, Figure 32 presents a birds-eye view of the OpenXP framework. This illustrates the conditions under which the solution is best applied to specific target domains in practice. From this more holistic perspective, a broader structure can be seen to emerge consisting of the 9 steps, linked to the 3 phases, alongside the strategic functions interconnecting with each of the 4 broader facets that complete the framework.

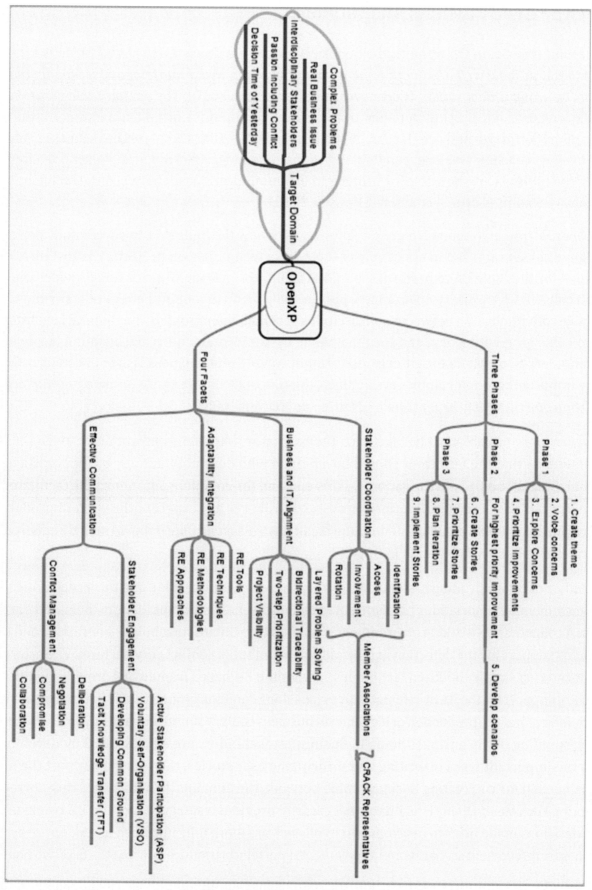

Figure 32 OpenXP birdseye view

## 10.7 The Agile Business Analyst Role

Successful transition from the traditional to the Agile Business Analyst (BA) role is largely dependent on *"how well BAs adapt to new ways of working with requirements, setting up teams and using group collaboration"* (Cottmeyer and Lee Henson 2010). The primary role of the Agile BA is to create a high trust environment by facilitating communication and understanding during elicitation (Cottmeyer and Lee Henson 2010), (Cooke 2013), (Hass 2014). Agile business analysis now involves coaching and team building, and with a greater degree of reliance on group facilitation skills, the BA is also responsible for bridging the communication gap between the business and technical domains (Cottmeyer and Lee Henson 2010).

The OpenXP framework offers a unique solution as to how the Agile BA can successfully perform this key skill set required to effectively execute agile techniques on projects. For instance, it is possible for the Agile BA to perform the role of facilitator in OpenXP, since this provides the BA with a collaborative working environment purposefully set up to support better understanding and effective communication between interdisciplinary stakeholder groups. The OpenXP facilitator is responsible for creating time and space, enabling dynamic interactions and encouraging diverse stakeholders to continue to self-organise around solving real business issues of concern. Once these important group dynamics are in place, the role of facilitator then *"becomes most effective by sitting quietly, simply being there and letting go"* (Owen 2008).

However, extreme care must be taken that the facilitator role is not compromised. Owen (2008) recommends that the facilitator should be a person who does not have any particular stake in the outcome of the OST investigation. To this end and for complete autonomy, the facilitator is not permitted to contribute, interfere or exert control over any aspect of the content produced. Therefore, an Agile BA could only adopt the facilitator role *if and only if* the BA strictly adhered to the rules for effective facilitation in OpenXP.

A number of clear advantages stand out for the BA in successfully adopting this crucial role. For instance, member associations consisting of relevant stakeholder groups identify themselves at the start. A collaborative working environment is created to facilitate stakeholder interaction and this includes support for the detection and resolution of potential conflict very early on. The artefacts produced (via simple tools and techniques) across the 3-Phased framework provide significant practical support for the BA in automatically establishing common ground to bridge the gap between the domains, and the production of higher level business context aims to equally improve developer understanding of the business domain. Business stakeholders are also assisted by developers with the important tasks of writing and prioritizing user stories, this aims to support the joint effort needed for co-creating business value between the domains. In addition to this, correctly adopting the role of OpenXP facilitator necessarily provides a safeguard for the BA by ensuring that decisions made prior to development in phase 3 are more fully informed as evidenced by the business improvement scenarios and supplementary artefacts produced during the first two phases.

## 10.8 Summary

Chapter 10 focused on presenting the broader elements of the OpenXP solution. This began by describing the four OpenXP facets in-depth detailing the strategic functions of each. The primary functions for the stakeholder coordination facet are identification, access, involvement of stakeholders, and rotation between groups on projects. While the two-step approach to prioritization, bi-directional traceability and project visibility function primarily under the business and IT alignment facet; the effective communication facet then focuses on engaging stakeholders and embracing conflict during elicitation on projects. Finally the adaptability integration facet recommends a set of guidelines for adapting existing known RE approaches, models, methods and techniques for use within the OpenXP framework. Existing approaches for instance, can be adapted for use in in this context as long as the models produced are agile according to the Ambler (2007) criteria. The extent to which OpenXP supports the adoption of a number of lean principles was also discussed. These include amplifying learning, empowering the team, building integrity in, making informed decisions and eliminating waste from the communication process during development.

Clearly, moving from traditional to agile business analysis requires a much greater emphasis on facilitating effective interactions to improve communication between vastly diverse stakeholder groups. The OpenXP solution offers a unique approach where Agile BAs can further develop the key skill set required to operate effectively on XP teams. This can be achieved when the BA adopts the role of facilitator in the framework. This provides a strong support structure for the BA in coordinating stakeholders and promoting effective communication throughout development.

# Chapter 11 Conclusions

## 11.1 Overview

Chapter 11 concludes with a review of the findings related back to the original research question, aims and objectives. The primary strategic functions of the four facets in the OpenXP solution are then briefly summarised. This is followed by a short review relating back to the original requirements derived for an evolutionary approach to be developed in RE as set out earlier in section 3.8. Finally, the conditions under which the OpenXP solution can be applied in practice are briefly discussed.

## 11.2 Review of the Findings

The goal this research was to develop an evolutionary framework to facilitate requirements elicitation to support the role of the customer for agile software development. The research question addressed was *"How can an evolutionary framework be developed to improve the facilitation of agile requirements elicitation?"* This was achieved by addressing the following objectives.

> ***Objective one:*** Investigate and classify the factors that affect the communication of requirements between developers and other stakeholders;
>
> ***Objective two:*** Investigate and classify agile software development approaches with particular relevance to the customer role;
>
> ***Objective three:*** Develop a suitable solution;
>
> ***Objective four:*** Evaluate the solution in an appropriate environment.

The following sections present how each objective has been fulfilled.

### 11.2.1 Factors Affecting Communication of Requirements

The first objective outlined was to *investigate and classify the factors that affect the communication of requirements between developers and other stakeholders.* In addressing this objective, a review of literature focusing on elicitation was first conducted. This revealed that it is critical to conduct effective elicitation as the failure of many software projects has been attributed back to insufficient attention being paid to the requirements phase on projects. Where projects had not failed, the impact including the cost of rectifying requirements problems increased exponentially. Existing elicitation techniques were considered inadequate and a novel approach to RE was in demand.

The problems highlighted surrounded lack of user involvement, inadequate communication and problems relating to the understanding of requirements. Challenges that were consistently reported in the literature were identified in this research as representative of the set of factors that affect the communication of requirements between developers and other stakeholders. A consistent pattern among the factors identified was that each related to the human aspect of requirements elicitation. As such these factors were subsequently classified as the set of *human related issues* affecting the communication of requirements during the process of elicitation.

### 11.2.2 AMs and the Customer Role

The second objective outlined was to *investigate and classify agile software development approaches with particular relevance to the customer role.* In line with this objective, the literature review also found that for the role of the customer in XP, a series of initially unanticipated pitfalls in performing this role had emerged since the agile method was first introduced. Problems including understanding, communication and regular engagement with the customer role were evident. This further exacerbated after the concept of the single onsite customer more recently began to develop into teams of diverse customer representatives charged with the responsibility of communicating problem space content to the software team. This strongly suggested that a support structure was required to facilitate more effective interaction between the customer role and the team.

What was clearly evident from the literature was that a means with which to efficiently communicate an agreed and representative perspective of the necessary requirements was in demand. The challenges also exhibited highly unpredictable and situationally specific characteristics not readily identifiable prior to early encounters with the customer role. This presented a considerable overarching challenge for agile teams in managing unpredictability during requirements activities surrounding this particular role. Recommendations thus included further support for self-organisation and more effective and efficient team-customer interaction on agile projects.

An exploratory case study was subsequently conducted. In this case study a single unit of analysis was defined at the beginning which focused on *the process of how requirements are elicited.* Considering that this was an exploratory study, it did not proceed with a set of predefined propositions. As part of the exploratory study conducted, Section 4.2 examined the roles and challenges for an agile team. During this project communication difficulties emerged both between team members and also during team-customer interaction. This was further exacerbated after time was wasted when it emerged that the same user stories had been duplicated by different team members. Difficulty had been experienced after an overall project goal had not been initially established. At the end of the project, the problem statement was explained to an independent reviewer from a technical rather than a business perspective. Despite the utilization of simple tools and additional artefacts as recommended by Scrum in this project, a common language between participants had not been successfully established. This study thus provided additional context into the types of problems that can be experienced for an agile team.

Also as part of the exploratory case study, a series of interviews were then conducted to develop a deeper insight into how requirements are elicited from the perspective of practitioners working with requirements in industry. This study found that requirements had been successfully communicated through the use of dynamic collaborative group based tools and techniques. However, practitioners confirmed that these collaborative interactions were also supported by additional practices surrounding the management of stakeholders on software projects. The notion of involving the *right* stakeholder representative was considered *key* to the successful communication of requirements. While the industry study was unable to ascertain a clear definition of the right stakeholder representative, what could be discerned was that this concept also included the necessity to involve stakeholders with *direct experience* of the problem to be addressed. This strongly suggested that effective facilitation of direct interactions between relevant roles was *imperative* to the successful communication of requirements.

Further support was required to *build strong relationships* between business and technology domains which included the use of a *common language* to successfully communicate requirements. Also, the necessity for practitioners to *widen perspectives* was evident where a *narrow viewpoint* of the requirement in question had been detected. This required the inclusion of additional stakeholders and in all cases where this occurred, this could not be anticipated prior to the commencement of the project. It was also necessary to specify requirements at *different levels of abstraction* for the purposes of supporting reusability. In addition to this, the notion of a *rotating stakeholder group* was evident where *priority shifted* between stakeholders depending on the quality of stakeholders, resource availability, vertical scope and the project timeline. This strongly suggested that practitioners required support to manage the *changing priorities* of a multiple diverse stakeholder group.

## 11.2.3 Key Results

The main findings that subsequently emerged from the literature review and the exploratory case study are as follows: Requirements need to be elicited from multiple diverse stakeholders. Conflict must be identified and resolved as early as possible. The changing priorities of a diverse group need to be more effectively managed. Stakeholders may not be sure of what is required, have difficulty communicating and developers may lack implicit domain knowledge. These factors represent a set of *human related* problems that affect the communication of requirements between developers and other stakeholders during the process of elicitation.

A suitable structure was therefore required to support:

- Participatory elicitation between multiple diverse stakeholder groups;

- Early identification and resolution of conflict;

- Management of multiple changing stakeholder priorities;

- Identification and access to the appropriate stakeholders;

- Understanding and communication through the development of a common language;

- The development of a representative perspective of requirements to be addressed.

The findings presented here contributed to addressing the research problem which sought to investigate how an evolutionary framework could be developed to improve the facilitation of agile requirements elicitation.

## 11.3 Developing the OpenXP Solution

In addressing the third objective, to design a suitable solution; a novel evolutionary framework called OpenXP was developed. The framework was designed to create an appropriate support structure to improve communication and understanding and to encourage a more proactive engagement during team-customer interactions. The first two phases facilitate:

1. The inclusion of multiple diverse stakeholder viewpoints in collaboratively developing a representative perspective of the problem domain;

2. The collaborative development of appropriate business improvement scenarios;

3. Early conflict identification, negotiation and resolution;

4. The prioritization of high level business improvement scenarios;

5. The collaborative development of additional business level context for creating user stories.

The third phase of the framework consists of linking prioritized business improvement scenarios with XP activities by supporting a continued collaborative effort toward creating and prioritizing user stories for development.

## 11.4 Evaluating the performance of OpenXP

The final objective was to *evaluate the proposed solution in an appropriate environment*. In order to achieve this objective, two confirmatory case studies were conducted. For each study conducted final year computing students were divided into two teams. Each team was given the same problem statement to be addressed within the same time frame. One team followed the OpenXP framework while the other team followed XP-only. Throughout each study observations were recorded and questionnaires and interviews were used to collect feedback. For each case study the unit of analysis remained focused on *the process of how requirements are elicited.* However, at the start of each study propositions were predefined. The key results that emerged from this are presented in the following sections. The results that emerged from the initial confirmatory study are presented first.

### 11.4.1 Results of confirmatory case study one

With reference to the propositions defined at the start of this study, proposition one was confirmed indicating that it was not difficult for developers to understand and use OST. The OpenXP team appeared apprehensive at first since the initial investigation commenced at a slow pace. However, it is not unusual for participants who have not previously participated in OST to feel a slight discomfort with the self-organising aspect of using the technique.  This dissipated as the focused discussion progressed and a more interactive discussion gradually unfolded. This suggested that the OpenXP team had independently self-organised around the concern to be addressed. The simple tools provided were used by the team and communication between members was dynamic and collaborative. This also indicated that activities conducted prior to phase three had supported the team in finding a common language without introducing a steep learning curve.

The analysis of proposition two confirmed that the developers would use the steps as described. An unexpected discussion commenced prior to voicing concerns, however, this appeared to help rather than hinder the process since the interaction was short and provided context for the first concern raised. The remaining steps proceeded as expected indicating that overall the developers had adhered to the steps as described.

Finally, the analysis of the third proposition confirmed that activities conducted prior to phase three had assisted the OpenXP team in understanding the problem background. Scope had been clarified after misunderstandings were aired with the team consistently exchanging multiple viewpoints. The high level prioritization of business improvements focused the team on only creating user stories for a singular aspect that had been explored and discussed in advance. The scenario diagram produced, revealed unanticipated complexity having captured the broader perspective of the problem and the team interpreted the user stories subsequently created as the detail required to satisfy the wider business perspective. An overlapping requirement had also been detected prior to creating user stories.

In addition to the confirmation of the set of predefined propositions, a number of subsequent results emerged indicating that OpenXP supported:

- The development of a quick and usable design;

- The clarification and management of scope;

- Detection of ambiguous requirements prior to commencing XP activities;

- Whole team collaboration including regular team-customer involvement;

- The development of a collective understanding through the use of a common language.

Finally, the framework assisted the OpenXP team with the clarification of misunderstandings, creating and prioritizing user stories.

## 11.4.2 Results of confirmatory case study two

In the second confirmatory case study, the first proposition was disconfirmed indicating that the developers did not use the steps as described. For instance, although prioritization occurred, it did not occur in the sequence in which this was expected. Also, although improvements were interpreted as scenarios, a separate set of scenarios were not created at step 6 as expected. However, this deviation from the steps as described did not appear to have a negative impact on the team or the project. Also, since the steps commenced differently, this confirms that OpenXP could be used differently depending on the project context, the concerns raised, the particular group involved and perhaps the number of people involved on a project.

Proposition two was also confirmed suggesting that outputs generated prior to phase three could be perceived as agile models. This confirms that the OpenXP framework can facilitate the generation of agile models as artefacts that support the creation of user stories on XP projects.

Proposition three was confirmed after OpenXP successfully brought the new team member up to date twenty five minutes in advance of the XP-only team and without communication problems occurring. This suggests that the new member successfully integrated within a significantly shorter space of time. It was also evident that the new team member understood the problem to be addressed considering that no delays or communication problems emerged on the OpenXP team for the remainder of the project. This indicates that the artefacts generated prior to phase three had assisted the team in effectively communicating progress to date to an unexpected stakeholder joining the project late.

A number of additional results emerged as follows:

- Extra activities did not impose a time delay for the project;

- Support was found for whole team collaboration including regular team-customer involvement;

- The project was developed on schedule and within scope;

- Activities conducted prior to phase three could continue to streamline concurrently alongside XP activities for the purposes of resolving unexpected problems that can emerge as an XP project proceeds;

## 11.5 Expert Validation

As part of the fourth objective, two expert reviews were conducted with independent industry practitioners in order to validate the OpenXP framework. This involved an interactive interview demonstrating each step in the framework using the physical artefacts created by each team during the two confirmatory studies. Overall, a positive response to the framework was received with a number of tentative revisions for future versions of the framework suggested.

### 11.5.1 Linking high level with low level requirements detail

Based upon the artefacts generated, clear links were visible depicting a logical path between high level business requirements and lower level requirements detail needed for implementation. It was predicted that OpenXP would assist stakeholders in prioritizing requirements and making informed decisions earlier in the development process. Addressing potential issues in advance was perceived as a means to support the detection of problems earlier and this was considered essential during the identification of high level business requirements.

### 11.5.2 Benefits of the focused discussions

Creating an opportunity to negotiate concerns during the focused discussions was considered invaluable since the potential problems associated with high level requirements could be sufficiently investigated by the relevant stakeholders in advance. This was also considered important for performing root cause analysis on existing problems and determining the impact of integrating new requirements into an existing system. Negotiations are regularly needed since problems are often unforeseen and approaching a requirement from multiple development roles could assist in developing a more representative perspective of a given requirement. The focused discussions could also assist in refining the requirement to the appropriate level of depth needed for implementation.

### 11.5.3 Prioritization

The two step approach to prioritization was welcomed in the case where stakeholders need to collaborate and negotiate. For instance, it was considered valuable to create a means with which to appropriately visualise high level business requirements aligned with the technical complexity involved during their development.

### 11.5.4 Potential issues for developers

Potential issues for developers were also pointed out, these include difficulty involving stakeholders post elicitation when issues emerge that must be resolved with the involvement of the relevant people. Collaborative online forums were suggested as a means to overcome problems associated with the availability of stakeholders. It was also suggested that if artefacts generated prior to phase three could be identified using a numbering scheme then stories could be traced upward to their associated usage context and a bidirectional trace could be clearly made between the tangible artefacts produced.

### 11.5.5 Application of the OpenXP framework in practice

In relation to how the framework might be applied in practice, it was expressed that OpenXP could direct stakeholders towards specifying requirements at the appropriate level of depth needed for implementation. It was also considered particularly beneficial to investigate a single high level aspect of a given problem in-depth first. The importance of identifying problems first in a software project was considered valuable. The framework could focus stakeholders on the importance of the business problem being addressed. It was also pointed out that the OpenXP framework has the capacity to encourage both business stakeholders to consider the technical perspective and developer stakeholders to consider the business perspective of a given problem space to be addressed. The concerns of multiple diverse stakeholders could be addressed across both business and technology domains if the framework were to be applied in practice.

## 11.6 OpenXP Facets

The OpenXP solution also consists of four broader facets, each of which is responsible for one or more strategic functions required for elicitation. These facets involve *Stakeholder Coordination, Business and IT Alignment and Integrating Adaptability and Effective Communication*. The following points briefly summarise the main functions for each.

### 11.6.1 Stakeholder Coordination

The Stakeholder Coordination facet is responsible for strategically assembling interdisciplinary stakeholder groups via member associations affected by a common issue of concern. This is achieved by viewing the existing groups that participate in focused discussions (in phase 1) as new *"member associations"*. The Agile BA can then identify the roles and relationships between stakeholders on member associations by organising them using the stakeholder onion model. Convenors emerging from the focused discussions are ideally suited for customer representation since they automatically exhibit the required skills and qualities needed to successfully play this role. Convenors are therefore identified as candidates for customer representation since they are Collaborative, Representative, Authorised, Committed and Knowledgeable (CRACK).

Later when development commences, customer inclusion on the XP team is managed by only involving CRACK representatives specifically associated with stories linked to the business improvement scenarios they have created themselves. This supports real customer involvement because it ensures that developers have a direct communication line with stakeholders who 'own' the requirements themselves. In the event of limited access to a CRACK representative, the customer role can rotate between the remaining stakeholders in the members association. This ensures that developers still have a direct link with a number of other CRACK sources of information to mitigate the risk of delayed feedback.

Larger stakeholder groups can be managed in OpenXP by taking the convenor from each focused discussion/member association and forming a CRACK customer team. Each CRACK representative on the team has a direct relationship with at least one set of business improvements under development. CRACK teams could regularly assemble in the business domain to manage the broader level developments of the project as a whole.

## 11.6.2 Business and IT Alignment

The third facet in the OpenXP solution concerns Business and IT Alignment. This important aspect of project management is addressed by dynamically generating a set of agile models that represent upper level business context which are then organised hierarchically into layers. Artefacts produced are logically linked upwards to create a bidirectional trace from the requirements relating back to their specific business improvement scenarios. These outer layers provide a means with which to organise additional context for business and technical stakeholders in writing stories.

The requirements of business and technical stakeholders are aligned using the two-step approach to prioritization. This helps to ensure that the requirements developed consistently relate back to the business value they intend to address. Particularly for business and IT alignment, project visibility is greatly improved by being able to step through a series of artefacts organised into broader layers, each of which represents a higher level of business abstraction. As evidenced by the findings from the industry study presented in chapter 4, specifying requirements at differing levels of abstraction was indeed a challenging task in practice. OpenXP offers a lightweight solution to this problem where requirements can be specified at differing levels of granularity, this can also be used to support reuse.

## 11.6.3 Effective Communication

While stakeholder identification, access, involvement and rotation on projects is managed under the Stakeholder Coordination facet; the Effective Communication facet focuses more on creating the ideal conditions for successful communication to prevail during team-customer interactions. As such it is primarily concerned with effectively engaging multiple interdisciplinary stakeholder groups during elicitation. One primary function of the effective communication facet is to provide hands-on practical support for ASP by motivating stakeholders to voluntarily self-organise around real business issues of concern and accept responsibility for developing improvements to these concerns. Only simple tools and techniques are used for problem solving and solution development, this aims to quickly create common ground for stakeholders to begin effectively communicating.

The second strategic function is to embrace conflict. Conflict is encouraged to emerge since deliberation, negotiation, compromise and collaboration are all activities that can be supported during the focused discussions at step 3. OpenXP embraces conflict under the assumption that conflict simply represents differing versions of reality that simultaneously exist in a given domain. For emergent systems development it is important to air conflict as soon as possible since this contributes positively to stakeholders shared understanding of the domain to be modeled. This in turn supports the emergence goal to facilitate the continuous reconstruction of the organisations reality. This must be embraced in order to maintain consistent focus on *the key factors of the current state* for dynamically changing business environments.

## 11.6.4 Adaptability Integration

To successfully develop emergent software systems, adaptability orientation is a fundamental goal that dynamic business domains must now strive to achieve. The Adaptability Integration facet enables existing requirements methodologies and techniques to be used within the framework. This is important for reusing known techniques (and/or practices) from the business stakeholders existing knowledge base and continuing to adopt approaches that stakeholders are familiar with themselves. Known methodologies leaning more so toward heavyweight approaches, however, must be adapted for use within the framework. A prerequisite for successfully achieving this in OpenXP is that known existing approaches must be applied in a lightweight JIT manner. This also requires that any artefacts produced as outputs from the steps in OpenXP must fit the criteria for determining that the models produced are agile. The OpenXP solution is concerned with integrating existing adaptable methods and techniques or indeed parts of these where it has become clear to stakeholders that in doing so the business problem can be better defined, understood and improved.

OpenXP is an evolutionary approach to RE that recognises the extent to which projects are directly dependent on a set of potentially unknown volatile factors impacting the development process. This solution therefore welcomes new versions of the framework to be implemented *if* steps are added or the sequence in which they take place has been altered, *and* this results in success in practice. This is important since the changes made in a particular environment have contributed toward producing a successful solution surrounding the peculiar circumstances for a specific situation. The advantage here is that other future development efforts that appear to consist of a similar set of imperatives and constraints may be better managed by implementing or continuing to tailor a newer version that has already proved successful in such settings in practice.

Additionally, OpenXP practically applies a number of lean principles that target the elimination of waste in the communication process. Learning is also amplified, team empowerment encouraged and integrity built in from the start. Finally, the OpenXP solution ensures that decisions made are delayed until the last responsible moment. Implementing this lean practice ensures that the BA is in a stronger position to make more fully informed decisions in advance of the commencement of development activities.

## 11.7 OpenXP: An Evolutionary Approach to RE

Relating back to the ten specific characteristics (as discussed in section 3.2.1) for an RE approach to succeed in the HCS, Table 19 illustrates where the performance of AMs can now be improved by adopting OpenXP as a means with which to assist in addressing the remaining seven characteristics that received only partial compliance earlier in Table 4. These characteristics are reproduced here for clarity in Table 19, column 1 presents a summary of the desirable HCS characteristics, column 2 then demonstrates the extent to which AMs comply with these. Two ticks indicate that AMs comply fully with the characteristic, one tick indicates partial compliance and an 'x' indicates that no compliance exists for the characteristic.

*Table 19 Compliancy mapping of RE characteristics vs. AMs*

| HCS Characteristics | AMs |
|---|---|
| Iterative development | ✓✓ |
| Prioritization | ✓✓ |
| Correlation with other processes | ✓✓ |
| Appropriate stakeholders | ✓✓ |
| Participatory elicitation | ✓✓ |
| Identification of conflict | ✓✓ |
| Resolution of conflict | ✓✓ |
| Retention and traceability | ✓ |
| Annotation (negotiation and traceability) | ✓✓ |
| Distributed elicitation | ✓ |

As Table 19 illustrates, with the OpenXP link, AMs are now in a position to comply with an additional five of the ten original characteristics. Here, full compliance can now be achieved for identification of appropriate stakeholders; participatory elicitation; conflict identification and resolution; and upper level business context is dynamically generated in advance of development which supports negotiation, traceability and annotation of the artefacts produced. This shows that AMs can now be considered fully compliant with eight of the ten desirable characteristics for an RE approach to HCS in the DAS domain. It is worth noting that while OpenXP does produce a set of tangible artefacts that can be bi-directionally traced, it does not directly address software tool support for traceability over time. For this reason AMs used in the OpenXP framework are still considered partially compliant with this characteristic. Likewise, OpenXP is specifically suited to elicitation conducted in co-located settings, and as such, AMs used as part of the OpenXP framework are still considered partially compliant with respect to the final desirable characteristic to support distributed elicitation.

With reference to the requirements for an evolutionary approach to RE as defined in section 3.8, Table 20 illustrates where each of these requirements have been addressed by the OpenXP Solution. The first column identifies each requirement while the second column gives a brief description, two ticks '✓✓' in the third column then indicate the extent to which the OpenXP solution complies with each. The following points then briefly describe how the OpenXP solution has addressed the requirements for an evolutionary approach to RE.

*Table 20 OpenXP as an Evolutionary RE Approach*

| Requirements for an Evolutionary Framework | | OpenXP |
|---|---|---|
| 1. | The candidate approach will exploit brainstorming, scenario analysis or prototyping | ✓✓ |
| 2. | Support stakeholder interaction and involvement through a visioning phase prior to writing requirements | ✓✓ |
| 3. | Support iteration as a prerequisite | ✓✓ |
| 4. | Exploit the use of simple tools and support the development of a common language | ✓✓ |
| 5. | Support the identification, access, engagement and involvement of appropriate stakeholders | ✓✓ |
| 6. | Support the identification and resolution of requirements conflict | ✓✓ |
| 7. | Support the development of additional context needed for writing user stories | ✓✓ |
| 8. | The candidate approach should make every effort to maximise design capability | ✓✓ |

**RQ1:** First OpenXP positively exploits the benefits of adaptable techniques such as brainstorming, scenario analysis and prototyping. In addition to this further guidance is provided for any other adaptable techniques or indeed a combination of these to be used within the framework.

**RQ2:** The first two phases in the framework address the second requirement since these phases are responsible for supporting stakeholder interaction and continuous involvement through a visioning phase that takes place prior to writing stories.

**RQ3:** All three phases in the framework expect iteration considering that this is a prerequisite for success in dynamically changing business environments.

**RQ4:** The first two phases in OpenXP are responsible for incorporating the use of simple tools in support of developing a common language for stakeholders to effectively communicate.

**RQ5:** The identification, access, engagement and subsequent involvement of relevant stakeholders, is addressed across all three phases in the framework. The stakeholder coordination and effective communication facets are primarily responsible for implementing this requirement.

**RQ6:** OpenXP provides practical support for the identification of conflict to emerge as early as possible during elicitation. This is achieved through shared reality reconstruction during the focused discussions which embraces conflicting viewpoints as valuable contributions and offers direct support for the development of amicable resolution.

**RQ7:** The first two phases purposefully generate upper level business context specifically to provide additional support for writing user stories. Artefacts created at the upper level are agile models which can be used to inform and supplement development.

**RQ8:** OpenXP purposefully makes every effort to maximise design capability as early as possible. This is achieved by supporting stakeholders in expanding initially on the multiple possible paths that could lead toward a solution.

## 11.8 When can OpenXP be used

In relation to the generalizability of this work as a whole, it is very important to understand the conditions under which OpenXP can be implemented in practice. Described in this research as the *most difficult* and *critical* aspect of software engineering, requirements elicitation can be considered a complex task for any problem domain that has not yet been well defined.

The OpenXP framework predominantly supports effective and efficient communication between stakeholders in situations where a set of diverse viewpoints must be consolidated immediately prior to agreeing the set of requirements for development. It is therefore not recommended in cases where existing perspectives on the requirements do not need to be amalgamated and where the problem to be investigated is considered somewhat trivial. Rather, OpenXP can be applied in any software project where the following conditions are present:

1. The problem can be described as a real business issue of concern;

2. The problem is considered to be complex;

3. Multiple diverse stakeholders are involved;

4. The potential for conflict including passion is present;

5. A situation of genuine urgency must exist in terms of the time frame available to solve the problem.

This is important considering that OST alone is *not* recommended in cases where some or all of the above conditions are absent. Particularly critical to the successful implementation of phase one activities in the framework, the OST investigation, this must consist to some degree, of a combination of the aforementioned conditions for mutually beneficial interactions between stakeholders to prevail. This is also an instrumental component for the seamless integration between phase one and two activities in the framework.

In addition to this, OpenXP has favoured agile practices such as *user stories*, *prioritization* and *iteration planning* in line with the XP development process. Considering that agile development teams in general consist of ten developers at most, and due to the fact that the confirmatory case studies involved seven developers at most, the framework can thus be considered applicable to small teams currently practicing AMs.

In this research, OpenXP was implemented with all participants situated in a co-located setting. It is therefore considered unsuitable in its current form for situations when stakeholders involved are geographically dispersed. As reported in the exploratory case study presented in chapter 4, physical meetings proved most beneficial in the cases where *pertinent issues* or *unknowns* needed to be quickly addressed during elicitation in practice. This point may also limit its applicability to handling the set of *critical* or *pertinent issues* that must be resolved *only* when stakeholders need to physically meet during requirements elicitation on agile software projects.

## 11.9 Research Limitations and Validity

A number of limitations should be acknowledged in the research conducted here. First, the sample of industry participants who contributed to the exploratory case study should be considered. Although numerous companies were initially contacted, it was only possible to interview nine participants across seven companies in total. This was mainly due to the time constraints of practitioners. It is therefore possible that the findings may differ beyond those presented here if either a larger or a different sample could have been recruited.

With ten or more years of experience in RE, seven of the industry practitioners who participated in the exploratory case study can be classified as experts in the domain. The remaining two participants had four and five years of experience respectively. Overall, the synthesis of results for the industry interviews comprises a total of one hundred and twenty five years of collective participant expertise in requirements engineering practice.

Due to the fact that practitioners predominantly reflect how requirements are elicited in the Irish software engineering industry, it should be acknowledged that the findings may be specific to within a single geographical location. For instance, results from the exploratory study interviews are broadly representative of bespoke software development in the *Irish* Industrial Goods and Services, Telecommunications, Healthcare and Pharmaceuticals and Financial market sectors. Further research on the process of requirements elicitation in practice could therefore expand the subject beyond the geographical boundaries of the work conducted here.

It should also be noted that students training in software development may not reflect the reality of an XP project conducted by a professional software development team. For instance, different results may have emerged with more experienced developers if the confirmatory studies had been conducted in practice rather than in an academic setting. As a precaution to minimize this threat, in all cases, student participants were recruited from their final computing course year. This ensured that each participant had completed at least one mandatory work placement module developing software in industry prior to the commencement of this research.

The type of development activity included implementation of a timetabling system for the exploratory case study, a student registration system for the first confirmatory case study and a tax collection system for the second confirmatory case study. Since the learning outcomes of computing degrees delivered are formally aligned to the necessary skill set required for students to later gain employment in the software engineering industry, it can therefore be stated that the types of development activities involved in the case studies conducted in this research, are closely aligned with the types of development activities that would be typically assigned in commercial software engineering practice.

In agile development projects, software is developed incrementally over a number of short iterations. For each case, development activities assigned were conducted over a period of at least two or more short iterations. As such, the duration of the development activities assigned is considered representative of the time frame typically allocated for agile practitioners to produce some level of working software in the form of a prototype for demonstration to stakeholders in live development settings.

It is both possible and likely that as this research reports, a customer representative or indeed a suitable representative may not be readily available in reality. However, in the context of this research, the use of a student setting in testing the implementation of the framework presented the ideal situation of a Collaborative, Representative, Authorised, Committed and Knowledgeable (CRACK) customer representative who was available for regular communication with each team during each confirmatory study. The results could thus be considered valid given this condition. Finally, although it is theoretically plausible for large numbers of multiple diverse groups to be involved on an OpenXP project, the research conducted here has evaluated the integration of the perspectives between a limited number of eight participants (including the customer representative) at most.

## 11.10 Summary

Requirements elicitation is a fundamentally important activity in software development. It is clearly evident that this process must be conducted effectively and efficiently in order to develop successful solutions, that adequately meet the needs of those affected by the outcome of software developed. Although, a number of complex problems associated with this particular activity have been widely acknowledged, significant challenges with communication and understanding during elicitation have remained unaddressed.

The research question addressed in this work was: *How can an evolutionary framework be developed to improve the facilitation of agile requirements elicitation?* This question was addressed by fulfilling four main objectives. First, the research question was constructed after a review of the literature in RE strongly suggested that a distinct problem was the lack of a clear understanding of a collective and agreed upon statement of the requirements that must be developed for multiple diverse stakeholder groups. This problem has been considerably amplified by the fact that stakeholder needs are expected to continuously evolve overtime. This research thus began by first identifying and classifying the factors that affect the communication of requirements between developers and other stakeholders. AMs were then evaluated for their suitability in addressing this problem with particular attention paid to the customer role. While AMs clearly promote continuous interaction with the role of customer throughout development, a significant problem is the effectiveness of this interaction and how this could be accommodated when multiple groups are involved.

With the most thorough set of guidelines including values, principles and practices defined, XP was selected here as the most suitable AM, with the foundations in place to support the challenges relating to multiple diversity between stakeholders on projects. A number of challenges in relation to the role of the customer, however, suggested a series of high risk pitfalls that remained unaddressed by XP in managing effective interaction between the development team and this role.

A review of the literature illustrated that existing research had not yet endeavoured to effectively determine how consensus between stakeholders could be achieved. Nor had it focused on how multiple diverse stakeholder interactions could be successfully integrated with a software development method. The research conducted here has concentrated on filling this gap. Primary research was conducted which determined the conditions under which requirements are successfully communicated based upon the experiences of practitioners in industry. This subsequently informed the development of an evolutionary framework to improve the facilitation of agile requirements elicitation. OpenXP is a three phase framework that links OST, an evolutionary group interaction technique, with XP through the development of Usage Scenarios. The framework was evaluated using two confirmatory case studies with the main findings as follows:

OpenXP assisted the team in providing additional support for developing a quick and usable design, clarification of scope, early detection of ambiguous requirements, team-customer collaboration and a collective understanding of the problem background. This was achieved through the use of simple tools and a common language. The framework also assisted the team in effectively communicating progress to date to an unexpected stakeholder joining the project late. Activities conducted prior to phase three facilitated the generation of agile models as artefacts that support the creation of user stories. Additional activities required at the start did not impose a time delay on the project. It also emerged that OpenXP could continue to be useful throughout projects to resolve unexpected problems that can emerge as the project proceeds.

Although OpenXP steps can be followed, they may not proceed in the sequence in which this is initially expected. In the second confirmatory study prioritization had occurred earlier than expected with concerns prioritized before improvements. This study also revealed that developers may not proceed with a separate set of scenarios as recommended by the framework. Instead the outputs from the OST investigation may be interpreted as scenarios and used to create user stories directly. This has shown that the framework may be implemented differently depending on the group involved, the problem to be addressed and the type of concerns raised. In the second confirmatory study this was not viewed as problematic since participants self-organised and this deviation from the steps as described did not have a negative impact on the team or the project.

On the contrary, this particular OpenXP team developed a fully functional prototype on schedule and within scope.

The framework may therefore evolve in practice provided that any change made to the steps or sequence in which they take place, results in benefitting the team, and in the production of business valued software for the project. Briefly documenting new versions is a considerably advantageous move for planning future development efforts in specific business environments. For example, this enables OpenXP development teams to openly acknowledge and more accurately map the steps that emerged (through process enactment in practice) where previous OpenXP implementations have resulted in a successful development effort. Variations that develop can be used to support future innovative development projects based on a similar set of situationally specific characteristics, circumstances and constraints.

In addition to the nine specific steps, the OpenXP solution also encompasses four broader facets. Essentially these include Stakeholder Coordination, Business and IT Alignment, Effective Communication and Adaptability Integration for elicitation on projects. Each facet is thus responsible for one or more strategic functions aimed at providing a support structure to facilitate activities involved in agile business analysis. The Agile BA may therefore be in a good position to adopt the role of the OpenXP facilitator. However, the role of the facilitator in OpenXP differs significantly from that of other typical group interaction techniques. In OpenXP, for instance, topics on the agenda for discussion are dynamically generated on the fly by participants in attendance themselves. The role of the facilitator in this respect is not to ensure that participants adhere to a predefined list of topics or a fixed schedule. Instead the facilitator is primarily responsible for continuously encouraging stakeholders to self-organise around the development of improvement scenarios for business concerns raised under a broader theme of common significance.

There are a number of distinct advantages for the BA in adopting this role: The OpenXP framework creates a collaborative working environment for identification, access to, and effective interaction between multiple diverse groups. The roles and relationships between stakeholders are also identified as early as possible; this includes those who exhibit the ideal characteristics for effective customer involvement (needed later for development). Direct ownership for business improvement scenarios with associated user stories can be established upfront and in many respects the Agile BA is also protected from making important decisions too early in the requirements process, this is clear since decisions are made by stakeholders who effectively create and 'own' the business improvements themselves. While care must be taken to ensure that the BA correctly adopts the rules for effective facilitation in OpenXP, it is clear that in doing so, the framework offers a strong support structure for the effective implementation of many agile business analysis activities.

The OpenXP solution has been designed to address the requirements for an evolutionary approach to RE. Underpinned by emergent systems thinking this framework expects dynamically changing business environments to continuously undergo consistent levels of adaptation. As such, practical support for elicitation and analyses as continuous activities on projects has been developed; a constant redevelopment perspective is adopted with dynamic requirements negotiation expected to continue throughout development; incomplete but usefully ambiguous specifications are practically supported by *only* generating artefacts that fit the criteria for developing agile models; Adaptability Orientation is embedded with a set of guidelines to support the integration of existing adaptable approaches to RE; Parallel Development is favoured over the traditional assumption that development stages must commence in sequence i.e. OpenXP recognises that while all stages of development are important, the order in which they take place is not. As such, the framework can also be used to provide amethodical software practitioners with an appropriate support structure for business innovation coupled with the flexibility to improvise while still using a software development process.

The OpenXP solution offers a unique and lightweight evolutionary approach to the purposeful elimination of waste in the communication process during elicitation on projects. This is achieved by linking software development with effective stakeholder interaction. This is the first framework to take advantage of the benefits of engaging potentially large groups of multiple diverse stakeholders by embracing existing business concerns as opportunities for change, and positively nurturing the early identification and resolution of potential conflict. This contribution is among the first to attempt to detect, nurture and channel unpredictability during elicitation surrounding the set of human related factors that affect the communication of requirements between stakeholders on software projects.

Clearly, as evidenced by the research conducted here, interaction is one thing, but achieving a high quality interaction between relevant representatives is quite another. This work has created an environment for successful dynamic informal communication to flourish in order to take advantage of the potential to recreate the conditions under which effective communication succeeds during requirements elicitation on software projects in practice. On this common ground, only then can we see the potential for *lean value stream interactions* between culturally diverse stakeholders to begin to develop in practice.

# References

Abrahamsson, P., Salo, O., Ronkainen, J. and Warsta, J. (2002). *Agile software development methods: Review and analysis.* VTT Technical Report 478.  VTT Electronics and University of Oulu. Espoo, Finland.

Abrahamsson, P., Warsta, J., Siponen, M.T., and Ronkainen, J. (2003). New Directions on Agile Methods: A Comparative Analysis. In: *25th International Conference on Software Engineering (ICSE' 03), 3-10 May. Oregon, USA.* IEEE, pp. 244-254.

Abrahamsson, P. (2003). Extreme Programming: First Results from a Controlled Case Study. In: *29th Euromicro Conference (EUROMICRO'03).* Belek-Antalya, Turkey, pp. 259–266.

Agile Open (2013). *Open Space Conferences on Agile Software Development* [online], Available from: <http://www.agileopen.net/node> [Accessed: 21 March 2013].

Akif, R. and Majeed, H. (2012). Issues and Challenges in Scrum Implementation. *International Journal or Scientific and Engineering Research.* Vol. 3 (8).

Alatalo, T., Oinas-Kukkonen, H., Kurkela, V and Siponen, M. (2002). Information Systems Development in Emergent Organisations: Empirical Findings. In: Kirikova et al. (eds), *Information Systems Development: Advances in Methodologies, Components, and Management.* Kluwer Academic Publishers.

Ali, I. (2011). Coexistence or Operational Necessity: The Role of Formally Structured Organization and Informal Networks during Deployments. In: *16th International Command and Control Research and Technology Symposium (ICCRTS 2011),* Canada.

Alexander, I. and Beus-Dukic, L. (2009). *Discovering Requirements.* New York, John Wiley & Sons.

Alspaugh, T.A., Tomlinson, B. and Baumer, E. (2006). Using Social Agents to Visualise Software Scenarios. In: *ACM Symposium on Software Visualization (SOFTVIS) Brighton UK. New York, USA,* ACM, pp. 87-94.

Ambler, S.W. (2002). A*gile Modeling: Effective Practices for Extreme Programming and the Unified Process.* New York, John Wiley & Sons.

Ambler (2009a). *Agile Requirements Modeling* [online] Available from: http://www.agilemodeling. com/essays/agileRequirements.htm#Challenges [Accessed: 25 October 2009].

Ambler, S.W. (2009b). *The Agile Unified Process (AUP)* [online], Available from: http://www. ambysoft.com/unifiedprocess/agileUP.html [Accessed: 03 November 2009].

Ambler, S.W. (2009c). *Examining the Agile Manifesto* [online], Available from: http://www.ambysoft.com/essays/agileManifesto.html [Accessed: 15 March 2009].

Anderson, D. J. (2012) *Lean Software Development* [online], Available from: http://msdn.microsoft.com/en-us/library/hh533841(v=vs.110).aspx [Accessed: 15 December 2012].

Anderson, D. J., Concas, G., Lunesu, M.I., Marchesi, M. and Zhang, H. (2012). A Comparative Study of Scrum and Kanban Approaches on a Real Case Study Using Simulation. In: *13th International Conference on Agile Processes and eXtreme Programming (XP2012), Malmo, Sweden, May 21-25.* Berlin, Springer, pp. 123-137.

Andrews, T. (2012). What is Social Constructionism? *Grounded Theory Review* .Vol.11 (1).

Anton, A. (1996). Goal-based Requirements Analysis. In: *2nd International Conference on Requirements Engineering (ICRE '96), 15-18 April, Colorado Springs, Colorado, USA.* Washington DC, USA, IEEE Computer Society, pp.136-144.

Arao, T., Goto, E. and Nagata, T. (2005). "Business Process" Oriented Requirements Engineering Process. In: *13th International Conference on Requirements Engineering, August 29th - September 2nd, La Sorbonne, France.* Washington DC, USA, IEEE Computer Society, pp. 395-402.

Archer, M., Collet, P., Fleury, F., Lahire, P., Moisan, S. and Rigault, J.P. (2009). Modeling Context and Dynamic Adaptations with Feature Models. In: *International Workshop Models@runtime, Models 2009 (MRT'09).*

Astels, D., Miller, G. and Miroslav, N. (2002). *A Practical Guide to Extreme Programming.* Prentice Hall.

Atkinson, P. and Hammersley, M. (2007). *Ethnography: Principles in Practice.* 3rd Edition. New York, Taylor and Francis.

Awazu, Y. (2004). Knowledge management in distributed environments: Role of informal network players. In: *the 37th International Conference on System Sciences, Hawaii.* IEEE.

Azevedo Santos, M., Souza Bermejo, P., Tonelli, A. and Zambalde, A. (2011). Challenges of Teams Management: Using Agile Methods to Solve the Common Problems. In*: International Conference on ENTERprise Information Systems (CENTERIS'11), October 5-7, Portugal.* Springer Berlin Heidelberg, pp. 297-305.

Babar, A., Zowghi, D. and Chew, E. (2010). Using Goals to Model Strategy Map for Business IT Alignment. In: *5th International Workshop on Business/IT Alignment and Interoperability, (BUSITAL'10). June 07, Hammamet, Tunisia.* Vol. 599, pp. 16-30.

Barnes, J. (2008). Strategies from bringing Agility to RUP in Large organisations [online], Available from: http://www.ibm.com/developerworks/rational/library/edge/08/feb08/lines_barnes_holmes_ambler/ [Accessed: 21 May 2013].

Baskerville, R. and Pries-Heje, J. (2002). Information Systems Development @ Internet Speed: A New Paradigm in the Making! In: *10th European Conference on Information Systems (ECIS), Gdansk, Poland,* pp. 282-291.

Bazerman, M. (1994). *Judgment in Managerial Decision Making.* New York, John Wiley and Sons.

Beck, K., Beedle, M., Bennekum, A. v., Cockburn, A., Cunningham, W., Fowler, M., Grenning, J., Highsmith, J., Hunt, A., Jeffries, R., Kern, J., Marick, B., Martin, R. C., Mellor, S., Schwaber, K., Sutherland, J. & Thomas, D. (2001). *The Agile Manifesto* [online], Available from: http://www.agilealliance.org/the-alliance/the-agile-manifesto/ [Accessed: 06 October 2008].

Beck, K. (1999). *Extreme Programming Explained: Embrace Change.* Addison-Wesley.

Beck, K. and Andres, C. (2004). *Extreme Programming Explained: Embrace Change.* 2nd Edition. Addison-Wesley.

Beedle, M. and Schwaber, K. (2001). *Agile Software Development with SCRUM.* Upper Saddle River, NJ, Prentice Hall.

Begel, A. and Nagappan, N. (2007). Usage and Perceptions of Agile Software Development in an Industrial Context: An Exploratory Study. In *1st International Symposium on Empirical Software Engineering and Measurement (ESEM '07), Washington DC, USA.* IEEE Computer Society, pp. 255-264.

Bell, S. (2006). *Poor requirements-definition equals ICT failure* [online]. Available from: http://computerworld.co.nz/news.nsf/news/0A6111812D30F9D2CC25721B000A22A4 [Accessed: 18 April 2012].

Bello, M., Sorrentino, M., Virili, F. (2002). Web Services and Emergent Organisations: Opportunities and Challenges for IS Development. In: *10th European Conference on Information Systems (ECIS), Gdansk, Poland,* pp 439–449.

Berry, D.M., Cheng, B.H.C. and Zhang, J. (2005). The Four Levels of Requirements Engineering for and in Dynamic Adaptive Systems. In: *11th International Workshop on Requirements Engineering: Foundation for Software Quality (REFSQ),* pp. 95-100.

Berry, D., Czarnecki, K., Antkiewicz, M. and Abdeirazik, M. (2010). Requirements Determination is Unstoppable: An Experience Report. In: *18th International Conference on Requirements Engineering, September 27 - October 1, Sydney, Australia.* Washington DC, USA, IEEE Computer Society, pp. 311-316.

Biggam, J. (2002). Exploiting Soft Systems Methodology (SSM) and Knowledge Types to Facilitate Knowledge Capture Issues in a Web Site Environment. In: *35th International Conference on System Sciences, Hawaii, (HICSS'02),* IEEE, pp.2602-2608.

Bjarnasan, E., Wnuk, K. and Regnell, B. (2011). Requirements Are Slipping Through the Gaps – A Case Study on Causes and Effects of Communication Gaps in Large-Scale Software Development.

In: *19ᵗʰ international Conference on Requirements Engineering, August 29-September 2ⁿᵈ, Trento, Italy.* Washington DC, USA, IEEE Computer Society, pp.37-46.

Bjerke, O.L. (2008). *Soft Systems Methodology in action: A case study at a purchasing department.* Thesis (MSc.), Universtiy of Gothenburg, Sweden.

Blomkvist, S. (2006). User-Centred Design and Agile Development of IT Systems. (M.Phil.) thesis. Uppsala University, Sweden.

Boehm, B. W. (1981). *Software Engineering Economics.* Prentice Hall.

Boehm, B.W. and Papaccio, P.N. (1988). Understanding and Controlling Software Costs. *IEEE Transactions on Software Engineering,* Vol. 14 (10), pp. 1462-1477.

Boehm, B. (2002). Get Ready for Agile Methods with CARE. *IEEE Computer Society,* Vol.35 (1), pp.64-69.

Boehm, B.W., Turner, R. (2003) Using Risk to Balance Agile and Plan-Driven Methods. *Computer,* vol. 36 (6), pp. 57-66.

Brekkan, E and Mathison, E. (2010). Introducing Scrum in Companies in Norway: A Case Study. In: *Informing Science and IT Education Conference (InSITE '10), June 19-24, Cassino, Italy.* pp. 331-351. Informing Science Institute.

Bresciani, P., Perini, A., Giorgini, P., Giunchiglia, F. and Mylopoulos, J. (2004). Tropos: An Agent-oriented Software Development Methodology. *Autonomous Agents and Multi-Agent Systems,* Vol.8 (3), pp.203-236.

Brooks, F. P. (2010). *The Design of Design: Essays from a Computer Scientist.* Addison-Wesley.

Bruegge, B., Creighton, O., Reiß, M. and Stangl, H. (2008). Applying a Video-based Requirements Engineering Technique to an Airport Scenario. In: *3rd International Workshop on Multimedia and Enjoyable Requirements Engineering - Beyond Mere Descriptions and with More Fun and Games,* Barcelona, Spain. IEEE, pp. 9-11.

Burke Johnson, R. and Onwuegbuzie, A.J. (2004). Mixed Methods Research: A Research Paradigm Whose Time Has Come. *Educational Researcher.* Vol.33 (7), pp.14-26.

Bustard, D.W. and Greer, D. (1997). *SERUM - Software Engineering Risk: Understanding and Management* [online], Available from: http://www.cs.qub.ac.uk/~des.greer/serum.pdf [Accessed: 15 February 2014].

Buxton, B. (2007). *Sketching User Experiences.* Morgan Kaufmann.

Caine, M. (2011). *Experience Report: DSDM Atern delivers more than just Agility* [online], Available from: <http://www.mcpa.biz/wp-content/uploads/2011/12/PMI-Experience-Report-DSDM-Atern-Delivers-More-than-Just-Agility.pdf> [Accessed: 25 May 2013].

Cao, L. and Ramesh, B. (2008). Agile Requirements Engineering Practices: An Empirical Study. *IEEE Software*, Vol. 25 (1), pp. 60-67.

Cardozo, E., Neto, J.B.F.A., Barza, A., Franca, A. and Da Silva, F. (2010). SCRUM and Productivity in Software Projects: A Systematic Literature Review. *14th International Conference on Evaluation and Assessment in Software Engineering (EASE '10), UK.* British Computer Society, pp. 131-134.

Carmel, E., George, J. F., and Nunamaker, J. F. (1995). Examining the process of electronic-JAD. *Journal of End User Computing.* Vol.7(1), pp.13-22.

Carnes, W.E. (2011). *Highly Reliable Governance of Complex Socio-Technical Systems* [online], Available from: http://ccrm.berkeley.edu/pdfs_papers/DHSGWorkingPapersFeb16-2011/HighlyReliableGovernance-of-ComplexSocio-TechnicalSystems-WEC_DHSG-Jan2011.pdf [Accessed: 01/09/13].

Cau, A. (2005). Exploring XP's Efficacy in a Distributed Software Development Team. In: *International Conference on eXtreme Programming (XP 2005), 18-23 June, Sheffield, UK*. Berlin, Springer, pp. 317-318.

Chan, Y. and Reich, B. (2007). IT alignment: what have we learned? *Journal of Information Technology*. Vol. 22, pp.297–315.

Charmaz, K. (2006). *Constructing Grounded Theory: A Practical Guide through Qualitative Analysis.* Sage Publications.

Checkland, P. and Scholes (1990). *Soft Systems Methodology in Action*. New York, John Wiley and Sons.

Cheng, B. H. C. and Atlee, J.M. (2007). Research Directions in Requirements Engineering. In: *Future of Software Engineering (FOSE '07), 20 – 26 May, Minneapolis*, USA. Washington DC, USA, IEEE Computer Society, pp. 285–303.

Chow, T. and Cao, D.B. (2008). A survey of critical success factors in agile software projects. *Journal of Systems and Software*. Vol. 81 (6), pp. 961-971.

Chung, K. L., Nixon, B., Mylopoulos, J. and Yu, E. (2000). *Non-Functional Requirements in Software Engineering.* 5, Springer US, Kluwer Academic Publishers.

Chung, L., Weimin, M. and Cooper, K. (2006). Requirements Elicitation through Model-Driven Evaluation of Software Components. In: *5th International IEEE Conference on Commercial-off-the-Shelf (COTS)-Based Software Systems (ICCBBSS'06), 13-16 February, Orlando, Florida.* pp.187-196.

Clarke, A. (2005). *Situational Analysis: Grounded Theory after the Postmodern Turn.* Sage Publications.

Cockburn, A. (2004). *Crystal Clear: A Human-Powered Methodology for Small Teams.* Pearson Education.

Cohen, D.H. (2010). *For arguments sake* [online], Available from: http://www.ted.com/talks/daniel_h_cohen_for_argument_s_sake/transcript?language=en [Accessed: 27/01/2015].

Cohn, M. (2003). *Toward a Catalog of Scrum Smells* [online], Available from: http://www.serena.com/docs/agile/papers/Scrum-Smells.pdf [Accessed: 25 March 2013].

Coffin, R. and Lane, D. (2006). *A Practical Guide to Seven Agile Methodologies* [online], Available from: http://www.devx.com/architect/Article/32836/0/page/ [Accessed: 19 May 2013].

Conboy, K. and Duarte, V. (2010). Scaling Agile to Lean -Track Summary. In: *1st International Conference on Lean Enterprise Software Systems (LESS), Helsinki, Finland.* Berlin, Springer, pp.1-2.

Conger, S. (1994). The New Software Engineering. USA, Wadsworth publishing company.

Corrigan, C. (2012). *Consulting in Organizational and Community Development* [Online], Available from: http://www.chriscorrigan.com/openspace/whatisos.html [Accessed: 30 January 2012].

Cooke, J.L. (2013). *The Power of the Agile Business Analyst: 30 surprising ways  a business analyst can add value to your Agile development team.* IT Governance Publishing.

Cottmeyer, M. and Lee Henson, V. (2010). *The Agile Business Analyst.* Whitepaper. The Agile Project Management Company, VersionOne.

Coughlan, J., Lycett, M. and Macredie, R.D. (2003). Communication Issues in Requirements Elicitation: A Content Analysis of Stakeholder Experiences. *Information and Software Technology.* Vol.45 (8), June, pp. 525-537.

Coughlan, J. and Macredie, R.D. (2002). Effective Communication in Requirements Elicitation: A Comparison of Methodologies. *Journal of Requirements Engineering.* Vol.7(2), pp. 47-60.

Coulin, C., Sahraoui, A. and Zowghi, D. (2005a). Towards a Collaborative and Combinational Approach to Requirements Elicitation within a Systems Engineering Framework. In: *18th International Conference on Systems Engineering (ISCEng '05), 16-18 August, Toulouse, France.* IEEE, pp.456-461.

Coulin, C., Zowghi, D. and Sahraoui, A. (2005b). A Lightweight Workshop-Centric Situational Approach for the Early Stages of Requirements Elicitation in Software Development. In: *1st International Workshop on Situational Requirements Engineering Processes (SREP '05), August 29-30, Paris, France.* University of Limerick, Ireland, pp.136-151.

Coutaz, J., Crowley, J.L., Dobson, S. and Garlan, D. (2005). Context is Key. *Communications of the ACM.* Vol.48(3), pp 49-53.

Cox, K., Hall, J.G. and Rapanotti, L. (2005). Editorial: A Roadmap of Problem Frames Research. *Information and Software Technology,* Vol. 47 (14), pp.891-902.

Coyle, S. and Conboy, K. (2009). A Study of Risk Managements in DSDM. In: *10th International Conference on eXtreme Programming (XP2009), May 25-29, Pula, Sardinia, Italy.* Berlin, Springer, pp.142-148.

Creswell, J. (2009). *Research Design: Qualitative, Quantitative and Mixed Methods Approaches.* 3rd Edition. Sage Publications.

Cross, N., Dorst, K. and Roozenburg, N. (1992). *Research in design thinking.* Delft University Press.

Cross, R., A. Parker., Prusak, L. and Borgatti, S.P.(2001). Knowing what we know: Supporting knowledge creation and sharing in social networks. *Organisational Dynamics.* Vol. 30(2), pp.100-120.

Crystal, A. and Ellington, B (2004). Task Analysis and Human-Computer Interaction: approaches, techniques, and levels of analysis. *In 10th Americas conference on Information Systems, New York.*

Cumps, B., Martens, D., DeBacker, M., Haesen, R., Viaene, S., Dedene, G., Baesensd, B. and Snoecka, M. (2006). *Predicting Business/ICT Alignment with AntMiner+.* KBI0708 Department of Decision Sciences and Information Management (KBI), Catholic University of Leuven.

Cutter Consortium. (2000). *Poor Project Management Number-one Problem of Outsourced E-projects* [Online], Available from: http://www.cutter.com/research/2000/crb001107.html[Accessed: March 24 2009].

Darke, P., and Shanks, G. (1996). Stakeholder Viewpoints in Requirements Definition: A Framework for Understanding Viewpoint Development Approaches. *Requirements Engineering.* Vol.1 (2), pp.88-105.

Davis, A., Dieste, O., Hickey, A., Juristo, N. and Moreno, A.M. (2006). Effectiveness of Requirements Elicitation Techniques: Empirical Results Derived from a Systematic Review. *In: 14th IEEE International Conference on Requirements Engineering, September 11-15, Colorado Springs.* Washington DC, USA, IEEE Computer Society, pp.176-185.

Davis, C.J., Fuller, RM., Tremblay, M.C. and Berndt D.J. (2006). Communication Challenges in Requirements Elicitation and the Use of the Repertory Grid Technique *Journal of Computer Information Systems.* Vol.46 (5), pp.78-86.

Dearborn, D. and Simon, H. (1958). Selective Perception: A Note on the Departmental Identification of Executives. *Sociometry.* Vol.21, pp.140-144.

Decker, B., Ras, E., Rech, J., Jaubert, P. and Rieth, M. (2007). Wiki-Based Stakeholder Participation in Requirements Engineering. *IEEE Software.* Vol. 24 (2), pp. 28-35.

Deemer, P. and Benefield, G. (2007). *The Scrum Primer. An Introduction to Agile Project Management with Scrum* [online], Available from: http://www.brianidavidson.com/agile/docs/scrumprimer121.pdf [Accessed 24 May 2013].

De Luca, J. (2007). *Jeff De Luca on Feature Driven Development* [online], Available from: http://www.it-agile.de/fileadmin/docs/FDD-Interview_en_final.pdf [Accessed: 26 May 2013].

Demchak, B. and Krueger, I. (2012). *A Model-Driven Engineering Approach to Requirement Elicitation for Policy-Reactive Cyberinfrastructures.* TR-CS2012-0988 University of California.

Den Hann, J. (2008). *8 Reasons Why Model-Driven Approaches (will) Fail* [online], Available from: http://www.infoq.com/articles/8-reasons-why-MDE-fails [Accessed: 15 February 2014].

Denscombe, M. (2003). *The Good Research Guide: For Small-Scale Social Research Projects.* 2nd Edition. Philadelphia, USA, Open University Press.

De Toni, A.F. and Nonino, F. (2010). Identifying Key Roles in the Informal Organisation: A Network Analysis Approach. *The Learning Organization Journal.* Vol.17(1), pp.86-103.

Dieste, O., Lopez, M. and Ramos, F. (2008). Updating a Systematic Review about Selection of Software Requirements Elicitation Techniques. In: *11th Workshop on Requirements Engineering (WER'08)* Barcelona, Spain. IEEE Computer Society, pp. 96 -103.

Dingsøyr, F. Bjørnsson, O. (2005). Using Open Space Technology as a Method to Share Domain Knowledge. In: Althoff, K.D., Dengel, A., Bergmann, R., Nick, M. & Roth-Berghofer, T. (eds), *WM 2005: 3rd International Conference on Professional Knowledge Management - Experiences and Visions, April 10-13. Kaiserslautern, Germany.* Kaiserslautern, DFKI, pp.102-106.

Dorst, K. and Cross, N. (2001). Creativity in the Design Process: Co-Evolution of Problem-Solution. *Design Studies.* Vol.22. pp.425–437.

DSDM Consortium. (2012). *Dynamic Systems Development Method* [online], Available from: http://www.dsdm.org [Accessed: 25 February 2012].

Duboc, L., Letier, E., Rosenblum, D.S. and Wicks, T. (2008). A Case Study in Eliciting Scalability Requirements. In: *16th International Conference on Requirements Engineering, 8-12 September, Catalunya, Spain.* Washington DC, USA, IEEE Computer Society, pp. 247-252.

Duggan, E.W. and Thachenkary, C. S. (2004). Integrating Nominal Group Technique and Joint Application Development for Improved Systems Requirements Determination. *Journal of Information and Management.* Vol. 41 (4), pp.399-411.

Dunne, C. (2011). The Place of the Literature Review in Grounded Theory Research. *International Journal of Social Research Methodology.* Vol. 14(2), pp. 111-124.

Dybå, T. and Dingsøyr, T. (2008). Empirical studies of agile software development: A systematic review. *Information and Software Technology.* Vol. 50 (9), August, pp. 833-859.

Easterbrook, S. (2004). *Requirements Elicitation Techniques* [Online], Available from: http://www.cs.toronto.edu/~sme/CSC2106S/slides/04-elicitation-techniques.pdf [Accessed: 20 October 2008].

Easterbrook, S., Yu, E., Aranda, J., Fan, Y., Horkoff, J., Leica, M., Qadir, R.A., (2005) Do Viewpoints Lead to Better Conceptual Models? An Exploratory Case Study. In: *13th International Conference on Requirements Engineering, 29 August- 2nd September Paris France.* Washington DC, USA, IEEE Computer Society, pp. 199-208.

Easterbrook, S. and Aranda, J. (2006). Case Studies for Software Engineering, Shanghai, China. In: *28th International Conference on Software Engineering (ICSE'06), May 20 – 28.* New York, ACM.

Easterbrook, S., Singer, J., Storey, M.A. and Damian, D. (2008). Selecting Empirical Methods for Software Engineering Research. In: Shull, F., Singer, J. and Sjøberg, D. J. K. (eds.) *Guide to Advanced Empirical Software Engineering.* London, Springer.

Elliot Sim, S., Alspaugh, T.A. and Al-Ani, B. (2007). Marginal Notes on Amethodical Requirements Engineering: What experts learned from experience? *16th IEEE International Requirements Engineering Conference, 8-12 September 2008, Barcelona, Catalunya, Spain.* Washington DC, USA, IEEE Computer Society.

Embrey, D. (2000). *Task Analysis Techniques [online],* Available from: http://www.cwsvt.com/ Conference/Functional%20Assessment/Task%20Analysis%20Techniques.pdf [Accessed: 15 October 2009].

Erdogmus, H., Morisio, M. and Torchiano, M. (2005). On the Effectiveness of the Test-First Approach to Programming. *IEEE Transactions in Software Engineering.* Vol. 31(3), pp.226-237.

Escalona, M.J. and Koch, N. (2004). Requirements Engineering for Web Applications - A Comparative Study. *Journal of Web Engineering.* Vol.2 (3), pp.193-212.

Feldt, R and Magazinius, A. (2010). Validity Threats in Empirical Software Engineering Research - An Initial Survey. In: *22nd International Conference on Software Engineering and Knowledge Engineering (SEKE 2010), July1-3, Redwood City, San Francisco Bay, CA, USA.* USA, Knowledge Systems Institute Graduate School, pp. 374-379.

Fennessy, G. and Burstein, F. (2000). Using Soft Systems as a Methodology for Researching Knowledge Management Problems. In: *1st International Conference on Systems Thinking in Management. Geelong, Australia.*

Finkelstein, A., Kramer, J., Nuseibeh, B., Finkelstein, L., Goedicke, M. (1992). Viewpoints: A Framework for Integrating Multiple Perspectives in Systems Development. *Journal of Software Engineering and Knowledge Engineering.* Vol.2 (1), pp. 31-58.

Finkelstein, A. (2000). Identifying and incorporating stakeholders in requirements engineering. *Magazine.* Department of Computer Science, University College London.

Finken, S. (2005). *Methods as technologies for producing knowledge: An encounter with cultural practices - reflections from a field study in a high-tech company.* (Ph.D.) thesis, Roskilde University, Denmark.

Fischer, G. (2004).Social creativity: turning barriers into opportunities for collaborative design. In Proceedings of the eighth conference on Participatory design. *Artful integration: interweaving media, materials and practices.* Vol.1. pp. 152–161.

Fox, J. and Clarke, S. (2009). Exploring approaches to dynamic adaptation. In: proceedings of the *2nd Workshop on Context-aware Adaptation Mechanisms for Pervasive and Ubiquitous Services, Lisbon,* June 12. ACM. pp 1-6.

Fraser, S., Alterhaug, B., Anderson, D., Larson, D. and Page, S. (2010). Collaboration in an Agile World. In*: 11th International Conference on Agile Processes in Software Engineering and Extreme Programming, (XP2010), Trondheim, Norway, June 1-4.* Berlin, Springer, pp.410-415.

Fredericks. E.M. (2013). Towards Run-Time Testing of Dynamic Adaptive Systems. In: Proceedings of the *8th International Symposium on Software Engineering for Adaptive and Self-Managing Systems SEAMS 2013, San Francisco, CA, USA.* IEEE. pp.169-174.

Fricker, S. (2010a). Requirements Value Chains: Stakeholder Management and Requirements Engineering in Software Ecosystems. In: 16th International Conference on *Requirements Engineering: Foundation for Software Quality REFSQ, Essen, Germany,* June 30 – July 02, vol.6182, pp. 60–66.

Fricker, S. and Glinz, M. (2010b). Comparison of Requirements Hand-Off, Analysis, and Negotiation: Case Study. In: *18th International Conference on Requirements Engineering, September 24th-28th, Sydney, Australia.* Washington DC, USA, IEEE Computer Society, pp. 167-176.

Fu, J., Bastani, F.B. and Yen, I.L. (2008). Model-Driven Prototyping Based Requirements Elicitation. In: Paech, B and Martell, C. (eds.). *Innovations for Requirements Analysis: From Stakeholders' Needs to Formal Designs.* Vol. 5320, pp. 43-61.

Gallardo-Valencia, R.E. and Elliot Sim, S. (2007). Planning and improvisation in software processes. *Crossroads Archive.* Vol.14(1).

Gauthier-Villars, D. and Michaels, D. (2007). EADS Considers a Simple Management Structure. *The Wall Street Journal.*

Gibbert, M. and Ruigrok, W. (2010). The "what" and "how" of case study rigor: Three strategies based on published research. *Organizational Research methods.* 13(4), pp. 710-737.

Giorgini, P., Massacci, F., Mylopoulos, J. and Zannone, N. (2006). Detecting and Mitigating Conflicts of Interest. In:*14th IEEE International Conference on Requirements Engineering (RE'06).* IEEE Computer Society, pp. 308-311.

Glaser, B.G. (1998). *Doing grounded theory: Issues and discussions.* Mill Valley, CA. Sociology Press.

Gleiberman, P. (2009). *Called to Community at Boeing* [online], Available from: http://www.oocities.org/athens/oracle/9215/bkboeing.htm [Accessed: April 25 2012].

Glinz, M. and Wieringa, R.J. (2007). Stakeholders in Requirements Engineering. *IEEE Computer Society*. Vol.24 (2), March/April, pp. 18-20.

Gnatzy, T., Warth, J., Von Der Gracht, H. and Darkow, I. (2011). Validating an innovative real-time Delphi approach - A Methodological Comparison between Real-time and Conventional Delphi Studies. *Technological Forecasting and Social Change,* Vol. 78, pp. 1681-1694.

Goedicke, M., Enders, B., Meyer, T. and Taentzer, G. (2000). *Viewpoint-Oriented Software Development: Tool support for integrating multiple perspectives by distributed graph transformation.* In: *6th International Conference on Tools and Algorithms for Construction and Analysis of Systems. (TACAS 2000), London, UK.* Berlin, Springer, pp. 43-47.

Goldsby, H.J., Sawyer, P., Bencomo, N., Cheng, B.H.C. and Hughes, D. (2008). Goal-Based Modeling of Dynamically Adaptive System Requirements. In: *15th IEEE International Conference on Engineering of Computer-Based Systems, Belfast, Northern Ireland, March 2008.* IEEE.

Gordon, T.J. (1994). *The Delphi Method [online],* Available from: http://www.gerenciamento.ufba. br/Downloads/delphi%20(1).pdf [Accessed: September 8th 2010].

Grenning, J. (2002). *Planning Poker or How to avoid Analysis Paralysis while Release Planning* [online], Available from: http://renaissancesoftware.net/files/articles/PlanningPoker-v1.1.pdf [Accessed: 05January 2013].

Grice, C. and Richards, K. (2010). *DSDM Atern Case Study: An Agile Approach to Software Systems Development for the Highways Agency* [online], Available from: http://agilekrc.com/wp-content/ uploads/2012/04/Highways-Agency-DSDM-Atern-Case-Study-2010.pdf [Accessed May 20 2013].

Grimm, F., Phalp, K., Vincent, J. and Beier, G. (2008). Enabling multi-stakeholder cooperative modelling in automotive software development and implications for model driven software development. In: *International Workshop on Business Support for MDA, (MDABIZ'08). July 03, Zurich, Switzerland.*

Grünbacher, P. (2006). Requirements Engineering for Web Applications. In: Kappel, G. Proll, B. Reich, S. Retschitzegger, W. (eds). *Web Engineering: The Discipline of Systematic Development of Web Applications.* John Wiley & Sons, pp.23-38.

Guba, E. G., and Lincoln, Y. S. (1994). Competing Paradigms in Qualitative Research. In Denzin, N. K., Lincoln, Y. S. (eds). *Handbook of qualitative research.* Thousand Oaks, CA, Sage, pp. 105-117.

Gunda, S.G. (2008). *Requirements Engineering Elicitation Techniques.* (Masters) thesis, University West, Department of Mathematics and Computer Science, Sweden.

Gunter, C.A., Gunter, E.L., Jackson, M. and Zave, P. (2000). *A reference model for requirements and specifications.* IEEE Software.

Gururajan, R. Gururajan, V. Soar, J. (2005). *A program for collaborative research in ageing and aged care informatics.* Centre for Ageing and Agedcare Informatics Research. University of Southern Queensland, Australia.

Hall, J.G., Rapanotti, L. and Jackson M. (2010). *Problem Oriented Software Engineering.* The Open University.

Harman, M., Burke, E., Clark, J.A. and Yao, X. (2012). Dynamic Adaptive Search Based Software Engineering. In: *6th International Symposium on Empirical Software Engineering and Measurement (ESEM'12), Lund, Sweden.* ACM.

Herman, M. (2002). *Inviting Organization: Evolution is now and open* space [online], Available from: http://www.michaelherman.com/publications/executive.pdf [Accessed: 04 June 2009].

Herman, M. and Corrigan, C. (2002). *Open Space Technology: A User's NON-Guide* [online], Available from: http://www.chriscorrigan.com/openspace/nonguide5.pdf [Accessed: 09 August 2009].

Herman, M. (2003). *Open Space Technology: Practice Resources for Inviting Organisation* [online]. Available from: http://www.michaelherman.com/publications/PracticeGuide.pdf [Accessed: 21 January 2012].

Herman, M. (2006). *Open Space Technology: An Inviting Guide 4th edition* [online], Available from: http://www.michaelherman.com/publications/inviting_guide.pdf [Accessed: 09 October 2009].

Herman, M. (2013). *Software in Open Space* [online]. Available from: http://www.michaelherman.com/cgi/wiki.cgi?SoftwareDevelopmentInOpenSpace [Accessed: 21 March 2013].

Hess, D. (2007). *Heterogeneous and homogeneous groups in the innovation process.* Oldenburg Studies for Europeanisation and Transnational Regulation, Vol.5. CETRO, Oldenburg, Germany.

Hibbs, C. and Jewett, S. (2010). Lean Software Development: One Step at a Time. *Systems and Software Technology Conference (SSTC '10), Salt Lake City, Utah.* Washington DC, USA, IEEE Computer Society.

Hickey, A. and Davis, A. (2004). A Unified Model of Requirements Elicitation. *The Journal of Management Information Systems.* Vol.20 (4), pp.65-84.

Hiekkanen, K., Helnius, M., Korhonen, J. and Patricio, E. (2012). Business and IT: Beyond Alignment. In: *8th European Conference on Management Leadership and Governance, 08-09 November, Pafos, Cyprus.*

Highsmith, J. (2002). What Is Agile Software Development? *Crosstalk: The Journal of Defense Software Engineering.* Vol. 15 (10), pp.4-9.

Hoda, R., Noble, J. and Marshal, S. (2010a). What Language Does Agile Speak? In: *11th International Conference on Agile Development, Trondheim, Norway.* Berlin, Springer, pp.387-388.

Hoda, R., Noble, J. and Marshal, S. (2010b). Agile Undercover: When Customers Don't Collaborate. In: *11th International Conference on Agile Development, Trondheim, Norway*. Berlin, Springer, pp.73-87.

Hoda, R., Noble, J. and Marshall, S. (2011). Supporting Self-Organizing Agile Teams: What's Senior Management Got To Do With It? In: *12th International Conference on Agile Software Development, Madrid, Spain*. Berlin, Springer.

Hoffman, J. J., M. L. Hoelscher, and Sherif, K. (2005). Social capital, knowledge management, and sustained superior performance. *Journal of Knowledge Management*. Vol. 9(3), pp.93-100.

Holman, P. (2010). Tools for Opening Space: A Collection of Open Space Technology Resources [online], Available from: http://peggyholman.com/wp-content/uploads/2010/04/OST-Outline-V3.pdf [Accessed: 09 March 2013].

Holmes, J. (2008). Geographic distributed agile teams: Enabling Individuals and Interactions with processes and tools [online], Available from: http://www.ibm.com/developerworks/rational/library/edge/08/feb08/lines_barnes_holmes_ambler [Accessed: 21 May 2013].

Hossain, E., Bannerman, P. L., Jeffrey, D.R. (2011). Scrum Practices in Global Software Development: A Research Framework. In: *12th International Conference on Product-Focused Software Process, (PROFES'11), Torre, Canne, Italy*. Berlin, Springer, pp. 88-102.

Hossain, E., Babar, M.A. and Hye-young, P. (2009). Using Scrum in Global Software Development: A Systematic Literature Review. *4th International Conference on Global software Engineering (ICGSE '09), 13-16 August.* Washington DC, USA, IEEE Computer Society, pp. 175-184.

Hughes, J., O'Brien, J., Rodden, T., Rouncefield, M. and Sommerville, I (1994). Presenting Ethnography in the Requirements process. SE/5/1994, Department of Sociology, University of Lancaster, Software Engineering Research Group. Institute of Electrical and Electronic Engineers IEEE. (1990). Standard 610.12:1990. *Standard Glossary of Software Engineering Terminology*. New York, IEEE.

IEEE. (2004). *Guide to the Software Engineering Body of Knowledge* [online], Available from: http://swebok.org [Accessed: 10/12/2014].

IIBA. (2009). *Business Analysis Body of Knowledge version 2.0* [online]. Available from: http://www.iiba.org/ [Accessed: 21/12/2014].

ISO/IEC 12207:2002/FDAM 2. (2004). *Information Technology - Software Life Cycle Processes.* International Organisation for Standardisation, Geneva, Switzerland.

Jablin, F. M. and L. L. Putnam (2001). *The new handbook of organizational communication: Advances in theory, research and methods.* Thousand Oakes, CA, Sage Publications.

Jackson. M. (1995). *Software Requirements and Specifications: A lexicon of principles, practices and prejudices.* Addison-Wesley.

Jackson, M. (2001). *Problem Frames: Analyzing and Structuring Software Development Problems.* Addison-Wesley.

Jaffee, D. (2001). *Organization theory: Tension and change.* Boston, McGraw-Hill.

Jain, A. (2012). *Cultural Influences on Software Development: Evaluation of the impact of having cross-cultural teams in software development projects* [online], Available from: https://www.google.ie/?gws_rd=ssl#q=Jain+A+2012+Cultural+Influences+on+Software+Development+Evaluation+of+the+impact+of+having+cross-cultural+teams+in+software+development+projects [Accessed: 21 January 2013].

Jatain, A. and Goel, S. (2009). Comparison of Domain Analysis Methods, in Software Reuse. *International Journal of Information Technology and Knowledge Management.* Vol. 2 (2), pp. 347-352.

Jeffries, R., Anderson, A. and Hendrickson, C. (2001). Extreme Programming Installed. Addison-Wesley.

Johnson, C.W. and Holloway, C.M. (2006). Questioning the Role of Requirements Engineering in the Causes of Safety-Critical Software Failures. In: *1st Institution of Engineering and Technology System Safety Conference, London, UK, June 2006.* Washington DC, USA, IEEE Computer Society, pp. 352-361.

Jorgensen, J.B., Norskov, K. and Ruben, N.M. (2011). Requirements Engineering and Stakeholder Management in the Development of a Consumer Product for a Large Industrial Customer. In: *19th international Conference on Requirements Engineering, August 29-September 2nd, Trento, Italy.* Washington DC, USA, IEEE Computer Society.

Kabbedijk, J., Brinkkemper, S., Jansen and Van Der Veldt, B. (2009). Customer Involvement in Requirements Management: Lessons from Mass Market Software Development. In: *17th International Conference on Requirements Engineering, August 31 - September 4th, Atlanta, Georgia, USA.* Washington DC, USA, IEEE Computer Society, pp. 281-286.

Kanyaru, J.M., Coles, M., Jeary, S. and Phalp, K. (2008). Using visualisation to elicit domain information as part of the Model Driven Architecture approach. *International Workshop on Business Support for MDA, (MDABIZ'08). July 03, Zurich, Switzerland.*

Keller, T. (2011). *Contextual Requirements Elicitation: An Overview* [online], Available from: https://files.ifi.uzh.ch/rerg/amadeus/teaching/courses/re_seminar_fs11/thomas_keller-contextual_requirements_elicitation.pdf [Accessed: 21 February 2013].

Kettelhut, M. C. (1993). JAD methodology and group dynamics. *Information Systems Management.* Vol.14(3), pp.46-53.

Kemmis, S. and McTaggart, R. (2005). Participatory Action Research: Communicative Action and the Public Sphere. In: Denzin, N. K. and Lincoln, Y. S. (eds.) *Handbook of Qualitative Research.* 3rd Edition. Beverley Hills, CA, Sage Publications.

Khurum, M. and Gorschek, T. (2009). A Systematic Review of Domain Analysis Solutions for Product Lines. *The Journal of Systems and Software.* Vol. 82, pp. 1982-2003.

Kieras, D. (2004). Task Analysis and the Design of Functionality. *In: Tucker, A.B. (eds). Computer Science Handbook.* 2nd edition. USA, ACM.

Kitchenham, B., Linkman, S., and Law, D. (1997). DESMET: A Methodology for Evaluating Software Engineering Methods and Tools. *Computing and Control Engineering Journal.* 8(3), pp.120-126.

Klein, H.K. and Myers, M.D. (1999) A Set of Principles for Conducting and Evaluating Interpretive Field Studies in Information Systems. *MIS Quarterly.* Vol.23 (1), pp. 67-94.

Kling, R. (1980). Social Analyses of Computing: Theoretical Perspectives in Recent Empirical Research. *ACM Computing Surveys.* Vol.12(1), pp.61–110.

Kniberg, H. (2007). *An Agile War Story: Scrum and XP from the Trenches. InfoQ Enterprise Software Development Series.* USA, C4media.

Koshy E., Koshy V. and Waterman H. (2010). *Action research for health care.* London, SAGE.

Kotonya, G., and Sommerville, I. (1992). Viewpoints on Requirements Definition. *Journal of Software Engineering.* Vol.7 (6), pp. 375-387.

Kotonya, G. (1997) *Practical Experience with Viewpoint-Oriented Requirements Specification.* CSEG/19/1997, Lancaster, UK, Cooperative Systems Engineering Group.

Kruchten, P. (2004). *The Rational Unified Process: An Introduction 3rd Edition.* Boston, Addison-Wesley.

Kujala, S. (2003). User Involvement: A Review of the Benefits and Challenges. *Behaviour and Information Technology,* Vol.22 (1), pp.1-16.

Kumar Gorakavi, P. (2009). *Build your Project Using Feature Driven Development* [online], Available from: http://www.asapm.org/asapmag/articles/A4_AboutFDD.pdf [Accessed: 18 December 2009].

Kurapati, N., Manyam, V.S.C. and Petersen, K. (2012). Agile Software Development Practice Adoption Survey. In: *13th International Conference on Agile Processes and eXtreme Programming (XP2012), Malmo, Sweden, May 21-25.* Berlin, Springer.

Kurland, N. B. and L. H. Pelled (2000). Passing the word: Toward a model of gossip and power in the workplace. *Academy of Management Review.* Vol. 25(1), pp. 429-458.

Kvale, S. (1996). *Interviews: An Introduction to Qualitative Research Interviewing.* Thousand Oaks, CA, Sage Publications.

Kivinen, T. (2008). Applying QFD to Improve the Requirements and Project Management in Small-scale Project. (MSc. ) thesis. University of Tampere, Finland

Lane, M.T., Fitzgerald, B. and Agerfalk, P.J. (2012). Identifying Lean Software Development Values. In: *21st European Conference on Information Systems (ECIS 2012), Barcelona, Spain.*

Langer, E. (1975). Illusion of Control. *Journal of Personality and Social Psychology.* Vol.32(2), pp.311-328.

Lavazza, L., Morasca, S., Taibi, D. and Tosi, D. (2010). Applying Scrum in an OSS Development Process: An Empirical Evaluation. In: *11th International Conference on Agile Processes in Software Engineering and Extreme Programming (XP2010)*. Berlin, Springer, pp. 147-159.

Leffingwell, D. and Widrig, D. (2003). *Managing Software Requirements: A Use Case Approach.* 2nd Edition. Pearson Education.

Leffingwell, D. (2011). *Agile Software Requirements: Lean Requirements Practices for Teams Programs and the Enterprise.* Addison-Wesley.

Lehtola, L., Kauppinen, M. and Vähäniitty, J. (2007). Strengthening the Link between Business Decisions and RE: Long-term Product Planning in Software Product Companies. In: *15th International Conference on Requirements Engineering, New Delhi, India, 15th-19th October.* IEEE Computer Society, pp. 153-162.

Lemaire, D. and Andersson, B. (2010). The Business Behaviour Model. In: *5th International Workshop on Business/IT Alignment and Interoperability, (BUSITAL'10). June 07, Hammamet, Tunisia.* Vol 599, pp. 31-45.

Lencastre, M., Araujo, J., Moreira, A. and Castro, J. (2006). Analyzing Crosscutting in the Problem Frames Approach. In: *International Workshop on Advances and Applications of Problem Frames (IWAAPF '06) New York.* ACM, pp.59-64.

Levina, N. (2005). Collaborating on Multiparty Information Systems Development Projects: A Collective Reflection-in-Action View. *Information Systems Research.* Vol.16(2), pp.109–130.

Letier, E. (2001).*Reasoning about Agents in Goal-Oriented Requirements Engineering.* (Ph.D.) thesis, Universite Catholique de Louvain, Belgium.

Li, Z. (2007). *Progressing Problems from Requirements to Specifications in Problem Frames.* (Ph.D.) thesis, The Open University.

Lines, M. (2008).Bringing Discipline to the Agile Lifecycle [online], Available from: http://www.ibm.com/developerworks/rational/library/edge/08/feb08/lines_barnes_holmes_ambler/ [Accessed: 21 May 2013].

Linstone, H. A. and Turoff, M. (2002). *The Delphi Method: Techniques and Applications* [online], Available from: http://is.njit.edu/pubs/delphibook/delphibook.pdf [Accessed: 24 February 2013]

Long, A. and Hughes, G. (2011). Users and Design Review – What Mock-ups Offer. In: *47th Annual Conference on Human Factors and Ergonomics Society of Australia (HFESA): Synergy in Sydney: Creating and Maintaining Partnerships.7-9 November, Australia.* Curran Associates Inc.

Luftman, J., Kempaiah, R. and Nash, E. (2006). Key Issues for IT Executives. *MIS Quarterly Executive.* Vol. 5(2), pp. 81–101.

Lunesu, M.I. (2013). *Process Software Simulation Model of Lean-Kanban Approach.* (Ph.D.) thesis, University of Cagliari, Italy.

Lussenburg, V., Van Der Storm, T., Vinju, J. and Warmer, J. (2010). Mod4J: A Qualitative Case Study of Model-Driven Software Development. In: Petriu, D.C., Rouquette, N. and Haugen, O. (eds.). *Model Driven Engineering Languages and Systems.* Springer, pp.346-360.

Lutters, W.G. and Seaman, C.B. (2007). Revealing Actual Documentation Usage in Software Maintenance through War Stories. *Information and Software Technology.* Vol. 49(6), pp.576–587.

Macaulay, L.A. (1996). *Requirements Engineering in Applied Computing.* New York, Springer.

Madsen, S. and Kautz, K. (2002) Applying System Development Methods in Practice—The RUP Example. In: Proceedings of the *11th International Conference on Information Systems Development, Methods and Tools—Theory and Practice, Riga, Latvia.*

Mahaux, M and Mavin, A. (2013a). A New Paradigm for Applied Requirements Engineering Research. In: *21st International Conference on Requirements Engineering, Rio de Janeiro.* IEEE. pp. 353-356.

Mahaux, M., Gotel, O., Mavin, A., Nguyen, L., Mich, L. and Schmid, K. (2013b). Collaborative Creativity in Requirements Engineering: Analysis and Practical Advice. *7th International Conference on Research Challenges in Information Science (RCIS), Paris France.* IEEE. pp.1-10.

Maiden, N. and Robertson, S. (2005). Integrating Creativity into Requirements Processes: Experiences with an Air Traffic Management System. In: *13th International Conference on Requirements Engineering, August 29th - September 2nd, France.* Washington DC, USA, IEEE Computer Society, pp. 105-116.

Mannio, M. and Nikula, U. (2001). *Requirements Elicitation Using a Combination of Prototyping and Scenarios.* Research Report 5. Telecom Business Research Center, Lappeenranta University of Technology, Finland.

Marchenko, A. and Abrahamsson, P. (2008). Scrum in a Multiproject Environment: An Ethnographically-Inspired Case Study on the Adoption Challenges. *Agile Conference (AGILE'08), Toronto.* Washington DC, USA, IEEE Computer Society pp. 15-26.

Marchesi, M. (2005) *The New XP* [online], Available from: http://laerer.rhs.dk/susanneru/agile%20 methodologies/TheNewXP.pdf [Accessed: 10 January 2013].

Martin, A. and Loos, P. (2008). Software support for the Computation Independent Modelling in the MDA context. In: *International Workshop on Business Support for MDA, (MDABIZ'08). July 03, Zurich, Switzerland.*

Martin, A., Biddle, R. and Noble, J. (2009a). The XP Customer Team: A grounded theory. In: *Agile Conference (AGILE'09), August 24-28, Chicago, USA.* Washington DC, USA, IEEE Computer Society, pp.33-40.

Martin, A., Biddle, R. and Noble, J. (2009b). XP Customer Practices: A grounded theory. In: *Agile Conference (AGILE'09), August 24-28, Chicago, USA.* Washington DC, USA, IEEE Computer Society, pp.33-40.

Martz, B., Neil, T. and Biscaccianti, A. (2003). TradeSmith: An Exercise to Demonstrate the Illusion of Control in Decision Making. Decision Sciences *Journal of Innovative Education.* Vol.1 (2), pp.273-287.

Marczak, S. and Damian, D. (2011). How interaction between Roles Shapes the Communication Structure in Requirements-driven Collaboration. In: *19th international Conference on Requirements Engineering, August 29-September 2nd, Trento, Italy.* Washington DC, USA, IEEE Computer Society, pp. 47-56.

Mathiassen, L. and Nielsen (1989). Soft Systems and Hard Contradictions: Approaching the Reality of Information Systems. *Journal of Applied Systems.* Vol.16.

Maurer, F., Hellmann, T.D. (2013). People-Centred Software Development: An Overview of Agile Methodologies. In: De Lucia, A. and Ferrucci, F. (eds.) *Software Engineering.* Vol. 7171, pp.185-215.

Maqsood, T., Finegan, A.D. and Walker, D.H.T. (2001). *Five case studies applying Soft Systems Methodology to Knowledge Management* [online], Available from: http://eprints.qut.edu.au/27456/1/27456.pdf [Accessed: 12 January 2014].

McBryan, T., McGee-Lennon, M. R., and Gray, P. (2008). An Integrated Approach to Supporting Interaction Evolution in Home Care Systems. In: *1st international Conference on Pervasive Technologies Related to Assistive Environments (PETRA'08), July 15-19, Athens, Greece.* New York, ACM, pp.1-8.

McGee-Lennon, M.R. (2008). Requirements Engineering for Home Care Technology. In: *SIGCHI Conference on Human Factors in Computing Systems (CHI'08), Florence, Italy.* New York, ACM, pp. 1439 - 1442.

McGhee, G., Marland, G.R. and Atkinson, J. (2007). Grounded theory research: Literature reviewing and reflexivity. *Journal of Advanced Nursing.* Vol.60(3), pp. 334–342.

McGill, T. (2005). The Effect of End User Development on End User Success. In: Mahmood, M.A. (eds), *Advanced Topics in End User Computing.* Vol. 4. Idea Group Inc.

Melis, M. (2006). A Software Process Simulation Model of Extreme Programming. (Ph.D.) thesis, University of Cagliari, Italy.

Miller, M.G. (2008). *IT Project Success & Failure - The Analysis of IT Project Success: Understanding Previous Performance to Create Future Prosperity.* (B.Sc.) Thesis, Loughborough University, Leicestershire UK.

Miller, G. and Williams, L. (2008) *Personas: Moving Beyond role-Based Requirements Engineering* [online], Available from: http://agile.csc.ncsu.edu/SEMaterials/Personas.pdf [Accessed: 21 May 2013].

Mnkandla, E. (2009). About Software Engineering Frameworks and Methodologies. In: *AFRICON'09*, Nairobi, September 23-25, pp.1-5.

Moe, N.B. and Dingsøyr, T. (2008). Scrum and Team Effectiveness: Theory and Practice. In: *9th International conference in Software Engineering and Extreme Programming (XP2008), Limerick, Ireland.* Berlin, Springer, pp.11-20.

Moe, N.B., Dingsøyr, T and Dybå, T. (2009). A Teamwork Model for Understanding an Agile Team: A Case study of a Scrum Project. *Information and Software Technology.* Vol.52 (5), pp. 480-491.

Mohammadi, S., Nikkhahan, B. and Sohrabi, S. (2009). Challenges of User Involvement in Extreme Programming Project. *International Journal of Software Engineering and its Application.* Vol.3 (1), pp.19-32.

Mohammadi, N.G., Alebrahim, A., Weyer, T., Heisel, M. and Pohl, K. (2013). A framework for Combining Problem Frames and Goal Models to Support Context Analysis during Requirements Engineering. In: Cuzzocrea, A., Kittl, C., Simos, D.E., Weippl, E. and Xu, L. (eds.). *Availability, Reliability, and Security in Information Systems and HCI.* Vol.8127, Springer, pp.272-288.

Molina, J. L. (2001). *The Informal Organisation Chart in Organisations: An Approach from the Social Network Analysis* [online], Available from: http://www.insna.org/PDF/Connections/ v24/2001_I-1_78-91.pdf [Accessed: 01/12/14].

Moniruzzaman, A.B.M. and Hossain, S. A. (2013). Comparative Study on Agile Software Development Methodologies. *Global Journal of Computer Science and Technology.* Vol.13(7).

Moreira, A., Araujo, J. and Rashid, A. (2005). A Concern-Oriented Requirements Engineering Model. In: *13th International Conference on Requirements Engineering, August 29th - September 2nd, La Sorbonne, France.* Washington DC, USA, IEEE Computer Society, pp. 293-308.

Müller, M.M. and Tichy, W.F. (2001). Case Study: Extreme Programming in a University Environment. In: *23rd International Conference on Software Engineering, May 12-19, Toronto.* Washington DC, USA, IEEE Computer Society, pp. 537-544.

Nasir, M.H.N. and Sahibuddin, S. (2011). Critical Success Factors for Software Projects: A comparative study. *Scientific Research and Essays.* Vol.6 (10), pp. 2174-2186.

Nathaniel, A.K. (2006). Thoughts on the literature review and GT. *Grounded Theory Review.* Vol.5(2/3), pp. 35–41.

Neill, C. and Laplante, A. (2003). Requirements Engineering: The State of the Practice. *IEEE Software.* Vol. 20(6), pp. 40-45.

Nerur, S., Mahapatra, R. and Mangalaraj, G. (2005). Challenges of Migrating to Agile Methodologies: Organizations must carefully assess their readiness before treading the path of agility. *Communications of the ACM.* Vol. 48 (5), pp.72-78.

Newell, A. F., Carmichael, A., Morgan, M., and Dickinson, A. (2006). The use of Theatre in Requirements Gathering and Usability Studies. *Interactive Computing.* Vol. 18 (5), pp.996-1011.

Nguyen, L. and Swatman, P.A. (2003). *Managing the requirements engineering process. Requirements Engineering.* Vol. 8, (1), pp. 55–68.

Nguyen, L. and Cybulski, J. (2008). Learning to Become a Creative Systems Analyst. In: Schmorrow, D., Cohn, J. and Nicholson, D. (eds), *The PSI Handbook of Virtual Environments for Training and Education: Developments for the Military and Beyond.* Praeger.

Niknafs, A. and Berry, D.M. (2012). The Impact of Domain Knowledge on the Effectiveness of Requirements Idea Generation during Requirements Elicitation. In: *20th International Conference on Requirements Engineering, September 24th-28th, Chicago, Illinois, USA.* Washington DC, USA, IEEE Computer Society, pp. 181-190.

Niu , N. and Easterbrook, S. (2007). So, You Think You Know Others' Goals? A repertory grid study. *IEEE Software.* Vol.24 (2), pp. 53-61.

Norfolk, D. (2011). *IT Governance: Managing Information Technology for Business* 2nd edition. London, Thorogood Publishing.

Nuseibeh, B., Easterbrook, S. (2000). Requirements Engineering: A Roadmap. In: *Conference on the Future of Software Engineering ICSE Limerick, Ireland.* New York, USA, ACM, pp.35-46.

Obendorf, H. and Finck, M. (2008). Scenario-based usability engineering techniques in agile development processes. *In: Extended Abstracts on Human Factors in Computing Systems Florence, Italy, (CHI '08) April 05 - 10.* New York, ACM, pp.2159-2166.

O'Connor, D. and Cooper, M. (2005). Participatory Processes: Creating a "Marketplace of Ideas" with Open Space Technology. *The Public Sector Innovation Journal*, Vol. 10(1).

OMG. (2014). *Object Management Group.* [Online]. Available from: http://www.omg.org/mda [Accessed: 15 February 2014].

Owen, H. (1995). *Tales from Open Space.* Maryland, USA, Abbot Publishing.

Owen, H. (2008). *Open Space Technology: A User Guide.* 3rd Edition. Berrett-Koehler.

Paasivaara, M, Durasiewicz, S. and Lassenius, C. (2008). Using Scrum in a Globally Distributed Project: A Case Study. *Software Process Improvement and Practice.* Vol. 13 (6), pp. 527-544.

Pacheco, C. and Garcia, I. (2012). A systematic literature review of stakeholder identification methods in requirements elicitation. *The Journal of Systems and Software.* Vol.85. pp. 2171-2181.

Pahl, G. and Beitz, W. (1996). *Engineering Design: A Systematic Approach.* Springer.

Palmer, S.R. and Felsing, J.M. (2002). *A Practical Guide to Feature Driven Development.* Upper Saddle River, NJ, Prentice Hall.

Pandey, S. K. and Mustafa, K. (2010). Recent Advances in SRE Requirements Research. *International Journal on Computer Science and Engineering.* Vol.2 (4), pp.1079-1085.

Pang, J. and Blair, L. (2004). Refining Feature Driven Development - A methodology for early aspects. In: Tekinerdogan, B., Clements, P., Moreira, A. and Araujo, J. (eds.). *Early Aspects: Aspect-Oriented Requirements Engineering and Architecture Design.* pp. 86-91.

Patel, N.V. (1995). Application of Soft Systems Methodology to the Real World Process of Teaching and Learning. *International Journal of Educational Management.* Vol.9 (1). pp. 13-23.

Peak, D. and Guynes, C.S. (2003). Improving Information Quality Through IT Alignment Planning. A Case Study. *Journal of Information Systems Management.* Vol. 20(4), pp. 22-29.

Perjons, E. (2011). *Model-Driven Process Design: Aligning Value Networks, Enterprise Goals, Services and IT Systems.* Ph.D. (thesis), Stockholm University, Sweden.

Petersen, K. (2012). A Palette of Lean Indicators to Detect Waste in Software Maintenance: A Case Study. In: *13th International Conference on Agile Processes and eXtreme Programming (XP2012), Malmo, Sweden, May 21-25.* Berlin, Springer, pp. 108-122.

Peterson, L. (2009). *Opening Space at the Bank of Montreal* [online], Available from: http://www.oocities.org/athens/oracle/9215/bkbom.htm [Accessed: 30 April 2013].

Phalp, K. and Cox, K. (2000). Picking the right problem frame - an empirical study. *Empirical Software Engineering Journal,* Vol. 5(3), 215–228.

Phalp, K., Jeary, S., Vincent, J., Kanyaru, J.M. and Crowle, S. (2007). Supporting Stakeholders in the MDA Process. In: *15th International Conference on Software Quality and Management, Tampere.* The British Computer Society.

Pietri, W. (2004). *An XP Team Room* [online], Available from: http://www.scissor.com/resources/teamroom.htm [Accessed: 06 October 2008].

Plickert, G., Cote, R.R. and Wellman, B. (2007). It's not who you know, its how you know them: Who exchanges what with whom? *Social Networks.* Vol. 29(3), pp. 405-429.

Poernomo, I., Tsaramirsis, G and Zuna, V. (2008). A methodology for requirements analysis at CIM level. In: *International Workshop on Business Support for MDA, (MDABIZ'08). July 03, Zurich, Switzerland.*

Poppendieck, M. (2002). *Principles of Lean Thinking* [online] Available from: http://www. gregoryneilassociates.com/articles/lean_thinking.pdf [Accessed: 24 May 2013].

Poppendieck, M. and Poppendieck, T. (2003a). *Lean Software Development: An Agile Toolkit.* Upper Saddle River, NJ, Addison Wesley.

Poppendieck, T. (2003b). *The Agile Customer's Toolkit* [online], Available from: http://www.torak. com/site/files/The%20Agile%20Customer%E2%80%99s%20Toolkit.pdf [Accessed: 21 April 2013].

Power, K. (2010). Software Development: A Stakeholder Approach. In: *11th International Conference in Extreme Programming, Trondheim, Norway, June 1 – 4.* Berlin, Springer, pp. 405-406.

Preece, J., Rogers, Y. and Sharp, H. (2002). *Interaction Design: Beyond Human-Computer Interaction.* New York, John Wiley and Sons.

Pressman, R.S. (2000). *Software Engineering: A Practitioner's Approach 5th edition.* McGraw-Hill.

Pries-Heje, J., Baskerville, R., Ramesh, B. and Levine, L. (2008). Advances in Information Systems Development: From Discipline and Predictability to Agility and Improvisation. In: Avison, D., Kasper, G.M., Pernici, B., Ramos, I. and Roode, D. (eds), *Advances in Information Systems Research, Education and Practice.* Vol. 24. pp. 53-75.

Qadir, M.M., Asghar, M.I. and Ghayyur, S.A.K. (2009). Scaling Critical Success Factors for Requirements Engineering in the Development of Large Scale Systems. *International Journal of Reviews in Computing (IJRIC).* Vol.1, December 2009.

Qasaimeh, M., Mehrfard, H. and Hamou-Lhadj, A. (2008). Comparing Agile Software Processes Based on the Software Development Project Requirements. In: *the International Conference on Computational Intelligence for Modelling Control and Automation (CIMCA '08), Vienna, Austria, 10 – 12 December.* Washington DC, USA, IEEE Computer Society, pp.49-54.

IBM (2001). *Rational Software - Rational Unified Process: Best Practices for Software Development Teams* [online], Available from: http://www.ibm.com/developerworks/rational/library/253.html [Accessed: 25 November 2012].

Raatikainen, M., Mannisto, T., Tommila, T. and Valkonen, J. (2011). Challenges for Requirements engineering – A Case Study in Nuclear Energy Domain. In: *19th international Conference on*

*Requirements Engineering, August 29-September 2nd, Trento, Italy.* Washington DC, USA, IEEE Computer Society, pp.253-258.

Racheva, Z., Daneva, M., Sikkel, K., Wieringa, R. and Herrmann, A. (2010). Do We Know Enough about Requirements Prioritization in Agile Projects: Insights from a Case Study. In: *18th International Conference on Requirements Engineering, September 27th - October 1st, Sydney, Australia.* Washington DC, USA, IEEE Computer Society, pp. 147-156.

Raghavan, S., Zelesnik, G. and Ford, G. (1994). *Lecture Notes on Requirements Elicitation.* CMU/SEI-94-EM-10.Software Engineering Institute, Carnegie Mellon University.

Rajagopal, P., Roger, L., Ahlswede, T., Chiang, C. and Karolak, D. (2005). A New Approach to Software Requirements Elicitation. In: *6th International Conference on Software Engineering, Artificial Intelligence, Networking and Parallel/Distributed Computing, Dalian, China.* Washington DC, USA, IEEE Computer Society, pp. 32-42.

Ralph, P. (2010). *The Fundamentals of Software Design Science.* Thesis (Ph.D.). The University of British Columbia, Vancouver.

Ralph, P. (2013). *The Two Paradigms of Software Design* [online]. Available from: http://dx.doi.org/10.2139/ssrn.2238571 [Accessed: 25/05/2013].

Rech, J. and Schmitt, M. (2008). Embedding Defect and Traceability Information in CIM and PIM-Level Software Models. In: *International Workshop on Business Support for MDA, (MDABIZ'08). July 03, Zurich, Switzerland.*

Regev, G. (2003).*A Systemic Paradigm for Early IT System Requirements Based on Regulation Principles: The Lightswitch Approach.* (PhD) thesis, Swiss Federal Institute of Technology, Switzerland.

Regev, G. and Wegmann, A. (2005). Where do Goals Come from: The Underlying Principles of Goal-oriented Requirements Engineering. In: *13th International Conference on Requirements Engineering, August 29th - September 2nd, France.* Washington DC, USA, IEEE Computer Society, pp. 253-262.

Reinhartz-Berger, I. and Sturm, A. (2008). Enhancing UML Models: A Domain Analysis Approach. *Journal of Database Management.* Vol.19 (1), pp. 74-94.

Reinikainen, L. (2001). *Elicitation of Customer Requirements with Group Methods in Software Engineering.* (MSc.) thesis, Lappeenranta University of Technology, Finland.Richards, K. (2010). *Agile Project Management: Integrating DSDM Atern into an existing PRINCE2 environment* [online], Available from: http://www.dsdm.org/wp-content/uploads/2012/08/Integrating-DSDM-Atern-into-an-Existing-PRINCE2-Environment-2010.pdf [Accessed: 22 May 2013].

Rising, L, and Jonoff, N.S. (2000). The Scrum Software Development Process for Small Teams. *IEEE Software.* Vol.17 (4), pp.26-32.

Robbins, S. P., B. Millett., Cacioppe, R. and Waters-Marsh, T. (2001). *Organizational behaviour.* Frenchs Forrest, Prentice Hall, Pearson Education.

Roberts, S., Basi, T., Drazin, A. and Wherton, J.(2007). *Connections: Mobility and Quality of Life For Older People In Rural Ireland.* Intel Corporation.

Robson, C. (2002). *Real World Research 2nd Edition.* Oxford, Blackwell Publishing,.

Rodriguez, P., Yague, A., Alarcon, P.P. and Garbajosa, J. (2009). Some Findings Concerning Requirements in Agile Methodologies. In: *10th International Conference on Product Focused Software Process Improvement (PROFES'09), Oulu, Finland, June 15-17.* Berlin, Springer, pp. 171-184.

Rodriguez, P., Markkula, J., Oivo, M. and Turula, K. (2012). Survey on Agile and Lean Usage in Finnish Software Industry. In: *International Symposium on Empirical Software Engineering and Measurement (ESIM'12).* New York, USA, ACM, pp. 139-148.

Rolland, C., Achour, C. B., Cauvet, C., Ralyté, J., Sutcliffe, A., Maiden, N., Jarke, M., Haumer, P., Pohl, K., Dubois, E., and Heymans, P. (1998). A Proposal for a Scenario Classification Framework. *Requirements Engineering.* Vol.3 (1), pp.23-47.

Royce, W. (1970). Managing the development of large software systems. In: *Proceedings of WESCON, the Western Electronic Show and Convention, Los Angeles, USA.*

Royce, W.W. (1987). Managing the Development of Large Software Systems: Concepts and Techniques. In: *9th International Conference on Software Engineering (ICSE'87), Monterey, California, USA.* Los Alamitos, CA USA, IEEE Computer Society, pp. 328-338.

Rundle, P.J. and Dewar, R.G. (2006). Using Return on Investment to Compare Agile and Plan-Driven Practices in Undergraduate Project Groups. In: *28th International Conference on Software Engineering, 20-28 May, Shanghai, China.* New York, ACM, pp.649-654.

Runeson, P. and Host, M. (2009). Guidelines for conducting and reporting case study research in software engineering. *Journal of Empirical Software Engineering.* Vol.14(2), pp. 131-164.

Russo, J. and Schoemaker, P. (1989). *Decision Traps.* New York, Doubleday.

Sabetzadeh, M. and Easterbrook, S. (2005). An Algebraic Framework for Merging Incomplete and Inconsistent Views. In: *13th International Conference on Requirements Engineering, August 29th - September 2nd, France.* Washington DC, USA, IEEE Computer Society, pp. 306-318.

Sabherwal, R. and Chan, Y. E. (2001). Alignment Between Business and IS Strategies: A Study of Prospectors, Analyzers, and Defenders. *International Journal of Information Systems Research.* Vol. 12(1), pp.11-33.

Salay, R., Chechik, M. and Horkoff, J. (2012). Managing Requirements Uncertainty with Partial Models. In: *20th International Conference on Requirements Engineering, Chicago, USA.* Berlin, Springer, pp.107-128.

Salem, M.A. (2010) Requirements Analysis through Viewpoints Oriented Requirements Model (VORD). *International Journal of Advanced Computer Science and Applications.* Vol.1 (5), pp.6-13.

Santana Tapia, R.G.,Van Eck, P.A.T., Daneva, M. and Wieringa, R.J. (2012). Key Success Domains for Business-IT Alignment in Cross-Governmental Partnerships. In: *From Government to E-Governance: Public Administration in the Digital Age.* IGI Global, Hershey, PA, USA, pp. 131-161.

Saunders, M., Lewis, P. and Thornhill, A. (2009). *Research Methods of Business Students.* Fifth Edition. Pearson Education.

Schön, D. A. (1983). *The reflective practitioner: how professionals think in action.* Basic Books. USA.

Schwaber, K. (1997). Scrum Development Process. In: *OOPSLA Business Object Design and Implementation Workshop, London.* Berlin, Springer, pp.170-175.

Schwaber, K. (2004). *Agile Project Management with Scrum*. Microsoft Press.

Seattle Area Software Quality Assurance Group (SASQAG) (2006). *Open Space Event on Software Quality* [online], Available from: http://www.sasqag.org/pastmeetings2006.htm [Accessed: 18 February 2009].

Séguin, N., Tremblay, G., Bagane, H. (2012). Agile Principles as Software Engineering Principles: An Analysis. In: *13th International Conference on Agile Processes and eXtreme Programming (XP2012), Malmo, Sweden, May 21-25.* Berlin, Springer, pp.1-15.

SEI. (2006). *CMMI for Development* (CMMI-DEV, V1.2). CMU/SEI TR-008. Software Engineering Institute. Pittsburgh, PA, USA.

Sensuse, I.D. and Ramadhan, A. (2012). Enriching Soft Systems Metholology (SSM) With Hermeneutic in e-Government Systems Development Process. *International Journal of Computer Science Issues (IJCSI).* Vol.9 (1). pp. 17-23.

Sharp, H., Finkelstein, A and Galal, G. (1999). Stakeholder Identification in the Requirements Engineering Process. In: 10th International Conference on Expert Systems Applications, Florence, Italy, September 01-03, Springer, pp. 387-391.

Sharp, H., Robinson, H., Segal, J. and Furniss, D. (2006). The Role of Story Cards and the Wall in XP teams: A Distributed Cognition Perspective. In: *Agile Development Conference (AGILE'06).* Washington DC, USA, IEEE Computer Society, pp.65-75.

Sharp, H. and Robinson, H. (2006). *Collaboration in mature XP teams* [online], Available from: http://www.ppig.org/newsletters/2006-09/4-study-sharp.pdf [Accessed: 24 may 2012].

Sharp, H., Rogers, Y. and Preece, J. (2007). *Interaction Design* 2nd Edition. John Wiley & Sons.

Shine Technologies (2003). *Agile Methodologies Survey Results* [online], Available from: http://www.shinetech.com/agile_survey_results.jsp [Accessed: 20 February 2013].

Shore, B. (2008). Systematic biases and culture in project failures. *Project Management Journal.* Vol.39(4). pp.5–16.

Siddiqui, F and Afshar Alam, M. (2012). Ontology Based Feature Driven Development Life Cycle. *International Journal of Computer Science Issues.* Vol.9 (2), pp. 207-212.

Silvius, A.J.G. (2013). *Business and IT Alignment in Context.* (Ph.D.) thesis, Information Sciences, University of Utrecht, Netherlands.

Simon, H. A. (1996). *The Sciences of the Artificial,* 3rd edition. MIT Press, Cambridge, MA, USA.

Sitou, W. and Spanfelner, B. (2007). Towards Requirements Engineering for Context Adaptive Systems. *31st Annual International Conference on Computer Software and Applications (COMPSAC 2007), Beijing, China.* IEEE. pp. 593-600.

Sjøberg, D.I.K., Johnsen, A. and Solberg, J. (2012). Quantifying the Effect of Using Kanban vs. Scrum: A Case Study. *IEEE Software.* Vol.29 (5), pp.47-53.

Sletholt, M.T. (2011). Agile Scientists? Investigating Agile Practices in Scientific Software Development. (Masters) thesis, Department of Mathematics, University of Oslo, Norway.

Sommerville, I. (2001). *Software Engineering.* 6th *edition*, Addison Wesley. p8.

Sommerville, I. (2007). *Software Engineering 8th Edition*, Addison Wesley.

Stake, R. (1995). *The art of case study research.* Thousand Oaks, CA. Sage.

Stapleton, J. (1997). *DSDM, Dynamic Systems Development Method: The Method in Practice.* UK, Cambridge University Press.

Stapleton, J. (2003). *DSDM: Business Focused Development 2nd Edition.* Harlow UK, Addison Wesley.

Staron, M, Meding, W. and Palm, K. (2012). Release Readiness Indicator for Mature Agile and Lean Software Development Projects. In: *13th International Conference on Agile Processes and eXtreme Programming (XP2012), Malmo, Sweden, May 21-25.* Berlin, Springer, pp.93-107.

Stephens, P. (2010). μServices2.0 - *An eBusiness framework for the management of micro-service businesses.* (M.Sc.) thesis, Kingston University.

Strauss, A. and Glaser, B. (1967). *The Discovery of Grounded Theory: Strategies for Qualitative Research*. Aldine Transaction.

Strauss, A. and Corbin, J. (1998). *Basics of Qualitative Research: Techniques and Procedures for Developing Grounded Theory*. Sage Publications.

Suddaby, R. (2006). From the Editors: What Grounded Theory is Not. *Academy of Management Journal.* Vol.49(4), pp. 633-642.

Sutcliffe, A.G., Economou, A. and Markis, P. (1999). Tracing Requirements Errors to Problems in the Requirements Engineering Process. *Requirements Engineering.* Vol. 4(3), pp.134-151.

Sutherland, J. (2007a). The Plan is the Problem! [online], Available from: http://www.gbcacm. org/sites/www.gbcacm.org/files/slides/1B%20-%20The%20Plan%20is%20the%20Problem. pdf [Accessed: 11 November 2010].

Sutherland, J., Jakobsen, C.R. and Johonson, K. (2007b).Scrum and CMMI Level 5: The Magic Potion for Code Warriors. In: *Agile Conference (AGILE'07).* Washington DC, USA, IEEE Computer Society, pp.272-278.

Sutherland, J., Shoonheim, G., Kumar, N., Pandy, V. and Vishal, S. (2009). Fully Distributed Scrum - Linear Scalability of Production between San Francisco and India. In: *Agile Conference (AGILE '09).* Washington, DC, USA, IEEE Computer Society, pp. 277-282.

Sutherland, J., Schwaber, K. (2011). *The Definitive Guide to Scrum: The Rules of The Game [online],* Available from: http://www.scrum.org/scrumguides/ [Accessed: 09 January 2012].

Sutherland, J. and Schwaber, K. (2012). *The Scrum Papers: Nut, Bolts, and Origins of an Agile Framework* [online], Available from: http://jeffsutherland.com/ScrumPapers.pdf [Accessed: 20 February 2013].

Syed-Abdullah, S., Holcombe, M. and Gheorghe, M. (2003). Practice makes perfect. In: *the 4th International Conference on Extreme Programming and Agile Processes in Software Engineering (XP'03), Genova, Italy.* Berlin, Springer, pp.354-356.

Tartaglia, C. M., Ramnath, P. (2005). Using Open Spaces to Resolve Cross Team Issue. In: *Agile Development Conference (ADC 2005).* Washington DC, USA, IEEE Computer Society, pp.173-179.

Tatum, R. (2005). Applying Lean Thinking Principles to Software Development. (MSc.) thesis, Applied Information Management, University of Oregon.

Taylor, A. (2000). IT Projects: Sink or Swim. *The Computer Bulletin.* Vol. 42 (1), pp.24-26.

Technology Research for Independent Living (TRIL). (2010). *Falls Prevention,* [online]. Available from: http://www.trilcentre.org/falls_prevention/falls_prevention.474.html [Accessed: 26/08/2012].

The Standish Group, (2010). *CHAOS Summary for 2010* [online], Available from: http://insyght. com.au/special/2010CHAOSSummary.pdf [Accessed: 26 June 2011].

Toçi, M. (2012). *Challenges in Market Driven Requirements Engineering* [online], Available from:

http://www.utdallas.edu/~chung/SYSM6309/SYSM6309-Spring2012-Presentations/Mairon_Toci%20-Final-Paper/Mairon_Toci-Challenges-in-Market-Driven-

Requirements-Engineering.pdf [Accessed: 25 May 2013].

Trochim, W. (2002). *Research Methods Knowledge Base* [online], Available from: http://anatomyfacts.com/Research/ResearchMethodsKnowledgeBase.pdf [Accessed: 25 May 2010].

Trochim, W. (2006). *The Research Methods Knowledge Base 2nd Edition* [online], Available from: http://www.socialresearchmethods.net/kb [Accessed: 21 April 2012].

Truex, D., Baskerville, R. and Klein, H. (1999).Growing Systems in Emergent Organizations. *Communications of the ACM.* Vol.42(8), pp. 117-123.

Truex, D.P., Baskerville, R. and Travis, J. (2000). Amethodical Systems Development: The Deferred Meaning of Systems Development Methods. *Accounting Management and Information Technologies.* Vol.10, pp. 53-79.

Truyen, F. (2006). *The Fast Guide to Model Driven Architecture* [online], Available from: http://www.omg.org/mda/mda_files/Cephas_MDA_Fast_Guide.pdf [Accessed: 15 February 2014].

Tudor, D. (2007). *An Agile Perspective Introducing DSDM Atern* [online], Available from: http://agile2007.agilealliance.org/downloads/presentations/DotTudor_1074.pdf [Accessed: 23 May 2013].

Turner, D.W. (2010). Qualitative Interview Design: A Practical Guide for Novice Investigators. *The Qualitative Report.* Vol. 15 (3), pp. 754-760.

Urquhart, C. (1999). Themes in early requirements gathering: The case of the analyst, the client and the student assistance scheme. *Information Technology and People. Vol.*12 (1), pp. 44-70.

Van Grembergen, W. and De Haes, S. (2010). A Research Journey into Enterprise Governance of IT, Business/IT Alignment and Value Creation. *The International Journal of IT/Business Alignment and Governance* (IJITBAG'10). Vol.1(1), pp.1-13.

Van Vleit, H. (2000). *Software Engineering Principles and Practice.* 2nd Edition. New York, John Wiley & Sons.

Van Lamsweerde, A. (2000). Requirements Engineering in the Year 00: A research perspective. In: *22nd International Conference on Software Engineering (ICSE '00), Limerick, Ireland.* New York, ACM, pp.5-19.

Van Lamsweerde, A. (2003). *The KAOS Meta-model: Ten Years After*. Technical report. Universite Catholique de Louvain, Belgium.

Van Lamsweerde, A. (2009). *Requirements Engineering.* John Wiley & Sons.

Verner, J., Cox, K., Bleistein, S. and Cerpa, N. (2005a). Requirements Engineering and Software Project Success: An Industrial Survey in Australia and the U.S. *Australasian Journal of Information Systems.* Vol.13 (1), pp. 225 – 238.

Verner, J.M., Cox, K.A., Bleistein, S.J. and Bannerman, P.L. (2005b). Predicting Good Requirements? A Pilot Study. In: *1st International Workshop on Requirements Engineering for Business Need and IT Alignment (REBNITA), 29-30 August, Paris, France.* University of New South Wales Press, pp. 85-92.

VersionOne (2013). *7th Annual State of Agile Development Survey* [online], Available from: http://www.versionone.com/pdf/7th-Annual-State-of-Agile-Development-Survey.pdf [Accessed: 30 May 2013].

Vijayan, J. and Raju, G. (2011). A New Approach to Requirements Elicitation Using Paper Prototype. *International Journal of Advanced Science and Technology.* Vol. 28, March.

Vijayasarathy, L.R. and Turk, D. (2008). Agile Software Development: A Survey of Early Adopters. *Journal of Information Technology Management.* Vol. XIX, (2).

Virili, F. and Sorrentino, M. (2008). The enabling role of Web services in information system development practices: a grounded theory study. *Information Systems Development Practice.* Springer.

Vlaanderen, K., Brinkkemper, S., Jansen, S. and Jaspers, E. (2009). The Agile Requirements Refinery: Applying SCRUM Principles to Software Product Management. In: *3rd International Workshop on Software Product Management (IWSPM '09), Atlanta GA.* Washington DC, USA, IEEE Computer Society, pp.1-10.

Voigt, B.J.J. (2004). *Dynamic System Development Method* [online], Available from: https://files.ifi.uzh.ch/rerg/amadeus/teaching/seminars/seminar_ws0304/14_Voigt_DSMD_Ausarbeitung.pdf [Accessed: 13 June 2009].

Walsh, S. (2014). *An OpenXP Framework for Agile Requirements Elicitation.* (Ph.D.) thesis, The Regulated Software Research Group (RSRG), Dundalk Institute of Technology. Co Louth, Ireland.

Waltzman, R., Winbladh, K., Alspaugh, T.A. and Richardson, D.J. (2007). In the Requirements Lies the Power. In: *International Conference on Automated Software Engineering (SEKE 2007) 7- 9 July, Boston, USA.* Illinois, USA, Knowledge Systems Institute Graduate School, pp. 185 – 190.

Wang, X., Lane, M., Conboy, K. and Pikkarainen, M. (2009). Where Agile Research Goes: Starting from a 7-year Retrospective (Report on Agile Research Workshop (XP 2009). *ACM SIGSOFT Software Engineering Notes.* Vol.34 (5), pp.28-30.

Wang, X, Conboy, K. and Cawley, O. (2010). "Leagile" Software Development: An Experience Report Analysis of the Application of Lean Approaches in Agile Software Development. *The Journal of Systems and Software.* Vol.85 (6), pp.1287-1299.

Wang, X., Wu, Z. and Zhao, M. (2008). The Relationship between Developers and Customers in Agile Methodology. In: *International Conference on Computer Science and Information Technology, Singapore, August 29 – September 2nd.* Washington DC, USA, IEEE Computer Society, pp.566-572.

Weiss, J.W. and Anderson, D. (2004). Aligning Technology and Business Strategy: Issues and Frameworks, A Field Study of 15 Companies. In: *37th International Conference on System Sciences, (HICSS'04) Hawaii.* Washington DC, USA, IEEE Computer Society.

Welsh, K. and Sawyer, P. (2008). When to adapt: Identification of problem domains for adaptive systems. In: Peach, B. and Rolland, C. (eds), Requirements Engineering: Foundation for Software Quality, *14th International Working Conference (REFSQ 2008), Montpellier, France.* pp.198-203.

Widya, I. and Bults, R.G.A. (2009). Scenario-Based Requirements Elicitation in a Pain-Teletreatment Application. *In 4th International Conference on Software and Data Technologies (ICSOFT 2009), 26-29 July, Sofia, Bulgaria.* INSTICC Press, Vol. 2, pp. 406-413.

Wiegers, K. (1999). Automating Requirements Management. *Software Development.* Vol. 7 (7), pp.1-5.

Wiegers, K. and Beatty, J. (2013). *Software Requirements.* 3rd edition. Microsoft Press.

Williams, L. (2007). *A survey of Agile Development Methodologies* [online], Available from: http://agile.csc.ncsu.edu/SEMaterials/AgileMethods.pdf [Accessed: 21 May 2013]

Williams, M. A., Alspaugh, T.A. (2008). Articulating Software Requirements Comic Book Style. In: *3rd International Workshop on Multimedia and Enjoyable Requirements Engineering - Beyond Mere Descriptions and with More Fun and Games. Barcelona, Catalunya, Spain.* Washington DC, USA, IEEE Computer Society, pp.4-8.

Winbladh, K., Ziv, H. and Richardson, D.J. (2009). Eliciting Requirements Characteristics for Usable Requirements Engineering Approaches. In: *ACM Symposium on Applied Computing (SAC'09) Honolulu, Hawaii.* New York, USA, ACM, pp. 360-364.

Wood, J. and Silver, D. (1995). *Joint Application Development.* 2nd Edition. New York, John Wiley and Sons.

World Health Organisation (WHO) 2010. *Public health implications of global ageing* [online]. Available from: http://www.who.int/features/qa/42/en/index.html. [Accessed: 03/02/2015].

Wright, H.K., Kim, M. and Perry, D.E. (2010). Validity Concerns in Software Engineering Research. *Workshop on the Future of Software Engineering and Research (FoSER), November 7-8, Santa Fe, New Mexico.* New York, USA. ACM, pp. 411-414.

Yin, R.K. (1994). *Case Study Research: Design and methods. Applied Social Research methods.* 2nd Edition. Vol. 5, Thousand Oaks CA, Sage.

Yin, R.K. (2003). *Case Study Research: Design and Methods. Applied Social Research methods.* 3rd Edition. Vol.5, Thousand Oaks CA, Sage.

Young, J.T. (2009). *Developing a Soft Systems Solution for Enhancing and Managing Change in Organisations.* (Ph.D.) thesis, RMIT, Melbourne, Australia.

Yu, E. (1997). Towards Modeling and Reasoning Support for Early-phase Requirements Engineering. In: *3rd International symposium on Requirements Engineering, Annapolis, MD, USA.* Washington DC, USA, IEEE Computer Society, pp.226-235.

Zhang, Z. (2007). Effective Requirements Elicitation Techniques - A Comparison of Requirements Elicitation Techniques. In: E. Berki, J. Nummenmaa, I. Sunley, M. Ross and G. Staples (eds.), *Software Quality Management XV: Software Quality in the Knowledge Society.* British Computer Society, pp.225-240.

Zheng, Y., Venters, W. and Cornford, T. (2011). Collective agility, paradox and organizational improvisation: the development of a particle physics grid. Information *Systems Journal.* Vol.21(4), pp.303–333.

Zowghi, D and Paryani, S. (2003).Teaching requirements engineering through role playing. In: *11th IEEE International Requirements Engineering Conference, CA, USA.* pp.233-241.

Zowghi, D., Coulin, C. (2005c). *Engineering and Managing Software Requirements. Requirements Elicitation: A Survey of Techniques, Approaches, and Tools.* Berlin, Springer, pp.19-46.

Zowghi, D., Firesmith, D.G. and Henderson-Sellers, B. (2005d). Using the OPEN Process Framework to Produce a Situation-Specific Requirements Engineering Method. In: *1st International Workshop on Situational Requirements Engineering Processes August 29-30 (SREP '05), Paris, France.* University of Limerick, Ireland, pp.59-74.

Printed in the United States
By Bookmasters